MW01093100

Light with No Shadow

My Life Bridging Two Cultures

Also by the author:

Transcendence: Saving Us from Ourselves
Economics and Nature

Note: In finding a title for this book, my scholarly friends helped. From initially eight suggested titles, the final selection was made from these four.

Light with No Shadow: Bridging East and West
Like Light, Life has a Purpose: Building Bridges
Light: The Reality of Everything
Light Reflections: Bridging Two Cultures

We all have a purpose in our lives, just as light has a purpose. The third title came to my mind after seeing the movie *The Theory of Everything,*telling the story of cosmologist Stephen Hawking. The first and fourth titles are from Mark Lee and my editor Margaret Dodd. Most of us agreed to combine the first and the last, so the final title selected was *Light with No Shadow: My Life Bridging Two Cultures*

Light with No Shadow

My Life Bridging Two Cultures

A Memoir by **Navin Doshi**

Balboa Press books may be ordered through booksellers or by contacting:

Balboa Press
A Division of Hay House
1663 Liberty Drive
Bloomington, IN 47403
www.balboapress.com
1 (877) 407-4847

Print information available on the last page.

ISBN: 978-1-5043-5469-1 (sc)
ISBN: 978-1-5043-5472-1 (hc)
ISBN: 978-1-5043-5473-8 (e)

Library of Congress Control Number: 2016905591

Balboa Press rev. date: 04/28/2016

I dedicate this book first and foremost with all my heart to my loving wife, Pratima, who has supported me in every endeavor I have pursued. I also dedicate this book to my parents and my brothers who helped me to stay on the right path.

"I feel very strongly that I am under the influence of things or questions, which were left incomplete and unanswered by my parents and grandparents and more distant ancestors. It often seems as if there were an impersonal karma within a family, which is passed on from parents to children. It has always seemed to me that I had to … complete, or perhaps continue, things which previous ages had left unfinished."

Carl Jung

CONTENTS

TABLE OF FIGURES

CHAPTER 4

CHAPTER 5

CHAPTER 6

CHAPTER 7

CHAPTER 8

CHAPTER 9

CHAPTER 10

CHAPTER 11

CHAPTER 12

APPENDIX A

FOREWORD

The foreword to the great Indian epic the Mahabharata reads:

What is here is found elsewhere,
What is not here is nowhere.

The story of the life of Navin Doshi, a virtual native of two cultures, has all the elements of an epic life lived so deeply and profoundly it is a whole literature unto itself. His memoir tells the truths of a self that is made transparent through honest self-revelation and detailed narration of more than seven decades of his life in India and America.

He draws out the harmonies of Eastern and Western cultures such that they portray a true culture of sensibility, grace, and generosity. In parallel are the realities of his life astraddle the complexities of education, business, spirituality, familial responsibilities, entrepreneurship, and philanthropy. As if it was a natural outcome of living so long in two cultures, and being able to realize and explicate the harmonies of both, Navin Doshi created a nano-Nobel Prize that draws attention to men and women who subtly but profoundly achieve bringing cultures closer together. In an era where the exaggerated and grand are commonplace at all levels of society, his Doshi Family Bridgebuilder Award elevates simple recognition and appreciation of lives dedicated to quality and goodness to a new standard of profundity.

Navin Doshi's narration of his life lends itself to the genre of slokas where he shares scientific, economic, familial politics, and spiritual truths he has experienced and understands. Not shy of giving advice to youthful family members or to his wide circle of friends and acquaintances, he speaks in the tongues of slokas, stories, and tales from the East and the West to illuminate his points. Scientific and spiritual light are recurring themes in Doshi's story, as are the truths of great seekers and characters from India's rich spiritual historical past.

I would normally refrain from suggesting or even hinting at giving value to one life or another, but my friend V. Ganesan, nephew of Ramana Maharshi, has looked at that inevitable process in a very different way. "Lives are more comparable to the mode of accountancy, than to the mode of arithmetic. For example, life is filled with punyam, merits, and paapam, demerits. If the amount of punyam is more than paapam, the lesser number of paapam does not get deducted and thus annulled. The effects of both have to be experienced, either in this life or in the lives thereafter. There is no escaping from it. As long as they are there, continuous rebirth is unavoidable, till both are exhausted, completely."*

The life of Navin Doshi could be seen as a continuous stream of fields he enters, exhausting each and every one; living fully through love, grief, appreciation, death, greed, jealousy, and the range of human conditions in any one of which a person could spend a lifetime. His are each and every one enlightening and then finished.

R. E. Mark Lee,
Former Director,
Krishnamurti Foundation of America
Ojai, California

---

* Ganesan V. *Drops from the Ocean.* Ananda Ramana, 2014, page 61.

PREFACES

The Light in the Path

We feel greatly honored to have read Navin Doshi's story of his life and to contribute a few comments. His warm sharing of his life experiences, the lessons learned, the eternal truths that shine through his life path, are illuminating, heartfelt and profound. Each one of us being a person of two cultures, born in the great countries of India and Greece, respectively, which gave so much to the world, and now living in the great new world country, the United States, we appreciate and cherish the biography of people who serve as bridge builders between different cultures. However, there is much more to the life of Navin than just the many experiences of two cultures: His upbringing, early years and in fact his entire life, are steeped in spiritual tradition and follow in the great teachings of others who came from India and had a high impact on western culture, influencing the thinking and lives of many. His direct experiences in meeting or later in association with Swami Nityananda, J. Krishnamurti, Maharishi Mahesh Yogi, Swami Muktananda, and other great luminaries, shaped the eternal truths that form so much of his life.

This book is a collection of wisdom gleaned over a lifetime spanning over seven decades. It's a memoir that will inspire anyone who wants to look beyond the narrow identity of nationalism, ethnocentrism, and religious identity. The book is complete with Navin's memories of childhood along with stories and people who influenced his life including Mahatma Gandhi, Swami Nityananda, and Swami Parthasarati, experts in Vedanta, and many others: dignitaries, persons of success and reputation. Page after page, the book provides great reading and personal touch. Navin's character was molded by a rich cultural heritage, but also his education in Poona, Ahmedabad, Ann Arbor, and Los Angeles. As a true bridge builder, he went beyond the surface to the depth of different fields, cultures and ancient teaching: Science and spirituality; business and culture; the East and the West, just to mention a few. He had a very successful business career, following which he turned his attention to the deeper understanding of science and spirituality. In fact one thing about Navin is that you cannot characterize him as just belonging to a single human endeavor, a single career, or a single path. As educators, we appreciate his commitment to education. He helped launch programs at the University of California, Loyola Marymount University, and the creation of the Bridge Builder Award through Loyola Marymount University. Over the years Navin has associated with luminaries and scientists including Thich Nhat Hanh, Vandana Shiva, Rupert Sheldrake and numerous others who have made a difference to the wellbeing of millions of people.

Reading about the H-E-A-R-T patchwork and his success in this business, one feels the great heart of Navin and at the same time his keen sense of business awareness and success in everyday activities. Doshi's "Laws for Raising Children" are a must read for young or aspiring parents. Being both of us parents, we enjoyed how down to earth and full of wisdom they are. These are just some aspects of this book which reflect the personality and life of this great bridge builder, a great being: Navin Doshi. We applaud Navin for writing the story of his life, which has inspired us. A must read.

Deepak Chopra, M.D., is the author of more than 80 books, with 22 New York Times bestsellers, including Super Brain, co-authored with Rudi Tanzi, Ph.D. He serves as the founder of the Chopra Foundation and co-founder of the Chopra Center for Wellbeing. He recently published The Future of God (Harmony 2014).

Menas C. Kafatos is the Fletcher Jones Endowed Professor of Computational Physics at Chapman University. He is a quantum physicist, cosmologist, and climate-change researcher and works extensively on consciousness. He has authored 300 articles; is author, co-author or editor of 15 books, including The Conscious Universe (Springer) and is co-author with Deepak Chopra of the forthcoming book Who Made God and Other Cosmic Riddles (Harmony).

A Fertile Cross-Cultural Exchange

Over the centuries, India and America have given one another a great deal of value. From the West, India has imported technologies, products and methods that have enhanced its economic development. In turn, the U.S. has imported not just fabrics, foods, spices and art forms, but treasures of India's heritage whose benefits are far less visible but far more profound and enduring: philosophical systems such as Vedanta, derived from the unparalleled insights of the Himalayan sages, and practical, far-reaching methodologies for mind and body adapted from the diverse repertoire of Yoga. These ideas and disciplines have transformed American healthcare, psychology and, most profoundly, the way we understand religion and pursue spirituality. They have come to the West through various means of transmission: first books, then gurus, swamis, yoga masters and other guardians of India's spiritual legacy, and then Americans and Europeans—both ordinary individuals and prominent scholars, writers, artists, scientists—who absorbed these teachings, integrated them into their own areas of expertise, and distributed them in modified form to a receptive populace.

The rivers, streams and tributaries through which India's ancient wisdom has penetrated American culture have been many, and new ones continuously arise. One in particular represents, I believe, a vital new chapter in this fertile cross-cultural exchange. I speak of the growing presence in mainstream American life of citizens of Indian descent, the majority of whom are Hindu. Because Indians now share workplaces and classrooms with Americans with other religious, ethnic, racial and national backgrounds; because they are, increasingly, neighbors, playmates, friends, lovers, spouses, colleagues and relatives of non-Indians; because Hindu temples have appeared in every major city and on far more rural and suburban landscapes than anyone would have predicted twenty years ago; because Indian Americans now run major companies, inhabit university faculties and medical facilities, appear in the media and seemingly win the National Spelling Bee every year—for all these reasons and others, prejudices and misconceptions have diminished, and the precepts of Hinduism arefar better understood byordinaryAmericans. This, of course, is a classic American immigrant story, as wc have seen with Jews, Catholics, and other religious minorities.

Only it's different, because India is vastly different from Europe and Hinduism is significantly different from the Abrahamic faiths. The assimilation of Hindus ushers in a new era in the globalization of American culture and a quantum leap toward a more complete and authentic religious pluralism. The evidence suggests that the impact of this phenomenon is transformative, and the direction of that transformation can only be regarded as a giant step forward toward a world where differences are not merely tolerated but understood, embraced and enjoyed, within an overall context of the unity to which India's spiritual traditions point. In a very real sense, Indian citizens are changing not just the face of America but its very soul.

Navin Doshi is one of the immigrants at the center of this saga, and the story he tells in this thoroughly engaging memoir is a vital contribution to our understanding of an important phenomenon. His tale is at once typical and illustrative of the Indian diaspora experience and, at the same time, different. Unlike most Indians in America, he is old enough to have lived through the uproar of India's independence (he actually met Gandhi as a youngster) and the immense tragedy of Partition. He also arrived in America as a student a full seven years before the landmark Immigration and Nationality Act of 1965 opened the door to immigrants from Asia. Hence, he was one of very few Indians, and fewer Hindus, in his new home for a number of years. He was also different because he started his U.S. life in typical fashion, as an engineer, but—in keeping with the spirit of both the American Dream and his native Gujarat—he went on to become a hugely successful entrepreneur. Finally, his story is significant because he used the wealth he acquired to foster the very cross-cultural fertilization and spiritual pluralism that his own life represents. His philanthropy has enriched the curricula of several universities and has given a growing number of students the opportunity to better understand the cultural and religious heritage of India. He has been a true bridgebuilder, like the recipients of the award given out annually by Loyola Marymount University thanks to Navin's dedication and generosity.

Historians in the future are likely to view the give and take of India and America as a significant development in the narratives of both nations. Navin Doshi's illuminating memoir will endure as an invaluable resource for those historians, and for ordinary readers a delightful journey through an uncommonly consequential life.

Philip goldberg, Author of *American Veda: From Emerson and the Beatles to Yoga and Meditation, How Indian Spirituality Changed the West*
(and 19 more books on spirituality and books for a better life)

In the Land of Opportunity

From before the time of Ashoka (3rd Century BCE) to past the time of Akbar (17th Century), immigrants came to India from

China, Japan, Indonesia, Thailand, Persia, Greece, Rome, Arabia, North Africa and Central Asia looking for opportunities to further themselves spiritually and materially. Scholars and pilgrims came from far and wide to the universities and monasteries of India, and the fabled wealth of the country drew traders and marauders through the centuries. Then intervened the colonial chapter and our entry into the modern age marked by science, technology, and the economic ascendancy of Western political and corporate power. The center of world civilization shifted to Europe and later, after World War II, to the United States of America. From the mid-'50s, people all over the world flocked to America to study in her universities and seek their fortunes in this "land of opportunity."

Navin Doshi was one of these people, coming to the U.S. in 1958 to study aerospace engineering but staying on to become an American citizen contributing to this nation's transcultural multi-ethnic heritage. Discovered by Christopher Columbus in 1492 while looking for a transoceanic passage to India, the American continent was immediately hailed as the New World, and granted the scope of a new beginning for world humanity beyond cultural histories and in keeping with the birth of humanism in the European Renaissance. At the same time it immediately became virgin territory to serve Europe's colonial ambitions. The destiny of America thus became inextricably linked from the start with India, colonialism, and an international humanism. These braided trajectories have shaped the history of the U.S., and in his own way Navin has served as an agent in furthering the resolution of these forces.

America's engagement with India outside of the commercial and colonial interests with which her discovery is linked, forms an integral part of her soul — the great bardic aspiration seeded by Walt Whitman in his "Passage to India," the transcendentalism of Emerson and Thoreau, the researches into the psychology of spiritual experience initiated by William James and his colloquies with Vivekananda, all founding the subjective core of the nation at the turn of the 19th and 20th Centuries, continue to live into our times, tracing a continuity through the counterculture of the '60s, the scholarship of Joseph Campbell and Houston Smith, and the succession of Indian yogis and teachers of a variety of denominations.

On the other side, America as a nation of immigrants attracted by the blazing torch of liberty held aloft by the statue on Ellis island has seen its continuing struggle between an identity dominated by European colonial powers and an increasingly multi-ethnic population, weaving its diverse cultural histories into the fabric of national belonging. Particularly, the representation of Asia on the west coast of America has brought significant new contributors to America's economic, intellectual and creative life. Yet one should not lose sight of the leveling action of corporate America, erasing cultural specificities or rendering them into commercial commodities. "Americanization" as a superficial lifestyle, a way of dressing and speaking and consuming stereotypes standardized through powerful arts of persuasion, is a malady that overtakes second-generation immigrants, with or without the willingness of their parents. Navin, as a first-generation Indian in the U.S., arriving with the first wave of non-Western postwar immigrants, has consciously engaged in the ethics and politics of all these issues. Aided by fortune but equally through hard work, financial intuition and wise choices, he has utilized America's material opportunities to enable himself to participate in the shaping of America's national trajectories. Growing up in India in the powerfully idealistic era of India's struggle for national independence, Navin's childhood was shaped in contact with great moral and spiritual leaders, such as Mahatma Gandhi and Swami Nityananda of Ganeshpuri. Thus made acutely aware of India's spiritual heritage and its potential to contribute to world humanity, he has been a lifelong student of both Indian and Western teachers of spiritual culture, and has empowered its furtherance through sponsorship. My own entry into Navin's life in the early '90s followed his life's passion in this direction, at a time when he facilitated group studies in Vedantic philosophy at his home. This period inspired and led to his major philanthropic activities, sponsoring scholarships in Indian studies through chairs, professorships, and scholarships in universities through the reputed annual Bridgebuilder Award and through the publications and scholarly activities facilitated by Nalanda International.

Navin's memoirs areherea testamentto this inspiration and contribution to bridgebuilding between the deep psychology of the Indian tradition and the egalitarianism and material organization of modern America, transforming and cross-fertilizing both cultures. The following lines from Whitman's "Passage to India" stand out in validation to this impulse:

> Passage to India!
> Lo, soul, seest thou not God's purpose from the first?
> The earth to be spann'd, connected by network,
> The races, neighbors, to marry and be given in marriage,
> The oceans to be cross'd, the distant brought near,
> The lands to be welded together.

But these memoirs are more than this. Full of the flavor of the earth and sap of lived environments, of times, places and subjectivities experienced, full of the human taste of mortal humor, they are oral history of the highest quality. It is this subjective continuity materialized and immortalized as text and offered with love to later generations that weaves its lasting legacy into the history of Indian Americans and their claim to this nation of immigrants. It tells us of an India and America swiftly vanishing into the mists of time, it tells us of the youth and adolescence and maturity of people and nations, and of the evolution of consciousness that seeks to be internalized for a responsible future to be born through our dreams and acts. It is entertaining, it looks behind and it looks forward. It is the celebration of a life lived fully and thoughtfully in engagement with its times.

Debashish Banerji, Ph.D., Dean of Academic Affairs,
University of Philosophical Research, Los Angeles

Transformational Vision

This profound and illuminating book transcends the conventional memoir. Navin Doshi's vivid, engaging, and deeply moving description of his life in India and America provides penetrating insights into both cultures and a transformational vision of the integration of East and West—one that promises a more enlightened and fulfilled humanity. In his extraordinary command of the depths of ancient Vedic wisdom, with its import for human fulfillment, and his inspiring success in the world of American business and technology, he has become an exemplar of "giving back" through groundbreaking educational opportunities and philanthropy. In the literature of Indo-American experience, his memoir reveals how these two cultures can most powerfully strengthen each other and open the door for humanity to know its roots in the innermost Self—the core of life. Each phase of his experience—childhood, marriage, parenthood, business success, educational outreach, global awards and recognition—exemplifies universality moving through an extraordinary individual life to bring about global change and cross-cultural unity for the well-being of the entire world.

John Hagelin, Ph.D., International Director,
Global Union of Scientists for Peace;
Professor of Physics and Honorary Chair of the Board
of Trustees, Maharishi University of Management

Building Bridges Between Science and Spirituality

It has been said by the sages of antiquity that the individual events of our lives are a reflection in large part of our own "pattern" of consciousness—the quality of our inner spirit and intelligence—at play with the world around us. In the light of

Indian philosophy, the goal of life is to refine our individuality to reflect in a pure and natural way the total intelligence of nature—Brahman. The Patanjali Yoga Sutras, an aspect of the Vedic literature, reveals that this can be achieved through repeated experience of the one true transcendental reality. This has been the life quest of Navin Doshi.

In thesepagesNavin wonderfully weaves a tapestry of his life. What is most remarkable is not so much the individual threads or fabrics of events that happened, in Mumbai or Michigan, but the underlying and quiet inner theme to take the individual stories and realize them in the context of the whole. This theme of connecting the individual to the transcendent, of uniting the ancient and the modern, of building bridges between science and spirituality, is a deep part of Navin's inner nature and being. It is an almost driving need to discover first for himself and then to share with others, how the timeless wisdom that lies like a treasure in mankind's oldest traditions can be an invaluable and integral aid to us in our modern world.

When Navin firstcameto the United States, hecamewith innocence, openness and a determination to make good. It musthavebeen quitea shock to him to find that, in theland of burgers and fries, no one had heard of yogurt! And it is therefore amusing and charming to read his college tales of trying to make Indian sweets with sour cream. America has changed a lot since the first waves of Indian immigrants (now nearly three million) came to study and begin new lives in this melting pot of the world. Now vegetarian restaurants, yoga studios, and meditation classes abound. Perhaps this is due in no small measure to the successful integration of Indians into the American mainstream. So successful was this integration that more than a decade ago there were over 223,000 Asian-Indian–owned firms in the U.S., generating close to 100 billon dollars in revenue. Navin and his lifelong inspiration, Pratima, are part of that tidal wave of successful immigrants who made the leap from India, the land of arguably mankind's most ancient continuous culture, to our relatively young country. Their stories are so numerous and varied that they would fill many thousands of pages. That is one reason why Navin's tale is wonderful to read, because we have the sense that in reading his own experience, while rich and unique, it also tells of the larger story of the Indian diaspora. By knowing well one of the individual "patterns," we can come to know the whole more completely.

One of the great branches of the Vedic literature is called "Smriti," which literally means "memory." In the Vedic understanding of the world, memory plays a crucial role in the emergence of the universe. It is through the memory inherent in natural law that the universe emerges again and again, as it says in the 10th Mandala of the Rig Veda, *Navo-Navo bhavati jayamanah.* And it is memory, or smriti in its purest form that allows us to "remember" who we truly are, the one pure infinite immortal bliss, the transcendental reality. That is why Arjuna says to Krishna at the conclusion of the Bhagavad Gita, "Smritir Labdha," "O infallible one, my illusion is now gone. I have regained my memory by your grace."

It becomes clear, as one turns the pages of this book and all the memories it contains, that Navin's greatest wish is to share with us the "memory" that unites all of us with the Supreme Reality, and thus link the eternal unity extolled by the Rishis of India to the diversity of our modern world.

Michael Busch
Maharishi Vedic City, Iowa

Traveller Between Worlds

Navin has written an interesting book, certainly of interest to his family and friends. But there is more to it than initially meets the eye. The writing is excellent, and the reader is treated to much attention to detail that many writers would have failed to include. The key to this work, and to Navin as a person, is not only is he a bridgebuilder, but he is also a traveler between worlds. This seems to run in his family's blood. The arc of his life connects not only the East and the West, but also technology, economics, and spirituality.

It is especially significant that his experience in America spans a unique period of history in a particular situation — the second half of the 20th Century. During this time America became the richest and also the most technologically advanced nation in the world. Because his story is told in such detail, his own experience as an immigrant and then as a U.S. citizen may well be of value to future economic and political historians. His descriptions of the cloth trade, and his experiences as part of it, comprise a history of a special moment and the economic realities of the times and places of which he writes. This may not seem very important, considering the larger cultural and spiritual themes he touches on in the book, but it is the very stuff of history, and the kind of document historians and students of history often search through libraries looking for.

Considering the book as a whole, one must also appreciate the total arc he describes, from his childhood in India, in which the reader is treated to detailed and concrete descriptions of his family life, on to his youth and college experience in India, and then to America for engineering school and quite a new life. I found his descriptions of the work he did as an engineer to be fascinating — especiallythe zero gravity fuel tank problem — but more special are his accounts of experiences and accomplishments financially, and especially in the cloth trade.

It is a fascinating and large span, starting somewhere far back in history and leading up through the present day. I was fascinated by his references to his father, grandfather, great-grandfather, and so on back five hundred years and more. Such lineages are unheard of in America, where we rarely even know who our great-grandparents were.

This is the story of a traveler between worlds who becomes a bridgebuilder between worlds — worlds of culture and worlds of the spirit.

Allan Leslie Combs, Ph.D., Navin and Pratima Doshi
Professor of Consciousness Studies Director, CIIS
Center for Consciousness Studies, San Francisco

Reflections on Navin Doshi's Journey

What an intriguing book! It is rare to find such a combination of personal narrative, family history, political history, philosophy, insights into thebusiness world, shocking glimpses of university politics, reflections on horses, amusing stories, and serious purpose all combined together. The writing style is clear and sincere, and amidst the flowing narrative, racy in places, are gems of wisdom and insight, both philosophical and practical. For me, the most intriguing passages werethosethatshowed the interplaybetween Indian traditions and themodern world, and oneof themostmoving sections is the description of finding a bride, ending with the tremendous success of marrying Pratima. This book builds many kinds of bridges between East and West, between practicality and idealism, between business and vision, and between family life and the wider world. Thank you Navin!

Rupert Sheldrake, Ph.D.

Candid Smiles and Invisible Tears

As I set about to write these words of welcome to Navinbhai Doshi's memorable book, a pleasant problem confronts me: how to welcome a book that is so delightfully honest and honestly delightful that it needs no formal words of welcome from anyone. His narrative recalls his own personal and private memories spanning some seven decades as well as of the collective social, political and economic roots of Indo-American society spanning over a century. Rich in details and engaging through its larger perspective, Navin Doshi's book is an important document of hard data and soft feelings, a deep, wide mine of many metals, each precious in its own way.

We live in times that tend to be disordered without warning. To work towards its sanity is as difficult as it is urgent. That is because the hugely destructive and largely unpredictable battles that erupt in a schizophrenic culture are not between the self and an external enemy but between self and self. Self divided against itself needs the touch of a healer who is compassionate and critical in equal measure. Navin Doshi's gripping account of our times and culture is marked by a sincere wish to heal and a remarkable capacity to balance compassion and criticality. As in his other books, the author consciously employs psychological insights and methodology that he sees as the unique strength of ancient Indian culture. Oneof thenotions so cultivated is theconcept of "clustering," the ability to group together when needed, and disperse when required. Navin Doshi understands, explains and presents such entities as the nuclear family, the extended family, caste, society, spirituality, immigrant groups, clusters at the sites of education, training and professional work, and the business world. With a razor-sharp memory and graphic descriptions of persons, places and periods, he recaptures and represents the many pasts of his life with courageous honesty and an infectious sense of humor.

Navin Doshi has been a bridgebuilder all his life and this book paints in lucid strokes a broad landscape of bridged distances, and of his ceaseless and affectionate efforts to provide access to the social, economic, educational, psychological and physical aspects of two cultures. The candid smiles and invisible tears of its author make his book all too human … Mywarm welcometo its adorablehumanity.

Sitanshu Yashaschandra, Ph.D., Former
Vice Chancellor, Saurastra University
(Recipient of many literary awards including Padmashree)

Vision for a Better World

Navin Doshi, from the time of his childhood, developed a profound capacity for introspection and the observation of externals. His memories of childhood include being made sleepy by bhaang, being nearly killed by an automobile, discovering his capacity for excellence in studies, and learning the generations-old stories of his merchant family. His parents inculcated in young Navin the importance of transcendence, bringing him into the presence of greatness. As a young boy in Ganeshpuri, he massaged the feet of the spiritual master Swami Nityananda. Mahatma Gandhi was a formative influence in his understanding of tolerance for all traditions. His wife Pratima cooked for Swami Muktananda during the Swami's stays in Santa Monica, and for Raj Kapoor, an all-time show man of Bollywood. Once the children had left the house, Navin and Pratima convened a regular series of philosophical study sessions based on Eliot Deutsch's insightful book on Advaita Vedanta. The Doshis welcomed into their home study group such luminaries as Swami Parthasarati, an expert on Vedanta and science, and Dr. Yajneshwar Shastri, then director of the School of Education, Psychology, and Philosophy at Gujarat University. They sponsored Dr. Shastri and his wife Dr. Sunanda Shastri, professor of Sanskrit, to visit Los Angeles on many occasions, where they interacted with the community and taught courses at Loyola Marymount University(LMU). Other scholars supported by the Doshis at LMU have included Drs. Purusottama and Renuka Bilimoria (Deakin University) and Ramprasad Chakravarti (Lancaster University). In the 1990s and 2000s, many leaders of the Indian community gathered at the Doshi home for splendid conversations, tea, and magnificent meals of both Western and southern Indian cuisine.

Navin's combined knowledge in science and philosophy, and his experience at home and in the marketplace, inspired the composition of two books and numerous online essays (www.

nalandainternational.org). With a deep appreciation of India's philosophy of interconnection, Navin articulates the reciprocal relationship between the ever-present witness consciousness (Purusa) and the ever-changing drama of life played out by the Divine Dancer (Prakrti). Reflecting on his own Rajput roots, he followed the course set out by his grandfather and father, being willing to move as opportunities presented themselves, but doing so in a reflective, measured manner. His choice of universities in Poona, Ahmedabad, Ann Arbor, and Los Angeles fostered not only a breadth of knowledge, but also the opportunity to learn about human nature as he carefully observed the professors and the underlying ethos of each institution. With great wisdom and energy, he conserved his money and diversified early, branching into real estate and textiles while pursuing a career in aerospace engineering and rearing two children in Los Angeles. The Doshis have engaged with many individuals in their realms of family, friends, work, and the intellectual arts.

After helping to launch three programs at the University of California at Los Angeles (UCLA) — the Doshi Chair of Indian History, the Sardar Patel Dissertation Prize, and the Dr. Sambhi Chair of Indian Music — Navin turned his attention to Loyola Marymount University and the creation of the Doshi Bridgebuilder Award. For more than a decade Navin Doshi has given scholarships, helped convene a major conference on the archaeology of the Indus/Sindhu River Valley, and bestowed the Bridgebuilder Award on leaders who have made significant contributions toward a deeper understanding in a variety of fields. By honoring Dr. Deepak Chopra, Navin heralded the ancient medical wisdom of India, inseparable from its meditative traditions. With Maestro Zubin Mehta, Navin acknowledged the greatness of a conductor of Parsi Bombay origin who helped shape the musical culture of Los Angeles, and also built bridges between Israelis and Palestinians. Venerable Thich Nhat Hanh, who brought more than 100 monks and nuns to lead more than

1,700 members of the LMU community in song and meditation, walked and ate with the attendees, demonstrating the gravitas of a master of Zen Buddhism who helped to negotiate the end of the Vietnam War. Professor Sardesai of UCLA reminded those gathered that two great deserving men of peace never received the Nobel Prize: Mahatma Gandhi and Thich Nhat Hanh. The Doshis' long commitment to education took center stage as Greg Mortenson, founder of schools for girls in remote areas of Afghanistan and Pakistan, addressed more than 4,000 people in LMU's Gersten Pavilion, describing how change can be effected with a minimum of resources and an abundance of good will. Professor Huston Smith, author of the million-copy book *The Religions of Man*, told stories of his upbringing in China, his years of training in Vedanta, and the life lessons that he shared with generations of students at Washington University, Massachusetts Institute of Technology, Syracuse University, and UC Berkeley. Dr. Vandana Shiva addressed a packed crowd, advising caution in the consumption of industrialized food, and telling of farmer suicides in India inflicted by the predatory lending practices of multinational fertilizer, seed, and pesticide companies. Dr. Rupert Sheldrake, a research botanist stationed for many years in India, shared his amazement at the interconnectivities to be found in Nature, and inspired all present with his childlike wonder. Over the years, so many thousands of people have been deeply and personally touched by the Doshi Bridgebuilder experience and awards made possible by the vision of Pratima and Navin for a better world.

In this memoir, Navin reminds us that when the historians centuries hence look back on the 20th Century, they will of course note the First and Second World Wars, but most likely find greater significance in the shrinking of national boundaries and the cross-fertilization of world cultures. The Doshi family, through their personal stories and their educational and philanthropic activities, has contributed mightily to this emergence of global culture. Like

Gandhi and those whom they have honored, the Doshis stand in a long line of peacemakers, retaining a quiet demeanor yet being actively engaged in good works.

Christopher Key Chapple, Ph.D.,
Associate Academic Vice President and
Professor of Theological Studies, Loyola
Marymount University, Los Angeles

INTRODUCTION

On my sixty-fifth birthday, our daughter Sonya asked me to write down the history of my "coming to America," for her children's reference. I was touched and daunted at the same time. Yet I realized that though we live in the 21st Century and most of us believe in an afterlife, we still want to live on in our children.

Then Professor Chris Chapple of Loyola Marymount University invited me to speak to a group of southern California teachers about my experience as an Indian and an Indian-American. It was a government-sponsored workshop on India and NRI's (non-resident Indians). My talk involved some research about my family of origin. After my presentation, Professor Chapple commented on how interesting my life had been.

My third prompting came from Rajmohan Gandhi, a visiting professor at UCLA's department of history during the fall quarter of 2001. Rajmohan is the grandson of Mahatma Gandhi and the author of eight books. He and I are almost the same age, and both of us have younger wives and grew up in a somewhat similar environment. In my first year at the University of Michigan in '58, we almost met at Mackinac Island where the headquarters of the MRA (Moral Rearmament Association) had been established. Rajmohan was an active participant and founder of the MRA, employing Gandhian principles of nonviolence and reconciliation to help change the world. When he and I eventually connected through UCLA, we became good friends, though with differing views in matters of politics. We often compared our life stories. I asked him for interesting tales of his life, possibly for a movie script. He retorted, "Why, you have had such a wonderful and interesting life, you ought to consider writing about yourself."

I wrote down some thoughts and later had them typed up. That was in 2003, and then I forgot about it. In fact, I gave priority to writing two books on subjects of my interest and life experiences: *Transcendence, Saving Us from Ourselves* in 2009, and *Economics and Nature* in 2012. Then my family and friends planned a celebration for my seventy-sixth birthday occurring on 12/12/2012, supposedly a day of great changes. For the occasion, a video was produced and projected, containing impressions by my good friends about our life experiences.

Later I remembered having started writing my life story, and I told Chris and Debashish about it. A few months later, while reciting one of the humorous events in my childhood, a fourth and fifth prompting came from Professor Debashish Banerji and former Vice Chancellor Sitanshu Mehta. In 2011, we were invited to visit Maharishi University in Iowa, thanks to our friends Gita and Mukesh Desai. There I met Michael Busch and we instantly became friends. A sage-like human being, Michael is totally devoted to Maharishi Mahesh Yogi's philosophy. He was responsible for the sixth prompting. Mark Lee, who helped me write my first book, also encouraged and supported me in all different matters in writing this book. Mark's experience in book publishing has been invaluable. God often speaks to us through the voices of others, so pondering the source of the voices, I took their advice.

There is a final reason for this book. In an effort to honor the request from our kids to provide a family history, it is also my hope that my history may inspire others to seek out their own histories and identities. The stories that follow are based upon stories told by my parents, grandparents, and from my own experience. I believe that these tales will help establish deeper roots for future generations, just as deeper, healthier roots underground give strong support to the trees above ground. One often has to go as far back as one can go. I believe knowing your history is good and advantageous not only for individuals and families but also for organizations, cultures and countries. When I wrote our family history, I discovered that we are all connected genetically, with the result that the whole of humanity is a big family. Every human being at the deepest level is identical. I discovered that we all have a purpose in life. My purpose lay in the gradings of light, transcending towards the brightest.

China under Mao, and Afghanistan under the Taliban tried to disconnect both countries from their pasts with terrible results that were counterproductive. I know a few friends who disconnected from their families in India, which resulted in a disadvantage for their children by depriving them of the good and bad experiences of their forefathers, and because of this they may have to "reinvent the wheel," so to speak, to help their children find their identities. Alex Haley's book *Roots,* which described his African past, gave back to African Americans their heritage and pride. My interpretation of evolution in a broad sense is that we need knowledge of our roots. The history of each one of us is just a tiny thread, though collectively it constitutes the whole of human history.

So much has happened since I first arrived in the United States from Bombay that I realized I had nearly forgotten part of it. As I began to ponder the elements of my own roots, I discovered a treasure of memories that just needed to have the dust shaken from their edges. From the soil of my native land, these treasures now unfold from India's "red earth" to mingle with the continuity of our legacy in California, and in some ways, my own immortality.

Navin Harilal Doshi
Los Angeles, California

CHAPTER 1

MY BEGININGS

"The land of India is unlike any other in the world, for it bears in it a spirit that has changed human hearts for thousands of years."

Rudyard Kipling

Like many Americans, I am an immigrant. However, being an immigrant from India, I bear a unique connection to America's roots because America's own native peoples, the Indians, were inadvertently named after my own people by the Italian explorer Christopher Columbus in 1492. Having convinced Queen Isabella of Spain he had figured out a cheap and quick way to get to India's precious silks and spices, Columbus was financially backed by the Spanish monarch, and the rest is, as they say, history.

Perhaps it is ironic that my journey to get to America runs in opposition to Columbus in his effort to get to India. Columbus died believing himself a failure for never reaching my country because he did not see the "vision" of what he had discovered. And though the people he mistakenly called "Indians" of the "West Indies" did not particularly share in the wealth of the later nation, these misnamed natives are perhaps a karmic connection to the successes myself and many Indians have enjoyed in recent decades in this "Land of Opportunity."

As you will see, Indians, whether they were natives of the Western Hemisphere or from the East, were originally never really welcomed by the dominant Anglo-European culture of America. But then neither were the Irish, nor the Italians, nor the Africans, nor the Mexicans, nor even the Jews. And yet if you remove this mosaic of world peoples from the cultural heritage of the United States, you would find a very bland and empty land.

To begin with, I am a Gujarati. I come from a region in India in the northwest, bordered by Rajasthan in the northeast, Pakistan in the northwest, Maharashtra in the south, and the Arabian Sea in the west. It is a beautiful land of contrasts with simple villages and several large city centers. Mahatma Gandhi and Sardar Patel, both Gujaratis, were sons of this soil. Current Prime Minister Narendra Modi and several of the richest businessmen of India are also sons of this soil. It is a region that characteristically has harbored a variety of communities and sects. Hindus, Muslims, Jains, Parsees, and Christians have all mingled in Gujarat or declined to mingle. The diversity of religious cultures is historic to the region.

Gujaratis are known mostly for being merchants. For centuries they have been acknowledged as hard working and industrious. They were some of the first expatriates from India to seek their fortunes in other lands like Africa, Asia, and Europe to better their lot in life. This movement to a new location is something in our blood. It is a theme that I have seen in my own life and in many of my fellow Gujarati countrymen; that is, a change of home may often bring a change of life. Even Gandhi lived this philosophy when one looks at the various locations to which his life took him, whether it was Gujarat, England, South Africa, and his several homes in India.

When I was born, the British still controlled India. India had become a prize for the Empire as a source of cloth, spices, soldiers, tea, and diamonds. Diamonds, for example, were first discovered in India in 400 BC, and sold all over the world for thousands of years. By the Middle Ages, diamond-cutting centers were established in Amsterdam and other locations of Europe due to a thriving trade that often involved Jews. These "jewelers," because of Christian Europe's anti-Semitism, were unable to own land. They therefore dabbled in precious stones and moneylending as a way of financial security.

By the 18th Century, when India was firmly entrenched as the "jewel" of the British crown, London had become the diamond-cutting center of the world. British cloth made from and by Indian craftsmen was the choice of the world. The saffron, pepper and teas enjoyed by people from the American colonies to Madrid were controlled by the British colonial occupation of India. They were also exporters of Afghan opium to China. It was this exceptional economic advantage of having India as a part of the British Empire that made Britain so resistant to India's later struggle for independence.

Gujarat, like other areas of India, had been divided up by the British into regions controlled by either the British Raj or the Princely States. Most of Gujarat was Hindu and composed of four divisions or castes: the Brahmins (priests or scholars), the Kshatriyas (nobles or warriors), the Vaisyas (merchants or farmers), and the Sudras (workers). From my earliest recollections, my family used to say that the Doshis were originally of the Kshatriyas or Rajput caste from Rajasthan. The family tree shows that one, Kasidas Doshi, some eighteen generations ago, migrated southwest to Gujarat (around 500 years or so ago). Rajputs are known as warriors who often took on the Moguls and Muslims when they invaded the subcontinent.

A group of Rajputs, probably our close cousins, who were defeated by the invaders left India, migrating toward the Middle East and Central Europe. Before they left, these Kshatriyas (warriors) made a vow that they would return when they were strong to retake the lands the Muslims took from them. However, the Rajputs, now known as gypsies, never returned to India. Instead they traveled throughout Europe, settling in Spain, Hungary, and then moving or relocating to various regions of Europe, from Rome and Naples to Vienna and Sarajevo. This migration is characteristic of the spirit of the Rajputs, a spirit that has mingled with many of the Gujarati Vaisyas who were Rajputs before conversion. It is a spirit found in my own family.

Kasidas and his fellow migrants became Vaisyas, also known as Vahanyas, based on economic needs. It is interesting to note that the name "banyan" came from the writer's caste "Bania," derived from the Gujarati name "va(ha)nias," meaning boat businessmen (vahan in Gujarati means sailboats), travelling as far as Java and Sumatra. Among Gujaratis, baniya or vanias implies they are grocers or merchants by profession. The last name Doshi comes from the word "dosh" in Gujarati, meaning a sin or serious offense. There is a popular Gujarati story recited by a Gujarati poet, Narsinh Mehta, claiming that Lord Krishna, one of the avatars of the Divine Being, appears as a doshi vanio (from vanias) wandering from village to village to sell cheap rough cloth.

The Portuguese picked up the word "banya" to refer specifically to Hindu merchants and passed it along to the English as early as 1599 with the same meaning. By 1634, English writers began to tell of the banyan tree (vad in Gujarati), a tree under which Hindu merchants (banias) would conduct their business. The tree provided a shaded place for a village meeting or for merchants to sell their goods. Eventually, banyan came to mean the tree itself. Even today children are schooled under the banyan tree in some tribal areas. The Times of India, one of the largest newspapers in India, has a column on spiritualism with the heading, "Under the Banyan Tree."

West Gujarat was also a business center that featured Kharvas. Kharvas, meaning sailors, sailed off to lands like Java, Sumatra and Burma in the 15th and 16th Centuries. Because Gujarat borders Rajasthan, many of the Rajputs migrated to this area of Gujarat and became part of the business community. Among Gujaratis, even today, on auspicious occasions, Brahmins recite stories, known as Satnarayan Katha, about merchants sailing to Java and Sumatra and avoiding sea storms or potential problems by performing Shree Satya Narayana Pooja and chanting God's name, not only during bad times, but also during good times. An overseas business of export and import was conducted by people from India during the first millennium; the spread of Hinduism and Buddhism in East Asia was one of the outcomes. However, Muslims took over the business of export and import from Indians during the second millennium.

However, Gujaraties never stopped travelling and even settling faraway places to these days to become more prosperous. They have formed prominent and prosperous communities, certainly in English speaking countries like America, England, Canada, Australia, and New Zealand. They are true believer of free enterprise economic system; business, indeed is the principal business of Gujaraties. This book is indeed a story of one Gujarati.

My ancestors wereShaivites from northwest Gujarat near a small town called Ghogha, around twenty kilometers from a major city called Bhavnagar where my mother was born. Ghogha in ancient times was a known port for the spice and textile trade. I recall my maternal uncle, Vadimama, affectionately calling me "Ghogha No Kharvo," meaning a sailor from Ghogha. We used to memorize the names of our forefathers; I still remember their names up to the sixth generation; the names start with my name, Navinchandra Harilal, Harilal Mohanlal, Mohanlal Panachand, Panachand Narsidas, and the last, Narsidas Jagjivandas. Note that the second name in the Gujarati tradition is always the father's name. Apparently my father and grandfather's names were popular in the Gujarati community, since they were also the names of Mahatma Gandhi and his first son.

People usually married among their castes or groups. Jains, a group of people that, like many Hindus, staunchly believe in nonviolence and respect for all living things, often married Hindus.

Rarely did Hindus marry a person from any other religion. I recall a family where the father was Hindu and the mother was Christian. They were very unhappy because of the vast cultural and religious differences in their marriage. Most of my community, wanting to avoid similar disenchantment, married among their own kind.

The Rajputs left India for the northwest, while my forefathers migrated from Rajasthan to the Ghogha/ Bhavnagar area of Saurashtra. My parents and grandparents were raised there. I was born in Bhavnagar in Gujarat, my mother's town, but was raised mostly in Bombay. Throughout my childhood I visited Ghogha, usually for family gatherings such as weddings. I recall traveling in the area by bullock cart, a primitive wooden carriage drawn by bulls. Though these carriages were bovine-powered, they could race as fast as if they were horse-drawn.

My grandfather, Mohanlal, was not happy in Ghogha. In the early 1900s, he migrated to the town of Bharuch. He did not leave on good terms with his family, so he received probably little or no financial support. My grandma, Muliba, used to say he survived in Bharuch on puffed rice, peanuts, and chana masala. Bharuch was a center for British tax collection.

My grandfather was a textile merchant and he, like other businessmen, profited in Bharuch, thanks to the World War One economy. Making money in textiles during the war has been the common theme for three generations; I happened to be the last one. Figure 1–1 shows the partial family my grandfather supported due to his success in the business. There was a time when he supported thirty-five members of his family, which included members of his own family and members of his brothers and sister in a large rented house shown in the background of the photograph. He was indeed magnanimous and a devout Shaivite who fasted every Monday of the week.

In the late '30s, my father, Harilal Doshi, moved to Mumbai. He was not happy working for his father in Bharuch. In the true "businessman Vaishia" spirit he wanted to be an independent businessman, where there was greater economic growth and opportunity. I was three to four years old when we moved to Mumbai, but my elder brothers, Jitubhai who was around seven, and Jasvantbhai who was around ten, stayed with my grandparents at their insistence. The word "bhai" is placed after a brother's name to show respect.

My mother's name was Kanchan and I was to keep her company in Mumbai, while my father prospered with the new WWII economic opportunities. With some help from my mother's cousins, my father hooked up with the Maffatlal Group as a textilemerchant. Once our family was doing better, my two brothers, I believe in '41, joined us in Mumbai. My maternal grandfather had passed away before I was born. My mother and I would visit my maternal grandmother, Rambhaba, in Bhavnagar; she passed away at the age of sixty-one, when I was around seven. Rambhaba lived in a "khadki," a three-story house with floors covered with dry mud and no electricity or running water.

My mother and Rambhaba made sure that I never jumped on the floor to avoid any damage to the floor. They would warn me that if I jumped high enough, I could go through the floor and go down to the bottom level hurting myself. She was a devout Rama and Krishna devotee who would ask me to recite God's name whenever we could remember, even when sitting on a toilet. Rambhaba looked and spoke like old Katherine Hepburn with a shaky voice. She would make sure that she had yogurt even if she had to get it from a local kandoy, a dairy retailer, because she knew that I was very fond of sweet yogurt with my lunch, the main meal of the day. Often Rambhaba would give a card to buy yogurt that looked like the cards in a monopoly game. I remember prominent merchants would issue their own cards in small denominations to be used as money because there was a shortage of coins. For example, if I gave a two rupees note to buy one rupee worth of yogurt, the merchant would give me a card denominated as one rupee. The card could have been issued by any of the prominent merchants.

There was another three story mud-house right across her house, where a couple and their twelve year old son were residing. I would watch husband and wife quarreling loudly with each other using abusive language. Rambhaba would explain to us that the wife was angry because the husband was lazy and stayed home. He did not want to work and expected their twelve year old son to support the family by working.

It was always fun for me to go to Bhavnagar, my birthplace, since my cousins and I would have a wonderful time going places; in fact I had learned to ride a bicycle in Bhavnagar. I even remember that my cousin Kanti would hold first and then push the bicycle for me to go forward. Then when I was on my own bicycling away, without my knowledge he would run behind me and jump on the back of the bicycle. Luckily I would not lose my balance. Our other activities included playing with a wooden spinning top, going to movies, and eating jalebi and gathya, a Bhavnagar specialty.

There is a Gujarati saying, "Chantar Tyaa Vantar," which translated means, "The birds weave their nests where there is bird feed." As we all know, the strength of the economy is proportional to the flow or the velocity of money. The money flow in turn depends on the availability of goods and services, following one of the few extremely important laws, Adam Smith's Law of Supply and Demand. For a healthy economy, the flow of money is crucial, as is the blood flow in a human body. A strong economy with a strong flow of money also generates opportunities for the go-getters. I suppose my family, with their constant relocation, understood this law, and truly lived the saying. My father used to say to my mother, "All I need is 100,000 rupees and a small bungalow and I'll take it easy." Well, he exceeded that and carried on further to acquire and achieve more. Today, 100,000 rupees, after so many years of inflation, have very little value.

My family and Gandhiji were visiting Punchgini and Mahabaleshwar, hill stations near Poona, at about the same time so we had a chance to meet Mahatma Gandhi. I was about nine years

From left (seated and standing pairs): Myself (five years) and oldest brother Jasvantbhai (eleven years); my father and mother, cousin and his mother; my grandfather; two kid cousins (seated) and Aunt Ramuphai (standing); my grandmother and aunt; youngest uncle Mahendrakaka (seated), Uncle Himatkaka and aunt; second brother Jitubhai (eight years, seated) and cousin (standing), 1942.

old. I vividly recall running alongside a gaunt man in a white loincloth with a walking stick. He had his hand on a young woman's shoulder as he strode, eyes always forward, never really looking at the people he was conversing with, and yet deeply listening to their every word. Gandhi spoke very little as a Parsi woman walking with him spoke continuously, questioning him. There must have been twenty to thirty people walking with him. After the walk there was a prayer. My father gave me five rupees to give to Gandhiji. As I strode up to him and handed him the money, he smiled and turned to a woman next to him who kept track of everything. "Write it down," he said to her. "Five rupees and his father's name." The woman immediately marked a ledger indicating who gave him what and what amount they gave. Gandhiji was revered by all the people I knew. As I witnessed, he was also very meticulous.

During the '40s we were living in a three-story building called Yashodhan in Matunga, a suburb of Bombay. We occupied the front apartment with a balcony. We had a housekeeper named Balu who spent nights with other

Navin showing off with Jasvantbhai's big coat

My parents, devout Shaivites, at Amarnath (Ice Linga) Temple in Kashmir.

The three brothers in 1952. I was heavier and stronger, and would beat and win over Jitubhai anyday, though in this photo, I look quite skinny. Jitubhai always enjoyed dressing up. Jasvantbhai was the "king" in the neighborhood.

housekeepers in the common area of the building. My father was doing well in the textile business, and had invited his brothers (my uncles) to help him. He also had hired a few more men since the business was expanding around the WWII period. I recall once during Janmastami (Lord Krishna's birthday) by tradition, the office staff and my uncles were playing poker on a terrace located on the third floor of a building that my father owned. My mother, on her way to shop for vegetables, asked me to give a message to my uncles. I must have been about seven years old. I went upstairs to the terrace and gave the message, as I was supposed to do. I saw them not only playing cards, but also drinking bhaang and laughing non-stop. My uncle insisted that I drink bhang, so I drank this very tasty sweet drink and came down to my mother. I then complained to my mother that I could not keep my eyes open, wanting to sleep. Evidently she knew what had happened, and she was quite angry with the uncle who had made me drink bhaang. You see, bhaang is a drink made of marijuana, milk, sugar, and spices, and when it is made by grinding copper coins, it becomes even more potent. My mother immediately asked Balu to take me home. A few hours later, when my mother came home, she could not find me. After a search, they discovered me in deep sleep under my father's palang (bed) with an empty box of cookies.

We had a neighbor, Mr. Gore (pronounced Goray), a Maharashtran Brahmin from Poona and a member of the ultra-right wing Hindu Mahasabha. His three daughters were pretty, with green eyes, and the mother and daughters were quite friendly. One day I heard screams in the far distance coming from Gore's apartment. The story was that their young cook had made a sex-related comment to one of the daughters. Realizing that he had made a big mistake, he ran away, and later Gore was able to find him. They brought him home by force and he was beaten up. The impression I had of Gore was that he was a Hindu fanatic. The day Mahatma Gandhi was assassinated (January 30, 1948), we heard the news on the radio. I was about eleven. I recall almost every working person in our neighborhood coming home in the early evening around five or six o'clock. My father normally would be home around 8 pm, but this night his ears were glued to the radio.

Initially the announcement was that a crazy man named Godse had shot Mahatma Gandhi. A few hours later it was announced that Gandhi was dead. Pandit Nehru's speech was broadcast, Sardar Patel's was not. Elders, I remember, commented that Sardar Patel was devastated after Gandhi's death, while Pandit Nehru seemed to be more composed. The next day there was a crowd of people waiting on the street looking up towards our balcony. They were looking for Gore to beat him up, since Gore belonged to the Hindu Mahasabha, the same party from which Godse came. Later we came to know that after hearing that many Hindu Mahasabha members were beaten up, Gore had fled. All institutions, including schools, were closed for several days. We boys visited every nearby place of worship and prayed along with others. The places we visited included Hindu temples, the Jain Derasar, and the Sikh Gurudwara.

We took this action because Gandhiji would have wanted us to do it, to show respect for all religions.

Four incidents I still remember vividly. One was the tragic death of a child friend, about ten years old; while playing cricket and running for the ball, he was crushed under a double-decker English bus. Needless to say, my mother was much concerned about my state of mind at that age; I was about eight years old. But time heals all wounds, mental as well as physical, especially when one is young. About the same time, English teenagers with BB guns visited our neighborhood to shoot pigeons; that was quite a depressing sight. After a few pigeons were killed, one of the parents convinced the boys to go somewhere else.

The third incident happened probably when I was ten. Chiman, roughly the same age, absconded from his family because his father punished him. His family tried to find him without success. Six months later he showed up, darkened and skinny. Later he recited his story of living in Delhi with runaway kids his age. Once he was stabbed in the stomach, and he would proudly show his wound to his friends in Mumbai.

The fourth incident occurred when I was about twelve years old. Our merchant tradition followed the ritual of worshipping business books (Chopda Poojan), also known as Lakshmi Puja (worshipping the goddess of wealth) during Diwali, the festival of light. It used to happen late at night on Diwali and would last several hours, ending around four in the morning. During the early night, the employees would recite funny stories, and older folks with experience would boast about their overseas experience, particularly in Burma (now Myanmar) and Indonesia in matters of riches and beautiful girls with long hair.

Around six or seven in the morning of the Hindu New Year, we would go home to take a long nap. This particular morning, my brother Jasvantbhai was driving my father's Ambasador. I recall experiencing a jolt while driving through a crowded street; a child of six or seven had gone under the car. A big angry crowd gathered around us, punching the car. Luckily the child did not get crushed, and was alive with a few bruises. The father of the child was happy that the child had survived, praying and chanting God's name continuously. My brother offered money to help, but the father was just happy that the child was alive and would not accept any money.

Mumbai was a thriving business center. One of my father's closest friends during WWII was a man named Champakbhai, who helped my father in his work. Before India's Independence there occasionally were Hindu/ Muslim riots. One day while Champakbhai was returning on a horse cart from his office, he was attacked and killed near the mosque in Masjid Bandar. My father was devastated. Out of his own pocket he gave Champakbhai's widow 100,000 rupees, considered a very large sum at that time. It was all done anonymously.

Jasvantbhai always seemed to find his genealogy in a "princely" existence. He was quite precious and spoiled, being the first baby boy in my grandfather's family. As he was growing up, though intelligent, he did not do well in high school. He was more interested in participating in drama and dancing. He was a ladies' man, being fairer and good looking. He always watched out for his brothers, trying to keep us on the "right track." Once when I got lost, I must have been about five, and somehow separated from the family, Jasvantbhai began crying thinking I was gone for good. He was very attached to me when I was a baby. When I was about five years old, I came close to death when a car drove over my toes, missing me by a fraction of an inch. The driver was a doctor in a hurry. I remember being in pain, and my mother was furious at the driver. The candy man across the street came running to offer me candy to distract me from my pain. Luckily it took only a few days for me to recover.

Some of my fondest memories are of seeing American movies with my brothers at the Aurora Theater near King's Circle in Bombay. We enjoyed an array of Hollywood exports where the heroes always won, compared to Dilip Kumar films where the hero usually wasn't so successful. From Gary Cooper in High Noon to Gregory Peck in Duel in the Sun, to Burt Lancaster in The Crimson Pirate, and William Holden in Stalag 17 and Picnic, we reveled in these films. Their influence on me inspiring a desire to come to America one day cannot be underestimated. One of my favorites was The Thief of Baghdad with Sabu; we had a friend who went to see Hedy Lamar and Victor Mature in Samson and Delilah twenty times! Often my brother's friend Pratap Maniar, with good taste in movies and plays, would visit us and describe his experience of movies like Julius Caesar, with wonderful acting by Marlon Brando. Remember that my brother Jasvantbhai, very much in the business of entertainment, had produced and acted in many dramas. He had played the historic king Ashoka in one of the school plays. Tickets in those days were 5 annas for the first five rows, 10 annas for the center seats, and a rupee (16 annas) for the last half of the movie theater, which had cushioned seats. At that time 5 annas and 10 annas were equivalent to a nickel and a dime. The cheap seats always sold first and lines to buy tickets were usually chaotic. As a small nine-year-old boy, I was able to wiggle through the legs of most of the patrons waiting to buy their tickets and climb to the front of the line. I could then purchase tickets for my brothers and myself.

On occasion we'd have school field trips to the movies. Sometimes our teachers chose films that didn't always make sense for us to watch, like Lon Chaney Jr. in The Mummy's Ghost. Our whole school attended, possibly to learn some historical academics that related to ancient Egyptian history. But I got so scared, Jitubhai tied his handkerchief over my eyes so I wouldn't look at the movie screen. and I saw little of the film, crouched with my head in my lap. Then there was a 1951 movie, Bird of Paradise, starring Debra Paget and Andre Jourdan. My classmate, Indrajit, fell in love with Debra Paget, and could not get her out of his mind for weeks.

During the summer vacation of my middle and high school years, my uncle Mahendrakaka, about the same age as Jitubhai, who was quite fond of me, would visit Bombay from Bharuch. Our main activity would be to see Bollywood movies. Sometimes, during summer holidays, I would visit my paternal grandparents in Bharuch. My grandfather enjoyed feeding me the best mangoes in town. He would select the best langdo mangoes, a Bharuch specialty, from a karandio (a basket made out of cane/bamboo), cut them and hand me a slice at a time without stopping. This process would go on till I was completely full, and even then he would try to convince me to have more. My grandfather once lived like royalty, with his own horse-drawn four-wheel carriage. The carriage driver Mahmad worked for my grandfather for decades. We would join grandfather in the evening for his walk near the shores of the river Narmada, while Mahmad drove the Victorian carriage slowly behind. My grandfather had to let Mahmad go after he sold his horse carriage when he moved to Ahmedabad. Mahmad was devastated, being out of a job and not able to support his family. When Mahmad visited us in Mumbai to find work, it was depressing to hear my parents inform him that they could not employ him.

I recall a trip from Bombay to Nasik, a pilgrimage spot, with my grandparents, Jitubhai, Mahendrakaka, and Kasinath, a Brahmin cook. I had the best appetite among the three youngsters. One early afternoon lunch, I had six churma ladoos; today I cannot eat even two. The trip was memorable since I could have died. One late morning we were bathing in the holy river Godavari. I was probably around ten years old, Jitubhai and Mahendrakaka around thirteen. I was in the water up to my chest. Taking a couple of steps further into a ditch, I started to drown. I would drop to the bottom of the river completely submerged and then bob up with barely my nose above the water and ask for help. Mahendrakaka and Jitubhai started to laugh, thinking that I was monkeying around. After a few jumps, Jitubhai came near me wanting to have fun. He started to drown though he, being slightly taller, found it a bit easier to keep his nose above the water. Finally Kasinath realized the seriousness of the situation. He had a dhoti in his hand that he was washing (a dhoti is a cloth about 7 yards/21-feet-long); he walked into the water and threw it at Jitubhai. Jitubhai held my hand and caught the end of the dhoti with his other hand. Kasinath then pulled the dhoti, bringing us to a safer level. Needless to say none of us knew how to swim at that time.

Jitubhai was the skinnier of my brothers. He was eminently more popular among his friends. He often captained his school cricket team. In fact, shortly after India's Independence, a British cricket team in Matunga challenged the Indian boys to a cricket match. The match was like something out of India's movie Lagaan. Jitubhai sent boys to gather some of the best players he could find among our friends. The Indian boys ended up beating the British fellas by a close score. I was too small to play, but I remember the pride we had of actually defeating our British challengers.

Both my brothers helped me in many ways. Most importantly, they took care of my father's business so that I could pursue my own dreams and not get drafted into the family business. This ultimately allowed me to go to America to study. My father admired me from my early childhood. One day after lunch, he was very angry for some reason with my mother crying, and left for the office. I was about five years old, and asked my mother, "Who found such a husband that makes you cry? However he has the money to support us." My mother could not stop laughing. Another attribute my parents liked about me was that I was very careful about spending money. I had frugal habits. I think it came from the training of my mother. Jasvantbhai being the eldest, fairest, and best looking, was the darling of the family. They say in India that firstborns are spoiled. Later siblings get "used stuff," including clothes. My mother recognized the "over-spending" habits of Jasvantbhai, and made special efforts for both Jitubhai and me to be cautious in spending. My father echoed her instructions with his own words to me: "Be frugal and also be understanding of the plight of others. Visit the slums once a week to appreciate what you have." I never forgot the wisdom of my father's words.

My father's relationship with his three sons was somewhat remote. We had respect for him but we were fearful of him and most especially of his anger. He was satisfied with the communication skills of my brothers because they spoke with politeness in detailed conversation. But he complained that I spoke little, and if I did, it was usually in measured, diplomatic words. However he sometimes admired me for my answers to his questions. Once, after I had passed my Secondary School Certificate (SSC) exam, and first year college with first class (a feat no one had achieved in the whole family), he asked me to accompany him while he was having lunch. Then he asked me a question. "Who do you think is more responsible for your progress, your mother or myself?" I replied, "During my childhood years I would give credit to my mother. Now I would give credit to you during my teen years." He was very happy to hear that "diplomatic" answer.

During the freedom movement, there was a revolt in the Mumbai Navy yard in '46, a year before India became free. British troops with rifles in their hands in big trucks moved into the Navy yard, passing through Matunga on Vincent Road. Our residence was just a block away. When we saw the soldiers pointing rifles at us, everyone started running. But not Jasvantbhai; unafraid, he stood against a tree trunk, motionless. He was the one who inducted us into the Gandhian movement of Independence, away from the Hindu Mahasabha, a nationalist organization. Those were the days of idealism under Mahatma Gandhi's leadership that helped us form good samskaras.

I had the opportunity to see many plays in my young years, due to my elder brother's interest and frequent participation in plays. One play I distinctly remember; the title in Gujarati, *Philosophi No Bramm,* translated into English, was Mirage of Philosophy. The story was about a young man who was sent to a big city college for higher education after completing high school. The support came from the savings of his uneducated villager parents desiring a better life for their son. Their son learnt philosophy and acquired a taste for the higher Western way of life. He also had a rich girlfriend, whom he tried to impress with philosophical dialogue. When his parents visited him unannounced, he was angry and avoided them during their visit to ensure that the girlfriend did not meet them. The play ended with his disheartened parents questioning how their son could have lost the ancient cultural values, and blaming the modern Western education of the time. There was another perception about education among Gujaratis, who valued street smartness over school education. I recall my father, who had not completed even high school, who would say in Gujarati about a few unsuccessful educated friends, *"Bhanyo pan ganyo nia,"* meaning, getting a college degree is not sufficient to becoming street smart.

I recall a game we played as children on weekends and holidays in the '40s in India, before independence, a game of Non-Violent Resistance Movement (Satyagraha). Kids would get together in clusters, acting as freedom fighters. The objective for everyone was to get into a one-meter-square-sized area on the grass, called "the jail." The jail space would be a few feet away from about twenty-five kids who competed. Winners were those found in the square at the end of ten minutes. Smaller kids would not attempt to get into jail, since it was hard to compete with bigger and stronger kids. If I stayed with kids of my size, I could never get into jail. However, when I made an attempt, I succeeded in getting in the jail by finding a void, a little space for little me among the bigger kids. I was the happiest "contrarian" small kid to be part of a cluster of "giant" winners.

Jasvantbhai never finished his high school education and later joined my father in the family business. He was married by arrangement when he was twenty years old in 1950. My other brother, Jitubhai, was drawn to commerce as his area of studies. He married at twenty-three years of age. That was the end of his education.

Jasvantbhai around fifteen, and his future wife, Damu Bhabhi (Damu is a short form of Damyanti, and Bhabhi means sister-in-law) around twelve, were engaged in '45, because my mother was determined to bring her to our home when she saw her for the first time. She believed she had discovered the prettiest girl for her firstborn; she was also anxious to have the daughter that she never had. She came to stay with us after their marriage in '50, when we had already moved from Matunga to Sion into our own building. I remember she was a very bright young girl. Given an opportunity, she could have been a college graduate. She would teach me and help me solve my homework problems. I cannot forget her affection towards her two brothers-in-law.

The first year of marriage was rocky, which is not uncommon in joint families. There was friction between my mother and the newlywed couple. I do not remember the cause, but one late night we heard Damu Bhabhi crying and moaning. She had swallowed iodine medicine, normally used for external wounds, in an emotional attempt to end her life. Immediately my parents called the family doctor, Dr. Patadia, living just a few houses away. She was induced to vomit to get the stuff out of her system. I suppose my mother, appreciated and admired by the larger family, was also learning to be a caring mother-in-law.

Damu Bhabhi became so precious in the family after she became pregnant, my mother would ask us to go with her just to make sure that nothing happened to her. She gave birth to my niece, Bharti, in '52. Bharti quickly became the apple of the eye of our family. My mother, with the three boys, never had a daughter of her own, so Bharti became even more precious and a delight. My father appreciated getting "Laxmi," the Indian tradition of having a granddaughter bring even more good luck.

When Jitubhai was a teenager, he was connected to a penpal named Olga, a German girl, through a magazine. After WWII, because Germany had lost so many men in the war, the women were literally desperate to connect with men in other countries. Olga had a friend named Doris, and she became my penpal. Our letters became a sharing of feelings, dreams, and cultures. Initially I found it fascinating to communicate with someone who lived so far away in a country I had never visited. Jitubhai and I would sometimes even share our thoughts about the two women we were writing to.

Jitubhai while in college fell in love with a Punjabi girl named Kanta. When my mother and Jasvantbhai found out Jitubhai was thinking of marrying a Punjabi girl, they convinced him not to go forward, considering cultural complications. Jitubhai never married her, though they remained friends. In India at that time, parents had a much greater say about children's potential marital partners due to economic dependence, unlike in Western traditional families. Eastern cultures differed from Western cultures because kids listened to their parents because they respected their opinions and the wisdom of their elders. Extended family ties were stronger. Such family traditions existed once in the U.S., but much less today.

A few months later, Jitubhai married a Gujarati girl named Saroj, who attended the same school we went to. Soon I was welcoming three more nieces. Damu Bhabi gave birth to Daksha and Nayana. Then Saroj Bhabi gave birth to Jagruti almost immediately after Nayana was born. Saroj Bhabi and I were closer because we were almost the same age. I enjoyed culinary benefits from both my sisters-in-law because they were both great cooks. Since my brothers' marriages had been arranged by their families, I looked toward my future marriage also being arranged. However, our family tutor always thought I would go far. It was therefore natural for me to wait until I finished my education before I took a walk down the aisle of matrimony. We were a close-knit family. Imagine an old Ambassador car with Jasvantbhai driving, Jitubhai with Jagruti on his lap, Nayana on my lap on the front seat, the two bhabhi's, mother, Bharati and Daksha on the backseat. We travelled far and near.

I was the only one in my family drawn to math and science. When I told my father I wanted to go into engineering he was not really supportive, because for one thing, it meant I would possibly be going out of town to study. To satisfy his concerns, my father consulted a learned man in the community and asked him about my future plans. The wise man told my father, "You must not worry about engineers. They will never starve." His implication was that merchants usually suffer ups and downs in the market, but there is always a need for engineers, no matter what their line of work. This piece of advice always stayed with me. That is, a wise diversification will always allow one to navigate the ups and downs of the world's business moods.

At first I was an average student in high school with little ambition. But once I made up my mind I wanted to be an engineer, my SSC state exam reflected a committed student. I knew I had to do well because there were not a lot of engineering schools in India and they all had tough entrance requirements, usually looking for first-class applicants. Two of my best friends in high school had opposite philosophical outlooks on life. Harshad Mehta was a bright student and an ardent idealist. Another good friend and classmate, Kishore Tejura (Teju), was a refugee from Pakistan. He was also a good student, but he was a pragmatist because his family had lost so much during the Partition. He had seen atrocities committed by Muslims on Hindus and vice versa. I suppose I was a blend of Kishore and Harshad, part idealist and part pragmatist. Despite our different outlooks on life, we all got on quite well.

In my last year of high school I was fortunate to score first class and be in the top 10 percent of my class. Those of us who did were admitted to many of the best schools in Bombay, which included St. Xavier's College and Elphinstone College, both top-rated. I chose Khalsa College in Matunga, which was a good college established by the Sikh community, but not as esteemed as Xaviers or Elphinstone. However, Khalsa College was only ten to fifteen minutes from our house by bike. The other schools would have involved longer time-consuming commutes. Even as a young man I was concerned about budgeting my time. This conscious desire to save time and resources would stay with me in later life. For example, I still believe in living close to work. When I began investing in properties, I purposely chose places that were near where I lived. My wife and I have never moved our home far from our business to "Timbuktu" locations like Palos Verdes and Malibu, in spite of being able to afford it. Currently, with the clogged arteries of traffic in major cities like Bombay and Los Angeles, my friends complain that what took half an hour commute time now takes over an hour.

Choosing a college close to home helped me succeed. My classmate Harshad, who graduated with much better grades than mine, chose Elphinstone. Because of his long commute, the fact that many of his classmates at Elphinstone were very talented, and because students often made fun of those who were bookworms as a way of showing intellectual superiority, he did not do as well as he had hoped. I, on the other hand, by choosing Khalsa College, scored among the top of my class in my second year inter-science curriculum. I had the psychological boost of being among students who admired my abilities and did not make fun of me studying harder. In the end, Harshad could not secure the first class required to be admitted to an engineering college. Kishore, my other classmate got a degree in science. I got a degree in engineering.

My final exams in inter-science were memorably challenging by something that blind-sided me one night when my brother Jitubhai told me in confidence that my father had a Goan mistress. It was not uncommon in our community that after acquiring wealth, businessmen would have a mistress. I had heard of this going on in many families. I must have cried for a couple of hours at

Jitubhai's news. It was with a mixture of grief and resentment that I learned this family complication during the week of my exams. I was in many ways a naive young idealist, living in a new India. We had recently gained our national independence and though Gandhi had been killed, his exemplary life of moral truth was something all Indians admired. Gandhi was even compared to Jesus, Buddha or Mahavir. We didn't know about Nehru's escapades with other women at the time. This was an idealistic India where our teachers in school spent summers in the villages volunteering to teach village children to read.

Even our movies were idealistic. Films like Dilip Kumar's Shaheed, about a patriot, and Devdas, or Raj Kapoor's Jagate Raho about social flaws, and Balraj Sahani's Do Bigha Jamin, movies about poor men in a rich society, spoke to us about the beauty of our country and its limitless potential. As an engineering student, I had traveled with my professors to Punjab to see the tallest dam in the world. I had seen Tata's impressive iron mills in Calcutta and power stations in Gujarat. As high school students, we had visited the "Somnath" temple, built with the blessings of India's great statesman, Sardar Patel, which had been destroyed by the Muslims hundreds of years earlier. It was a vibrant time for a country whose future seemed unwritten and endless. The fact that my father had another woman on the side was a crushing blow at a very inopportune time. But life went on. I completed my exams and gained admission to India's top engineering school in Poona.

It was about this time that I stopped writing to my penpal Doris. Her letters had become more and more intimate, as if she had fallen in love with me. I realized the impracticality of such a long-distance relationship was not good for my ultimate goals. I therefore stopped writing her, thinking I would never hear from her again. Poona Engineering School was an Englishmen's college. Situated on the Moola Mutha River, it was a genteel campus of boat clubs, tennis, and cricket, all of which appealed greatly to us students. The climate was ideal. The professors were exceptional. Even the students represented a diversity of countries and religions. Soon after I arrived in Poona, I was told by my family I had also received admission to the Chemical Technology College (CTC) in Bombay. Because this college was close to my home, I reluctantly returned to Bombay to begin courses at CTC.

After a few days of attending classes at CTC, I got very depressed. I really didn't like the smell of chemicals, two of the professors, and the school. We were only four students in the class, and one of them was repeating the first year, since he had failed the first time. It was much smaller than Poona and the classes were terribly boring. I would read the Gita just to get out of my depression. Even my mother and Damu Bhabhi could see that something was wrong. When they asked me about my mood change, I confessed to them how much I liked Poona. After listening to my heartfelt longings, my mother suggested that I contact the Poona College and see if I could return. With much trepidation I wrote to Dalvi, one of my Maharastran classmates in Poona. Two days later Dalvi wired me saying, "Your seat hasn't been given away!"

I was exultant! Some of my happier moments in Poona still tower in my memory. Poona has historically been a learning center in India. It is a town of Brahmin idealists and intellectuals, influencing academia. It is significant that Gandhi was imprisoned by the British in Poona's Yerwada Prison. When I attended the Poona Engineering College, there was an expression, "Poona cha Paus Ani – Poona chi Pori, Visvas Nako Kara," which means, "Never trust Poona's rain and Poona's girls," meaning that both were so unpredictable.

Nikita Krushchev and Marshal Bulganin visited Poona from the Soviet Union when I was doing my first year engineering. They passed in a motorcade, with no security, going about 20 miles an hour down streets lined with students throwing flowers. I threw some flowers plucked from a nearby plant at them in celebration, and I can still see Bulganin wiping his right eye from the sap of the flower stem. It's amazing how openly great leaders traveled so freely, compared to the high security we see now post-9/11. The senior students at Poona threw water balloons at the freshmen as a sort of initiation at the beginning of the year. At the student hostel where I was staying, we had a fellow from Africa who ran for our track team. A Jewish student named Solomon was our team captain. The African student was so fast that during our Holi Festivals, where

Hindus slap colored powder on each other, he would tease us and say, "You want to color me? Then you've got to catch me!" No one even tried to catch him. During one of our track meets he beat all the competition, but unfortunately crossed the white boundary line too soon and the judges disqualified him. Solomon protested, but it was useless.

At Poona I had a classmate, Kumar Patel, who also came to America and invented the carbon dioxide laser, the workhorse of all laser technology, certainly in medicine and defense. During our field trips, political views would often be discussed. Kumar, a Gujarati, would put down a fellow Maharashtrian student, an admirer of a warrior king, Shivaji, stating that he also looted Surat, a thriving city of the time in Gujarat. Challavala, a Muslim from Bombay, stated the views of his imam that India would soon disintegrate, and Prime Minister Nehru would go mad. Then another student quoted Sardar Patel's words, heard by a close associate of Sardar, that a civilized country like India was ruled by "Jangali" people, meaning the boorish heartless British, and we Indians were stupid to be ruled by them.

After passing my first-year exams at Poona, my older brother Jasvantbhai moved from Bombayto Ahmedabad with his family. I was encouraged to follow him. I was not quite sure about it, but I was partly responsible for his relocation. My father had invested in a Bollywood studio making movies in those days. Invested is really the wrong word; he basically lost money in the studio and it siphoned off quite a bit of our family wealth. My brother Jasvantbhai got some assignments working around the studio and it was there that he met a Muslim actress named Naz, and started having an affair. When my father heard of it, he was very concerned, fearing this new woman could ruin not only my brother but the entire family's fortune. Seeking advice for the predicament, my father and mother ironically turned to me, the youngest of their three sons. By now I seemed to have the reputation for being moreintelligentand "stable." My opinion expressed to my father about this new female interloper was typically Rajput: "Move." Move my brother to Ahmedabad, away from Naz. Our grandfather gave the same advice.

My father liked the advice because part of his textile business was based in Ahmedabad. By sending his son there, my father could also support his business, in a way killing two birds with one stone. My parents suggested that I transfer to Ahmedabad in '56 to be with my brother, Bhabhi, and my nieces, for whom I had great affection. So I enrolled in LD Engineering College in Ahmedabad.

It was not easy at first. The food at the student hostel in Ahmedabad was terrible. The rotis in the mess hall in comparison to the rotis at Poona were like "kadi," rubber-like elastic and hard to chew. There were flies and ants in the sugar bowls. When we complained about the flies, the kitchen workers retorted, "Flies in the sugar? What do you expect, an elephant?" Professor Kulkarni was the rector of the hostel. He was also a corrupt man. He wouldn't let any student eat outside the hostel mess because he was getting a bribe from the mess food suppliers. The end result was that when I graduated from Ahmedabad, I weighed 120 pounds. When I was attending school in Poona, I weighed 140 pounds!

One of my friends at the hostel was Ravindra Badker, who remained a close friend and was in close proximity in Los Angeles for the rest of our lives. He had also moved to Ahmedabad when I returned to complete my schooling. With Ravindra, a Maharastran from Bombay, there was a common background. His father also had a mistress. Though Ravindra was older by a couple of years, we often went out for entertainment in Ahmedabad during the holidays. We were fellow travelers to Bombay. We studied together, we compared notes, and both of us planned to visit the U.S. after we graduated. Even transportation from Ahmedabad's LD Engineering College was a problem. Jasvantbhai purchased a German-made NSU scooter for me to visit them. After two accidents, one of which resulted in a burn on my leg from the scooter's silencer, the other being a fractured wrist, I gave the scooter back. Ravindra was with me when I had my first accident. He escaped injury, being taller.

It was about this time (post-Independence) that India was struggling with how it would divide the country into represented regions. There were two choices. Division would be based on language or on geographical sections. Because of strong language-based allegiances, many Indians wanted separate areas for Gujarati-speaking peoples, Punjabi-speaking, Tamilian-speaking, and so on. Sardar Patel, Gandhi's right-hand man, had convincingly argued earlier that language-based divisions in India would degrade nationalism. Nehru, Gandhi's chosen prime minister, had agreed with Patel. Patel had passed away in '50 due to heart failure. Nehru was touring India in '57, even visiting Gujarat to promote a division of India based on geographical regions of a north, south, east, center, and west respectively. How powerfully Nehru spoke to the crowds, standing up and emotionally proclaiming, "I am a child of the freedom fight! I spent time in jail with Gandhiji and I know what's good for India!"

But the pressure for language-based divisions was too great. Students were encouraged to strike for it. Some Gujaratis pushed for their own state more for political gain than anything else. Ultimately language-based regions were chosen, and the area of Bombay state, which under the British had included Bombay and Gujarat, was separated into the two regions of Maharastra (which included Bombay) and a separate state of Gujarat. I still believe these language-based regions throughout India have hurt the nation and its unity, just as Sardar Patel warned. For Gujaratis today in Bombay, it actually has become a disadvantage. This is because of people like Bala Thackeray, a "city boss" in the tradition of America's "Tammany Hall" days, who controlled a good part of Maharastra using hate or repelling outsiders rather than embracing a philosophy of inclusiveness.

We had good times in Ahmedabad. Besides Ravindra (Ravi), I made a number of good friends at the college and continued to play tennis and ping pong with players like Sudhir Kakkar. I became so good at ping pong I played against the university champions and did quite well. Had I not gone to Ahmedabad College, I would never have enjoyed special days playing with my nieces or the good home-cooked food of my extended family. The college social event of the year was the "engineers' banquet," which I helped organize.

But probably my most dramatic image of Ahmedabad College was my final exams. Finals were held during the months of March and April, just before the monsoon and the hottest months in the region. The building in which we would take our exams had an asbestos roof with 110-degree temperatures outside and 120-degree temperatures inside. To cool us down, peons moved up and down the aisles toting buckets of ice water that we drank every 15 minutes. The water was quickly lost through our pores as perspiration. This torture went on for three hours. When it was over, you felt as though you really had taken an exam. There was an oral exam conducted by a visiting examiner, Professor Gundda from Poona University. I was informed that he failed half of the class, including me, in his subject, machine design. He wanted to prove that the professors at LD Engineering College were not as good as in Poona. However, luckily the college made an exception and passed most of us.

After I completed my studies at Ahmedabad College, I was offered a job with a French shipping company based in Bombay. However, with too little time to think it over, I opted to take admission at Ann Arbor College in Michigan in the United States. I recall running into Kumar Patel, my classmate at Poona, at the United States Information Services (USIS) office, which was where many Indian graduate students went before going to the U.S. He had received a scholarship to Stanford as a first-class graduate from Poona. We would cross paths again in America much later.

In many ways, my choice to study in the United States was like my family's pattern of moving to better ourselves. Certainly America seemed like a land of opportunity. Also, I may have wanted to achieve my own success in going away from the imperfect world of my family. Note that I, an idealist, believed then in perfect marriages, not knowing that perfection in life is extremely rare. I was certainly ignorant of the flaws of my role models like Gandhi, Nehru, and Einstein. I had not even completed twenty-two years of my life on this planet. There was so much to learn, not just in fields of my interest like science, but also about sociology and even more important, human psychology. Decades later, I would learn that India had a lot more to offer about human psychology than anywhere else.

Three countries were usually chosen by students for advanced studies: the U.S., Germany, and England. Most students chose America, because to go to Germany, a student would have to learn the German language. England didn't seem to offer the financial support that American schools did. The report on U.S. schools was that you got your degree and you could get a job and pay off your tuition at the same time. I remember an advertisement at USIS that said, "In America you work for an hour and you have earned your food for the day. When you work for a month, after your expenses are paid, you have earned yourself a flannel suit." Indians also benefited coming from the country of Mahatma Gandhi. Gandhi was admired all over the world. People therefore saw Indians as being non-violent and honest. This brought other opportunities along with our future education. Still, my parents were reluctant to send any of their children out of India to school, much less to America. Part of the reason was that two local boys had gone overseas to study, with disturbing results. Natoo Doshi, a studious and bright boy who was the same age as Jasvantbhai, had gone to England. When he returned from his schooling he had become the "perfect Englishman," dressing, speaking, and acting like one. Unfortunately this included breaking almost all contact with his family, purposely ignoring them, and isolating himself in Delhi. Navinchandra Kothari was another young man who went to England to study medicine, and came back so depressed that he seemed to be mentally unbalanced. Eventually he recovered after some time and married a young girl in a local family. But both men made negative impressions in our community.

I was determined to go to America, to a state named Michigan. Michigan had a large Canadian immigrant population, and the second largest was Indian. It was a funny-looking state that on a map looked like a glove surrounded by several large bodies of water called the "Great Lakes." From India, Michigan was about 10,000 miles travel.

It was indeed an unforgettable journey.

With my father and mother at the departure dock, August 13, 1958.

Mother, Sarojbhabhi, aunts, and a cousin on my right, Damubhabhi with Nayana and aunts on my left; most of them, including the kids from the Doshi clan, were curious to see the ship Vietnam, August 13, 1958.

CHAPTER 2

THE JOURNEY

"I love the sea and have always found my journeys by ship a strange parallel to my life. It is this journey that we all must make to find our truth ..."

Mahatma gandhi

I had never traveled by boat, other than travelling in a sailboat to cross the Narabada River in Bharuch, as we used to fondly call the big river Narmada, literally "river of joy", that flows across three western-central regions of India. That was a scary experience, when the boatmen had difficulty controlling the boat sails in a very windy, typhoon-like afternoon; that could have been a disaster for my grandfather and most of his family. I had also never been out of the country before. Now I was going to America, following in the footsteps of many Indians before me, and even more who would soon follow.

I had traveled by plane in India from Bombay to Bhavnagar, a short flight of about an hour, with my father and his partner, Pranjivandas Gandhi, on Mistri Airlines, one of the first airlines in India. I recall the smell of airconditioning on the plane and luxurious seating. It was a three-wheeler DC-3. To go to your seat you had to literally climb uphill. They were the noisy aircrafts with radial piston engines that drove the propellers. We often put cotton balls in our ears to make the ride more comfortable. This was, of course, before I took up studies in aerospace engineering in the USA!

In many ways my coming to America by boat was an experience where I fully encountered the adventure of travel. As so many immigrants to America had arrived by boat to Ellis Island on the East Coast and Angel Island on the West Coast, I felt it was natural that much of my journey was by sea. The last leg of my travel to the United States would be by the famous "clipper ship of the sky" airline, Pan Am. To thoroughly appreciate my entrance into America, a bit of a history lesson is in order about Indians who had previously migrated to the U.S. The earliest recorded Indian coming to "the Land of Opportunity" was a man from Madras who visited Massachusetts in 1790. Since he was from South India, we can only imagine that he was most likely looked at with some curiosity as being a blend of dark-skinned African with European features. I only make this point because as late as 1920, an American judge from New Orleans wrote that he was troubled to see Indians looking like Europeans only with dark skin. This fact apparently rattled certain whites who based much of their apparent "Social Darwinism" on a belief that justified the white races of the world controlling the dark races.

Whether we want to admit it or not, much of American history is riddled with persecution or prejudice against immigrants. Americans' prejudices were often shown in their attitudes toward darker-skinned people. True, some light-skinned immigrants, like the Irish, suffered blatant "no Irish need apply" experiences on the East Coast, but this was probably encouraged by predominantly negative British propaganda about them. When I arrived in the U.S. in 1958, there existed a hierarchy of ethnic groups and races. Being from India, I was well aware of my country's caste system. I quickly recognized that America also had its own caste system; it was just "unspoken." In first place were the white, blue-eyed, English, Germans and Scandinavians. In second position were the slightly darker Irish, Italian, Spanish, Greek and Mediterranean groups. In third place came the Jews, Egyptians, Syrians, and Middle Easterners. In fourth place were the Chinese, the Indians, and other Asians. In the last and fifth position were the blacks. This "caste" system was essentially based on skin color. I remember a comment made by my fellow engineer at Hoffman Engineering in the early '60s stating that white Americans have more dislike of American blacks than the blacks from overseas. In his view black Americans are more violent. It reminds me of a similar situation in India or Nazi Germany or in the story of the Mahabharata.The hate and prejudice are much greater when both groups are culturally closer.

In the Asian category, Indians had an edge due to their education, which was comparable to a British education and that too in English. These views about America's racial caste system were based upon conversations in the early '60s that I had with fellow students and later fellow engineers in corporate America. There were plenty of exceptions to these racial rankings based on an individual's qualifications and capability. Two Indian exceptions that I can recall were Dr. Pravin Bhutta and Dr. Kumar Patel. They were more accepted because not only were they brilliant in their fields, but also they projected themselves with absolute confidence. I believe humility in those days, maybe even now, was often confused with timidity and lack of confidence. Those attributes ultimately gave them a greater economic and position advantage when they were looking for employment. Historically, a number of Indians had been brought to the U.S. by seafaring captains to serve in their households as servants. Indians were also used to work with the Chinese for Leland Stanford and Collis P. Huntington as they constructed the western side of America's transcontinental railroad through California's Sierra Nevada Mountains. Many Indians were working in America to send money home to their families. There are records of bright turbaned Indians participating in Fourth of July parades in the mid-1800s in some American towns. With exposure to these Indians, a number of American scholars became interested in Indian culture, history and philosophy. Terms like "Boston Brahmin" and "Pundit" came to be used in American literature.

The Indians found their greatest negative reception in the Asian Exclusion League (AEL), a movement that tried to prevent Chinese, Japanese and Indians from coming to America in the 1800s and early 1900s. Let me tell you a little more about this "League"! Some Sikhs came from India, for example, after their lands were taken from them by British landlords who had imposed heavy taxes on the land. Taxes were collected even if there was a drought, which often destroyed Indian farmers and was used as an excuse for the British to confiscate property. The movie *Lagaan*, starring Amir Khan, was based on such stories, and involved a cricket match between the British rulers and local peasants. The Punjabi Sikhs came to America from India's rich agricultural areas of the northwest. They were excellent farmers and well suited for the West's agricultural lands. However, the Sikhs were often given land in America that was not "fit for white men to farm." Sometimes whole towns, like Bellingham, Washington, conspired in 1907, together with the town's mayor, to kick Indians out of their cities. In this particular town, the AEL helped start a riot, and 500 white men attacked Indian dwellings and work places while the police stood by and did nothing. Songs like "White Canada" became popular with growing acceptance of the AEL in America's west and northern regions. For many years U.S. immigration laws only allowed whites to become naturalized citizens. Indian women were forbidden to immigrate because it was feared this would encourage Indians to establish roots in the U.S.

To get around immigration laws, groups of Indian farmers contracted land deals with white farmers as a co-op. However, sometimes these deals would be bitterly terminated when the white farmers claimed the whole crop was theirs at harvest time. Once Britain and America entered WWII, British spies in the U.S. often kept watch on Indians, fearing they were plotting against the British over Indian independence. This surveillance often got Indians deported from America. Towards the end of the Second World War, President Roosevelt started to lift immigration restriction on Asians. The Chinese Exclusion Act was eventually repealed, but the Indian Regional Exclusion Act got stuck in Congress's committee web. Roosevelt had to send his personal envoy to the Hill to lift the ban on Indians. Indian immigration didn't really pick up until after the Immigration Reform Act was passed, making immigration a little less racist and a little more equitable.

During the '40s and '50s many foreign students, including Indian students, had been coming to the U.S. However, the majority of Indian students had the intention of returning to India to work and to be with their larger families. It wouldn't be until the late '50s and '60s, when the space race with the Soviets was initiated and the Vietnam War was put in high gear, that Indian immigration picked up momentum. During this period, America found itself with a shortage of engineers and doctors, and well-trained Indian engineers and doctors coming from Indian universities established by British rulers were given an opportunity to establish roots in the U.S.

I was coming to America for postgraduate studies, leaving Mumbai on August 13, 1958. Often ignorance is bliss, since I had never thought about leaving my closely knit family and how I would miss the good home-cooked food prepared by my Bhabhis. I had never thought about the money I would need to support myself in a faraway country, and was still dependent on my family. I was carrying about $2,000 worth of traveler's checks and required tickets for the various modes of transportation. My brother Jasvantbhai helped me pack my bags. I would be traveling via a French shipping company. I had been informed to fill a large metal trunk with books and possessions, and this would be sent through freight storage by the shipping company all the way to America. The French line told us to limit our other baggage to three bags. I had one large bag that we filled with food for the journey. Another bag was filled with clothes. A third bag I used as a small carry-on. As a vegetarian, I had theplas, khakras, and sweets in my food bag. My older brother also put a sari (a garment women in India wear) in my clothing bag. What he had in mind for me I wasn't totally sure at that time. A rich gold-color, embroidered silk sari later on would come in so handy when making new girlfriends.

That summer Jasvantbhai taught me the four-step "fox trot" and the three-step "waltz," "rumba" and "samba." He thought it might be useful in America. He was himself an excellent dancer and a good teacher, so I became quite good. Later I attended classes at the Bombay dancing school. Before I left, my father took me aside one night and with a piercing glance said that I should be like Gandhiji on this trip. "What does that mean?" I asked. "You know what it means. It means don't indulge in alcohol, meat, and no relationship with women." My brother Jasvantbhai, who had already put the sari in my trunk, cut my father off, saying, "Motabhai, those days are gone!" And then turning to my father he said, "You shouldn't ask Navin to do something that will handicap him or will hinder his social interaction! Let him use his judgment. You know he is intelligent enough." My father wasn't too impressed, and reemphasized his advice to me. I already knew about Jasvantbhai's affair with a Muslim actress, because my father had sought my advice on what to do about it. Perhaps because of his affair, Jasvantbhai was feeling guilty and felt that I should also have fun in my life. Maybe my father saw in me the potential to become very successful in America. The last thing he wanted was some woman or drink to derail my success. As we left for the docks in Bombay, my father's words still rang in my ears. During those days, members of the whole family would come to wish a happy and safe journey, a journey to the country farthest away from Bombay. Members of the family included uncles, aunts, and their children. The Bombay dock, where the ship had arrived, was clean but crowded with people. There were at least twenty students leaving for England or America for higher education.

The name of the French ship taking us to Europe was the *Vietnam*. Looking back I suppose it was ironic. Here I was, an Indian man coming to America aboard a ship bearing the name of a war that was yet to involve America. Perhaps more ironic is that the Vietnam War would have a future destiny for me in my own business endeavors. I was in tourist class on the ship, in one of the bottom levels. The top levels were for higher-class passengers. The Vegetarian bill of fair on the boat was sadly wanting. My fellow vegetarian Indian travelers and I often went to the galley cooks and got them to give us potato soup, bread and apples to keep us from going hungry on the ship's non-vegetarian food we didn't and couldn't eat. The uncooperative French cook reminded me of the French cook played by Gerard Depardieu, in the movie, *The Life of Pi.* The kitchen and dining areas were stuffy and congested, with the smell of the dead fish I had experienced on the shore of the river Narmada. There were a few benches for boat passengers to sit and eat. The sound of the ocean waves was amplified in the lower economy compartment, caused by the resonating metallic walls.

With Jaswantbhai in the ship *Vietnam*, August 13, 1958, just before departure.

Three Gujjus (Gujaraties, Navin on the right) and one Sindhi (left) sharing jokes during the travel.

As it was August and summer, the journey was very warm. Some of my companions were a company of other Gujaratis. An older Parsi gentleman, probably in his late twenties, advised us all what to do and what not to do. There were two Muslim fellows from India who were always putting down Hindus for being weaklings or not being strong. Many Muslims in India consider themselves descendants from the Pastunes or Pathans in Afghanistan who had fought the British there. It is a pride they often wear on their sleeve, seeming to need to prove themselves all the time. My impression of these two fellows was that they were very aggressive and it would be wise not to cross swords with them.

We also had one American with us, a young man who enjoyed playing bridge with the Indians and Frenchmen. Two couples on board made quite an impression on me because they were racially mixed. One was a Frenchman with an African wife, which seemed very unusual to me. The other was a Frenchman with a Vietnamese wife, something I also found very different. Needless to say, the word around this part of the world was that many of the French were color-blind compared to other Europeans.

The Arabian Sea is often rough since it is relatively a shallow body of water. I got seasick quite a bit so I hardly stayed in my tiny cabin below the deck. The amplified noise created by the ocean waves made it quite difficult to sleep. Along with a few friends, I spent most of my time in the common area for all the passengers up on the deck. Sometimes we even slept there in the evenings when the night air was calm and balmy. For a while I was so afraid of the high waves of the ocean, or that I could be robbed or taken advantage of, that I would come back to my cabin and spend the night. These feelings dissipated with time on my trip. We had to be inventive to entertain ourselves on days with few activities, so we would share jokes of our time.

I remember even today how we tried to joke and laugh on the ship, even when there was not much else to be happy about! Some of the jokes we shared and found so funny then, even if I (and more so, you) might not even smile at now. Here are some of our "famously funny ones," basically sex-oriented.

A young couple in love, but not married yet, under the shade of a tree would describe their affections to each other. All the girl will allow is to let the boy hold her hand. Indian girls were well-trained to be disciplined, at least in those days, not to be physically interactive. So the more enterprising boy would propose, "Our mind and soul are one. Why don't we make our body one?" I do not think it is that funny, as we know the current generation is a lot more advanced in these matters.

How was the human alphabet discovered? During ancient times, elders wanting to devise methods of communication would observe people's activities. Vowels were discovered when a man and a woman were having sex. Consonants were discovered when a woman was delivering a baby.

A priest in a church proclaims, "I know that all of you are sinners; you must confess your sins so that the Lord can forgive you." He then pauses, and continues a few moments later, "Those of you, who are involved in 'He and She' physical activities, please gather in this corner." So a portion of the crowd gets separated in one corner. Then he repeats the same instruction about the activities of "He and He" and "She and She," and asks them to collect in two other corners. The priest is surprised to see one person left out. He asks, "Have you not committed any of these sins?" The man replies," Father, you did not mention 'Me and Me.'"

A Christian missionary, wanting to convert Hindus, stands on the steps of a temple and a crowd gathers around him. He then pulls out a photo of Krishna having the Raas Lila with Radha and Gopies (women devoted to Krishna) around him. He thunders, "Look at your God, a womanizer." Then he pulls out another photo of Hanuman, holding Gada with both hands, a weapon of the time, and his hands covering the lowest Kundalini chakra. He then says, showing some disgust, "Look at the hands of your monkey God, it is so shameful." Then he pulls out a photo of Christ, his arms extended with open palms, "And look at Lord Christ, so peaceful giving and wanting to love."

A mischievous Hindu from the crowd responds, "Sir, in reality your God is asking our God Krishna to share with him a woman or two, but Hanuman says your God needs to control his lowest chakra."

A note to my Christian friends and readers; my role model is Mahatma Gandhi. Therefore I share his views of having an equal reverence for all saints and gods of all traditions.

We used to share jokes with fellow students from Xavier College in Mumbai, while standing in line for a Hollywood movie playing in the Metro Theater close to the college. The humor of Indian Christians is quite well known. The famous tennis player, Vijay

Amritraj, an Indian Christian, was known for his joke sessions during the '70s in the tennis circle. I distinctly remember reading about Vijay's expertise in joke sessions, I believe, in *TIME* magazine. We Indo-Americans were so proud to see him play in torn shoes, almost winning the Wimbledon and the U.S. Open titles. Even more complimentary to Vijay were the words and expressions of the commentators, listened to and observed on the TV screen.

As stated earlier and later on, you will note my admiration for the blacks endowed with superior physical capability, and Americans for what they have achieved in America. However, Indians in India, and we on the boat, needed to feel good about ourselves. So I responded by telling the story of God's creation of humanity. "God started to make roti (human beings, metaphorically), but took it off from the fire in haste; it was uncooked and white. Then God tried again, and kept it longer on the fire. It was overcooked and turned quite dark. Only on a third try, the roti came out just right, golden-brown in color. So let us be happy with what God has given to us."

Sailing north of Somalia, Africa into the Gulf of Aden, we docked in Djibouti, a French colony on the coast of Ethiopia. Two Gujarati friends of mine hosted us there for the day and fed us quite well, which was an enjoyable experience for us starving men. This was because the ship's food was so unappealing. It was my first encounter with a "frozen culture," in other words, a Gujarati culture that had established itself and hardly changed for over fifty years. We were fed some wonderful food by the Gujarati community living there. But even though we would say we had had enough, "no" was an unacceptable answer to our hosts. As we were sitting in line on an 18-inch-wide long wooden plane (paatalo in Gujarati), we were forced to open our mouths and more food was stuffed inside. This was an old tradition in Gujarat that had long gone out of style, but in Djibouti, Gujarati culture from many years back seemed to be living on in a vacuum of time and space. The food was served on a large banana leaf, as they did in Gujarat. Everyone was wearing a Gujarati traditional dress, the women in saris and the men wearing dhoti.

Our ship officers had informed us with warnings that we should be very careful of our belongings and wallets. When we asked them to explain, they retorted that in some of the suburbs of Djibouti, thieves would take our wallets and because they run so fast we would never see our belongings again. I reflected on my old African track friend in Poona and how he taunted us on the Holi festivals. I realized that our hosts were telling us to be very cautious in matters of our valuables.

As we reached Port Suez, the boat was to continue to the Suez Canal while we embarked overland, to rendezvous with our ship on the Mediterranean. The next morning we were put into a car and brought close to the magnificent Egyptian pyramids at Giza. Many in the groups were not just Indians, but French and Vietnamese as well. We rode camels with red Muslim Egyptian caps on our heads. It was indeed a wonderful experience visiting one of the eight marvels of the world. Egyptians, like the car and camel drivers with whom we interacted, were very friendly, and kept repeating that the Egyptian leader Nasser and the Indian leader Nehru were good friends. The Egyptian music played in the car sounded so much like Bollywood music.

On camels and in automobiles, we were transported to Cairo in the evening. We had some of the best vegetarian meals there after being "starved" on the ship for so many days. For me, pita bread and spicy garbanzo beans was food from heaven. At the Cairo docks we reboarded the *Vietnam* and set sail for Marseilles. Sailing in the Mediterranean Sea was pleasant. I noticed that there were more women than men on board. On the calm seas, many of us students were invited to dance parties with the French women who had joined us on board from the French colony of Morocco. The French women were eager to dance with whoever they could. The foxtrot and ballroom dancing my brother Jasvantbhai had taught me before I left India suddenly came in pretty handy, though I could not converse with the dancing partners, since they spoke very little English and I could not speak a word of French. The next few days we compared our experiences on the dance floor. I remember a comment from the Parsi gentleman that he thought the legs of European ladies were a lot heavier than their counterparts in India. Just before our trip was to end, one of the Gujju friends asked me to loan him $150 so that he could travel safely to Florida, where he was to go to school. He promised that he would pay me back within a couple of months. That never happened. He would write a polite letter with unbelievable stories for not paying me back. That was my first lesson not to trust anyone in matters of money.

When we arrived in Marseilles and transferred to the train bound for London, I noticed the change in temperature. For the first time I enjoyed the cooler European climate. I reveled in the bread, cheese and pastries that we bought on our way. I noticed that the food in the food bag I had brought from India was all gone. With my budget always tight, I knew I'd have to be a bit frugal and watch what I spent on lodging and food from there to America. The differences in a European country and India were quite distinct — less populated, well-dressed people, much cleaner cities, luxurious trains, and lots of cars.

As I had a little time, I thought of visiting my pen-pal friend Doris in Germany. We had not communicated in several years, but I was curious to actually see her after having received so many letters from a country I could finally visit. Doris had sent me her photo when we started corresponding. Then I had sent her my photo with my three lifetime friends, Teju, Kishore Shroff, and Arvind. She responded, stating that my friends were good-looking, though not as handsome as me. My heart pounded reading those lines. However, it was not possible to visit her since I had to be in time at Ann Arbor to attend school.

four life long friends: Teju, myself, Kishore Shrof, and Arvind.

Photo of pen-pal Doris.

We boarded the French train from Marseilles going to Paris, exhausted from carrying our bags during the transition from the ship to the train. I recall removing my shoes in the train to stretch and maybe even take a nap. A middle-aged lady across from our bench closed her nose and stared at me. I recognized that she was signaling to me that it was not appropriate for me to remove my shoes, since my sweaty socks could smell bad. Note that it was understood that we could not communicate with each other. I immediately put my shoes back on, while getting her approval with a smile.

We had a few hours to spend in Paris, and we utilized them appropriately by visiting the Eiffel Tower, one of the Seven Wonders of the World, completed in 1889. Just in my first trip out of India, I was fortunate to have visited two manmade Wonders of the World: the Eiffel Tower in Paris and the Great Pyramid of Giza in Egypt. As an engineering student, all I can say about the Eiffel Tower was that it was indeed a magnificent sight to see and appreciate this modern engineering marvel, built by French engineers. I had already visited the Taj Mahal in India, one of the Seven Wonders, in 1957, so for a twenty-one-year-old young man, I thought myself to be quite fortunate.

To reach London, the French train was put into the bottom of a boat, known as a boat train. The boat then sailed across the English Channel to be unloaded at Dover. It was an intriguing sight to see an entire train in the belly of a ship. Reaching London, based on the tour planned by my travel agent, I had about a week before my departure to the States. I was advised by Jitubhai's friend Kishore Somani to stay at the YMCA because it was the least expensive residence. A young Englishman with a Cockney accent had traveled with us from Bombay, migrating back to England from India for good. He gave us all good advice on things to see and places to eat. I was also advised by another of Jitubhai's friends who had gone to London to study aviation. I met him on arrival and he was quite helpful. I was informed later that he had married an English woman and settled in England and become bald. Bald? "Marrying a demanding white woman and the climate are the causes," Jitubhai explained. I vividly remember wonderful South Indian food in London. In fact, I can't forget how good the masala dosas tasted in the restaurants there. My fellow travelers and I spent time in the London tubes en route to various sights like the British Parliament Building, Big Ben, the Tower of London, and Piccadilly Circus.

While in London I met a couple of German girls who were touring England, so we decided to see London together. They were quite pleasant travelers. I was complimented by some of the fellow Indians coming to America for graduate studies that I could have a "date with these girls" and cross the"barriers" of Indians mixing with Europeans. Certainly, my writings to Doris and getting to know her helped me find a connection to these German girls. Often it is in just finding a common ground of experience that allows people from different parts of the world to connect, regardless of culture, religion or creed. On my way to the airport from the YMCA, while waiting for a bus, I was obliged to get a ride from an unknown but very British English gentleman in his car. It was apparent that this polite gentleman admired Indian leaders like Gandhi and Nehru. Due to his curiosity, I had to answer his question, as well as I could, that I selected America over England because of better financial opportunities. I also had a positive impression of America based on the Hollywood movies I had seen in the Aurora theater near my home in Matunga, a suburb of Bombay.

As I headed toward Heathrow Airport to make my final journey to Michigan, I pondered the different lands and cultures I had already seen in my quest to study in America. In a way, I had touched a small part of some of the world's great civilizations. In coming from India, I had glimpses of Africa, Egypt, France and England. As an Indian, I brought with me an appreciation not only of my own rich culture, but I had seen a few others along the way. This new awareness or openness to cultures, even with its history of prejudice, is probably one of the keys to America's vibrancy. Unlike Djibouti, where I witnessed a community frozen in time, I was headed to a country that was always changing, and where so many roads converged for opportunities for immigrants to make something of themselves. Today I can distinctly differentiate India, a world within a greater world, from America, a country out of this world.

I had already spent about twenty days away from my family and my country, yet I was not homesick. However, I had mailed a postcard from London informing my family that I was doing well. Mentally I was enjoying every moment of these new experiences, meeting new people without getting bored. Physically, I was fortunate that I did not get sick even for a day. The fact that I can remember and write about these experiences indicates that the process was an important part of my life. Lifting off the runway in a blue-and-white Pan Am 707 enroute to Michigan, I wondered what challenges and successes awaited me in "the land of the free, and the home of the brave." It was indeed a wonderful and very pleasant experience traveling by plane compared to traveling on a French ship tourist-class, which was probably closer to the ship's lowest class.

CHAPTER 3

MY ARRIVAL IN AMERICA

"The United States is the end road of many dreams ... some are fulfilled ... some are changed ... some are shattered. But they still are dreams."

Thomas Edison

I had applied to several schools in the United States but ended up in Michigan. Why Michigan? Well, my friend Gunvant Mavani was trying to get a degree in chemical engineering there. We had attended junior college together in India so I took advantage of his help. I applied to Anne Arbor but also applied to a school in the UC system in California. The Illinois Institute of Technology and the University of Wisconsin were popular schools at the time because Midwestern universities seemed more helpful with scholarships for foreign students than schools on the East Coast. The California schools were popular because of the warm Mediterranean climate. Two of my other friends from India, Ravi Badker and Kumar Patel, were attending universities in California, at UCLA and Stanford respectively.

After I landed by plane in Detroit, toting a handbag and a suitcase, I grabbed a bus for Ann Arbor, which was a couple of hours journey from the Detroit airport. When we arrived, not too far from the university, the bus driver realized that I would need some help carrying the big bag to the International Student Center. The driver must have had some experience of bringing foreign students in the past. At that moment he saw a young black tall teenager walking down the road, and asked him to help me carry one of my bags. What struck me was that the young black man made no objection. I suppose the driver expected none; it was implied he would do it. Needless to say, I was very obliged to receive help from this young man.

The best experience right from the beginning, I recall, was meeting the student advisor, Mr. Klinger. Always smiling, very polite, and wanting to help, he was probably one of the most pleasant men I met during my stay in Ann Arbor. Perhaps he was trained to make foreign students feel at home and take good care of them. If that was the case, it worked. He then arranged for someone to take me to Gunvant Mavani's apartment, not far from the International Student Center. The university campus, with so many international students — and I must add, plenty of pretty girls compared to the engineering colleges of all boys in India — was quite inviting. Even the scenery of the campus, filled with colorful trees in the fall season and just the right temperature, was very attractive.

I recall my immediate shock about the costs of things in America. For example, a haircut in India would cost one rupee or less in 1958. In the United States the cost was a dollar, and that without any additional services like massage, as we would get in Mumbai! To give the reader an idea of the currency rate in '58, it was about 5 rupees to the dollar. So a haircut in the U.S. was five times the cost in India! If we include the time spent by the barbers in America and Mumbai (ten minutes and fifty minutes respectively), then the American barber made 25 times more than the one in Mumbai.

Most of the foreign exchange students tried to economize as best they could. I stayed with my friend Mavani for a few days. Mavani had three roommates, Dhorda, another Doshi, and Chadda; they were doing their PhD's in pharmacy. The five of us tried, like other Indian students, to simulate Indian cooking with what was available. The closest thing to chapatis was pita bread in those days. There was no yogurt available in Ann Arbor, so we would substitute it with sour cream, and make Gujarati shrikhand with sugar and spices like cardamom. We attempted to make bhel, which in the true sense was puffed rice with garbanzo noodles, peanuts, shredded onions, tamarind, brown sugar, cilantro, chutney, and other ingredients. In Ann Arbor, we made bhel with corn and wheat cereals, adding shredded onion and pizza sauce.

I enjoyed donuts, milkshakes, ice cream, and French fries. Within three months my weight jumped from 125 to 145 pounds. Ever since then, I've never gone below 150 pounds. Mavani's apartment was like Grand Central Station, where we enjoyed varieties of food based on the creativity of fellow Indian students. We bought the groceries in large quantities and when the food shopping was completed, we would call from a public phone and hang up immediately to save the dime used to call. A fellow student would then pick us up, with lots of grocery bags, in his car. The food Americans were eating in the early '50s, base upon my memory, is described with some humor below.

Pasta had not been invented. It was macaroni or spaghetti.

Curry was a surname. A takeaway was a mathematical problem.

A pizza was a leaning tower, though Shakey's pizza appeared in the mid-'50s.

Bananas and oranges only appeared at Christmas time.

All chips were plain. Rice was a milk pudding, and never a part of the dinner.

Brown bread was something only poor people ate. Oil was for lubricating, fat was for cooking.

Tea was made in a teapot using tea leaves and was never green. Cubed sugar was posh, and Americans had never heard of yogurt. Healthy food consisted of anything edible.

People who didn't peel potatoes were regarded as lazy.

Cooking outside was called camping; seaweed was not a recognized food. Sugar enjoyed a good press in those days, and was regarded as white gold.

Whisky a go-go was scotch and prune juice.

Muesli was readily available; it was called cattle feed.

Pineapples came in chunks in a tin, though pictures were seen in Hawaii.

Water came out of the tap. If someone had suggested bottling it and charging more than petrol for it, they would have become a laughing stock. Two things that families never ever had on their table in the '50s were elbows and hats!

Often I would call my family in India, person to person, then ask to talk to "Navin" (that is, me); they would get the desired message without expensive telephone costs. If a policeman caught us for any violation and tried to give a citation, we were told by the seniors to say, "No speak English"; then the policeman would often let you go.

Later Dhorda and I rented a room for 70 dollars per month (35 dollars per person) in a rooming house. The university asked me to take extra classes to qualify for graduate work. I renegotiated with them to take 32 units for a BS in electrical engineering. This would mean ten courses in electrical engineering, including the lab. When foreign students were admitted they were asked to take an extra semester, which was an additional 15 units to the 30 graduate-degree units required. So by renegotiating, I would receive first a second Bachelor of Science degree in electrical engineering in a year, followed by the Masters of Science in the electro-mechanical engineering program taking an additional 30 units of coursework. It would take one more year.

I was encouraged by seniors to put my name in for being invited for an orientation, Thanksgiving, and Christmas at the International Student Center. So I did. During the foreign students orientation in early September, we were taken to a wonderful park with giant Michigan trees in full bloom, a very pleasant experience. I was impressed with the diversity of the students. I remember a girl named Judy, part of a group of students that made sure foreign students were not only comfortable but learned the "American" way. She was a tall good-looking girl with dark hair, and always smiling. I had a good impression of students from the University of Michigan even before, since we had come in contact with them when the delegation from Ann Arbor visited Ahmedabad in 1957.

One of the things we were told was to speak clearly and slowly. In India, we always thought that to speak well in English, you needed to speak as fast as you could. The opposite is so in linguistics in the U.S. Pronunciation was quite different from that in India. Judy informed us that the habits of saying "thank you" and "much obliged" are the niceties of exchange in America and the lubricants of communication. Every foreign student had to take an English test, even engineering students, to see if we had a good grasp of the English language. It was a two-hour test with a multiple-choice section and an essay. I must have spent 50 percent of the test time on my essay on Mahatma Gandhi. I couldn't complete many of the questions I was asked. After taking the test, I thought I would fail, but to my surprise I passed and didn't need to take the English class. Perhaps it was because I wrote such a good essay on Mahatma Gandhi.

Later, as I came across students from different parts of America, I learned to distinguish the accent of students from New York, and students from southern states like Alabama. It was quite difficult for me to differentiate, for example, "all" and "oil" in the southern accent; they sounded the same to me. The southern accent also reminded me of the accent of Gujaratis coming from the place of my birth, Bhavanagar. They both are spoken leisurely. Another aspect I discovered was American slang in the English language. My parents would often address my grandfather as "Doha" in Gujarati, meaning an old man. A son in America often addresses his father as "old man." Often, American students would warn us not to use certain words like "rubber," that we called a pencil eraser in India. Rubber in America meant a condom. An Indian doctor friend visiting an elderly patient in Detroit hospital would inquire about his health. The patient would ask, "Come again?" since he did not understand the question. The doctor would leave thinking that the patient had asked him to come back again later. I am sure there were many more such misunderstandings between Americans and foreign students in the '50s.

Michigan and America were new experiences for me in many respects. It was a different climate and a different culture. Also, compared to what I went through in India, the educational system was very different. Overall it was enjoyable, because there was hardly any stress to pass the test. There was no need to memorize the stuff from the books, since often there were open textbook tests. There were over 350 students from India, mostly Gujaratis, and that was the second-largest foreign student population, after Canada. Having so many Gujarati students and some with their wives, there were occasionally dinner parties with delicious Indian food prepared by the ladies. My increased weight was one of the indicators of eating well. Eating very rich American food, including pizza, was the second reason. During the days of student orientation, when I played ping pong with Judy, her first reaction was that I was too aggressive as a player, since I *was* quite aggressive showing off my ping pong shots. She politely encouraged me to be more gentlemanly, especially playing games with ladies. Being frugal, my friends would tease me that for a date with a girl, I would spend only a nickel. Being friendship-based, a date would often involve drinking coffee and talking. Coffee didn't cost more than a nickel.

Up to this time I had never earned a penny in the U.S. Madhu was a fellow student renting a room in the rooming co-op. He was a muscular well-built Punjabi and a great cook. He made a very good potato curry by frying onions and then putting in slices of potatoes, eggs and spices. It was heavenly eating this with pita bread. One day Madhu asked me if I'd mop and clean the church floor in his place. It was more for the sake of experience than needing money. I agreed to do so. I was paid 1.25 dollars for four hours of mopping the floor of the church. I believe that was the first time ever in my life that I earned some money. The only time I made money in Mumbai was the money I received by selling a bundle of old newspapers given by my mother. Note that the minimum wage in America then was a dollar per hour, which was much better in terms of purchasing power compared to today's minimum wage, which is 7.50 dollars per hour. There is a bill in Congress to raise it to 10 dollars. I would argue that today's minimum wage should be over 35 dollars per hour if we were to measure using gold as a currency.

Many students were on stringent budgets and some were able to find work. But some foreign students had difficulties surviving. One extreme example was a Taiwanese student who had been missing for months. He had apparently arrived on a very stringent budget and then disappeared. Later on, he was found hidden in a nook of a church, feeding himself by stealing food from the church refrigerator. The church authorities and some NGOs later helped him to finish his education. This was the first experience I recall of American generosity.

Madhu later introduced me to a girl he knew named Sylvia Major, who wanted to go out with a foreign student. He thought she was unattractive and was not interested in taking her out. So I went out with Sylvia several times. She was a very pleasant girl, and the first girl I dated in America. I learnt a lot from her in matters of social interaction and dating. A year later, I discovered that Madhu had started going out with her and later married her. Madhu found her attractive later, probably because she had upgraded her looks with stylish clothing and makeup. It was only natural that as students experienced such a good lifestyle in the U.S., many wanted to settle there. However, the only way to do so was to acquire a green card. U.S. Immigration worked on the quota system in the '50s and '60s. Even with India's huge population, the U.S. only allowed 100 to 150 people legally in a year. It would take a decade to get a green card if you were lucky. One way around this was to marry a U.S. citizen. Indians were on the whole looked on somewhat favorably as law-abiding citizens. We never had problems of refugees in India, like other countries. We also had the advantage of coming from the land of Mahatma Gandhi, who was a sterling example of a decent Christ-like figure and a benevolent human being. Gandhi was one of the reasons the FDR administration pressured British Prime Minister Churchill to give independence to India.

During the Eisenhower administration and the time of John Foster Dulles as secretary of state, India's neutrality in matters of foreign affairs was not appreciated by the U.S. Dulles believed neutrality was unethical, since he thought there was no middle ground between right and wrong. America at that time carried the ball from the English as a superpower to maintain the balance in the Indian subcontinent, keeping Pakistan and India in check. Many foreign students didn't like the U.S. foreign policy. I remember two roommates in my co-op, Mario from Venezuela who was an art student, and another student from New York named Louie. They had a debate about who was more popular, Eisenhower or Picasso. Louie took votes from all of the co-op students and obviously Eisenhower won. Their debate went on for quite a while.

We would occasionally have dance parties in the co-op. One student from Algeria was an activist in political matters. He was elected president of the International Student Organization, designed in ways that resembled the United Nations. I learned a lot from him. For example, initially I was notcritical of Germany's rolein WWII because of my naiveté, because India had been ruled by the British, Germany's enemy in WWII. Later, when I learned about Nazism from this Algerian student and about the extermination of the Jews, I did not make the same mistake again.

One of the students living in the co-op was named Gary. He met a girl named Barbara at a party, fell in love with her, and they married and moved out to live together. A few months later we learned that Gary had killed himself because Barbara had left him. That was the first time I observed an unstable marriage that resulted in tragedy. Walter, another student living in our co-op, was also my classmate in an electrical circuit design course. A former army officer during the Korean War, he had a GI scholarship to get a degree in electrical engineering. The subject was very difficult for him to understand, in spite of my help in explaining some of the fundamentals of circuit design. Ultimately he gave up and left the school.

A few months later I received a phone call from an American fellow student, Marty Centala, introducing himself as my big American brother. This was because I had given my name to be invited for Thanksgiving and Christmas. We met for the first time at the International Student Center. He had a Polish background, and invited me for a milk shake and onion rings. This was a new delight for a vegetarian that I discovered, thanks to Marty. He was a student in mechanical engineering and was also a member of ROTC (Reserve Officers' Training Corps) in the Air Force. He was impressed that I could beat him so easily at ping pong. We became friends, double dated, and went to movies together. Marty always teased me about my old coat, an outer garment styled during the '30s and '40s. During my journey to the U.S., while in Cairo, I had bought a WWII coat for the cold climate. The vendor tried to sell it to me for 50 U.S. dollars. I told him I couldn't afford it at that price. He asked me how much would I pay. I said 20 dollars. So I was fooled by the vendor. Marty made fun of it, saying it was so old, from WWI. I later threw it away and got something more modern.

One thing I learned at this time was that a good way to attract girls for dating was to learn palmistry, because girls were always intrigued about Eastern traditions, and certainly were interested in knowing their futures. So I took out a book at the library by Charo on the subject. During that time it was also popular to compare people's faces to movie stars in Hollywood. It was natural for me to compare faces, and I became good at it. Predicting a brighter future and comparisons with Hollywood stars helped me make more friends.

Certainly Marty and his family appreciated my different offerings, like the reading of palms. So when I was invited for the first time to Marty's house for Thanksgiving dinner, I was asked to make an Indian dish. This was my first cooking lesson in Michigan. I decided to make shero, because it was the simplest preparation I had learned from experienced Gujarati students. To cook it, one first makes an oil of melted butter. Then you sauté cream of wheat and add milk and sugar, then heat this till it's a puree. Add cardamom and groundnuts, then let it cool down a few degrees above room temperature, and it is ready to eat.

It was the first thing I ever cooked, but people appreciated getting things from India. I gave a few gifts to Marty's family. During Thanksgiving vacation, Marty had invited quite a few girls and boys. We played shuffleboard. Marty wore a turban and became a snake charmer, playing an Indian flute I had given him as a gift from India. We had a rope with one end tied with an almost invisible fine black thread. I pulled the black thread when Marty played the flute. The rope rose magically against a dark background and in dim light, one would have to look very hard to discover the black thread. So we impressed a few girls and Marty's drunken uncles with the famous Indian rope trick.

One gift Marty's family loved was a hollow red bean (chanothi) about a quarter-inch in size, filled with small stamped ivory elephants, about twenty-five of them in the cavity. I had bought it from a handicraft store in Mumbai. Marty's father was a carpenter retired from the Ford Corporation and his uncle was a truck driver. During Christmas one year when I was invited to their house, Marty would walk over to the Christmas tree and pick off one of my tiny beans and open it to show Marty's relatives the tiny ivory elephants inside. His truck driver uncle, half-drunk, would exclaim in surprise, "Wow, do they grow those beans in India like that?"

Marty and I occasionally would double date. Once I had dinner with Ruth, a girl from the Netherlands majoring in biology, Marty and his girlfriend. After finishing dinner I took a few pieces of sopari (beetle nut). Ruth asked me for the same to try it out. Marty had tried it before.You could see that Ruth was laboring to chew the sopari with a funny expression on her face. Then she could not resist making a comment, "It is like chewing sweet wood; you and termites have similar food habits." Once I had double dated with a fellow student from the Middle East, Ali. Ali, with an overflow of hormones, started to be fresh with his date. She would politely say, "Stop it, Ali." Suddenly Ali became angry, stiff, and stayed quiet for the rest of the evening. Later, after dropping the girls, I asked him the cause of his anger. He replied, "I do not like she calling me stupid." So it does make sense to learn the right pronunciation, as we were told during the orientation. These are such good and pleasant memories.

Some unpleasant memories involved Dhorda while he struggled to get his PhD. At Michigan, I came across six students who had been studying for their PhD's for over five years. Some professors would use the foreign exchange students for cheap labor to do research work. Some of the students didn't mind because life in Ann Arbor was better than life in India. Some had no choice because they didn't have a green card. Dhorda had been doing his PhD in pharmaceutics for over three years. He was frustrated and he didn't like his advisor. Dhorda was paid meager wages, with the result that he was always short of money. In the summer of '59 he decided to go to New York and work for a drug company. He found a job but it didn't pay very well. Finally, after being frustrated with expenses in New York, Dhorda decided to come back to Ann Arbor. He tried to buy the plane ticket on his credit card at the airport. However, the airport officer wouldn't issue the ticket since there was not sufficient credit available. Dhorda lost his temper, claiming discrimination against him. The ticket officer called the police who took him into custody. Dhorda was taken away and brought back to Ann Arbor where he was put in a mental hospital. His friends and I were flabbergasted. How could they do that? We thought he had broken a law or had just gone crazy.

When we visited him at the hospital, we did not find any abnormality. However he was treated quite well. He certainly wasn't a mental patient. I suppose that was the policy of the university and the State. It reminds me of the movie, *One Flew Over the Cuckoo's Nest*, starring Jack Nicholson. The hospital treatment was quite mechanical with little love and care. It also reminds me of my childhood, where we had at least two families with disabled and retarded but grown-up kids. Natu, with no hands and only one leg, had adjusted so well, he would participate in some of the games we played. They were not institutionalized and lived with their families. They were brought up as if they were normal with some additional tutorials to alleviate their handicaps.

We met another Indian student in the same mental hospital named Mahendra. He, on the other hand, *was* mentally unstable. Though brilliant, Mahendra apparently couldn't take the competition at Ann Arbor. His instability also came from being lonely and having difficulties in dating. He would boast that a rich girl wanted to marry him, and he seemed to believe people were trying to kill him so he'd eat only canned foods directly out of cans.

Mahendra and Dhorda's families eventually came to get both of them to prevent them being deported. Uncle Sam would buy their ticket if they were deported. But the U.S. government never did buy their tickets and neither were they deported.

Part of Dhorda's loneliness came to him because he was married in India, though he would date, which caused his conscience to bite him. In fact I dated one of the girls he had dated, and I learned a lot from her about Dhorda. She said that he was totally stressed. He hated his advisor, Audian; he thought Audian was out to get him and wouldn't give him his PhD. Dhorda's conflict with his advisor seemed to build up in time, resulting in essence his going back to India without his PhD.

Loneliness was a major cause among students who came from a bigger family and those who came to study without their wives. One of my cousins, who came from a big family of a dozen brothers and sisters, was admitted in the sparsely populated Oklahoma University, and went back to Mumbai for the same reasons. Another story I heard was that of a brilliant Rajput student wanting to have his wife join him at the University of Chicago. He had a scholarship from the university, and was well funded to allow him to have his wife come to Chicago. Evidently, his advisor had recognized his loneliness, and tried to convince his father to let his wife come to stay with him. The father, an orthodox Rajput, did not allow it to happen. He probably was afraid that his son would never come back to India. The student ultimately committed suicide brilliantly by getting an electric shock and then falling down from the window of a multistory apartment building.

Most Indian students were shy and inexperienced in matters of dating. Few students married for love to get the green card. Those who left the U.S. usually had girls back in the U.S. Most of the rich Indians planned to return to India. Though I came from a higher middle-class family in India, I was too cautious to get married. In fact, I planned to go back to India and start an industry. Few of us went to Toledo, a city in Ohio, at the southern border of Michigan.

Toledo was famous for burlesque shows, known for female striptease. Visiting Toledo was considered shameful by Indian students; we would never publicize our visits to Toledo.

My second semester in the year of 1959 was easier. There were about four-and-a-half months per semester. I was working twenty hours a week and getting a 3.3 GPA. I landed a job with one of my professors named James Grimes. He taught a class in electro-magnetics, in which I received an A grade. I worked for two hours a day. My expenses and fees were running about 2,000 dollars a semester. With my new job, I bought a '49 Kaiser for 120 dollars, a discontinued car. I actually went into partnership with a student named Amin. Then we took turns using the car a week at a time alternately. It didn't work well, so I sold my share for 40 dollars and took a 20 dollar loss. Later, Amin and his friends drove the car to Canada where it broke down. So they just left it on a highway. The next car I bought was a '51 Chevy for 200 dollars. It gave me good service for about six months, then later I bought a '55 Chevy for 400 dollars. A '55 Chevy, even now, has been considered a classic car for its reliability.

About six of us rented a new '58 Chevrolet and drove to Mackinac Island, located between the American and Canadian border, for a pleasure trip. I was the only driver, since only I had a driving license from India. I did not know that Rajmohan Gandhi, the grandson of Mahatma Gandhi, was involved with the MRA (Moral Rearmament Association), located on Mackinac Island. MRA was instituted to resolve political problems employing Mahatma Gandhi's principles of non-violence. Visiting MRA was a good experience, where we were treated with a wonderful vegetarian lunch. We had also planned to visit the county fair, located in upper Michigan. As we drove along we would hear songs on the radio like "Itsy bitsy teenie weenie yellow polka dot bikini …," which was a popular song of the time. While we were visiting the grounds of the county fair, some Latin girls began talking to us in Spanish, thinking we were from one of the Latin countries.

En route to the county fair, we saw some huge horses seen in the Budweiser advertisements, and huge trees. One of my companions commented that everything in America was big, even the people. "Americans are the most favored sons of God," he would say. "How could it be otherwise?" I realized that socializing and speaking well were of value to succeed in life. Later, I invited two of my professors to an Indian movie, *Boot Polish*, produced by Raj Kapoor, to expose them to Indian art and culture. Socializing with professors had a minimal effect on my grades. Out of four classes I took in the second semester, one of the professors gave me a "C," one gave me a "B," and two gave me an "A." The "C" I got was in auto control systems. The professor was tough. My GPA for the Bachelor of Science was slightly less than 3.0. However I had no problem going for the Master of Science degree. The next two semesters were relatively easy. I was also working part-time as a research assistant for Professor Grimes. In the summer of 1960, Professor Grimes asked me to quit my job. As I was graduating and had only two units to complete, I transferred to Detroit University where Mavani had moved. Mavani had not been able to keep up his grades at Ann Arbor, so the university suggested he go to Detroit University to complete his Bachelor's in Engineering. It was an easier college to graduate from. I shared a flat with him and applied for a PhD at UCLA and the University of Massachusetts.

While in Detroit I dated an Italian girl for a few months. She was a few years older than me. I also met a pretty lady at one of the employment agencies. I thought she could help me find a job, since her husband was an executive of a big company. It did not work. I planned to go to LA, so I had sold my Chevy to a friend who had just got his driver's license.

In Detroit I first tasted Mexican food, which would later become a staple food in California. One of my first dates in Ann Arbor was a Puerto Rican girl. However I sensed it wouldn't work out as we were culturally so different. She wanted to settle in the U.S. and Puerto Ricans had to return to their country if they were not married. I noticed the difference in matters of marriage. Indian boys in India had help from the family in finding mates for marriage. But in the U.S., blatant "matchmaking" was not part of the culture, so everyone had to help themselves, first dating then falling in love, to get married.

One day I went to the medical center for university students, on the eighth floor, since I had a bad flu. After receiving an injection of antibiotics, the nurse warned me not to leave immediately and stay there for a while. I did not take her warning seriously and walked to an elevator to go down. The next thing I knew when I opened my eyes, I was being carried back to the medical center by a six-and-a-half-foot black man as if he was carrying a baby. It reminded me of the physical fitness of a fellow student from Africa in Poona, and if size is the criterion, then certainly Americans are blessed. The experience was frightening for me and it taught me something of the dangers of getting ill in a foreign country. It also impressed upon me the value of good health. So I prepared to go to California, a state at that time known for "good health" and a good climate.

Graduation, June 1959, Ann Arbor. I had gained weight from 135 to 150 pounds, thanks to doughnuts and milkshakes.

): (Back row) Roommates Dhorda, Body builder Manu, and Garry; Garry committed suicide after his newly wed wife left him. (Front row) Myself and widower Mr. Sud; all residents of a poorly built and managed six-bedroom house occupied by 10 students, with one-and-three-quarters baths, January 1959.

Thanksgiving at Marty's parents' house; Marty (second from left) and his friends, 1958. I am playing the flute.

CHAPTER 4

THE JOURNEY TO LOS ANGELES

"The West is the place where people who think they can be cowboys, aren't."

Will Rogers

My decision to come to Los Angeles in 1960 was filled with some restraint. I was very conscious about spending money and my mother's recommendation to be frugal seemed to follow me everywhere. I responded to an ad in the newspaper from a man who was driving to Los Angeles. I agreed to pay him 20 dollars for the transportation costs. He was a teacher. I asked him why he was leaving Michigan., and he responded that Michigan residents were so simple-minded that he was glad to leave the area.

It was a long trip. There were many things I wanted to see. For example, I wanted to visit Chicago but I couldn't because my traveling companion wanted to get to California as soon as possible. Needless to say, we had some disagreements about the trip. When we came to Cheyenne, Wyoming, I recall a lot of big hats and big boots on the locals. In Zion National Park I was impressed with the reddish mountain ranges of the region. We also drove through Las Vegas and I marveled at some of the early neon signs, which in comparison to today's Las Vegas, was a paltry lighting show.

We arrived in Los Angeles via the San Bernardino Freeway. It ended at the Harbor Freeway in those days; there was no Santa Monica Freeway. I called the International Student Center at UCLA and they said to just follow Wilshire Boulevard all the way to Westwood and then to the university. There were so many lights that it took us forever to come to UCLA. My travelling companion dropped me at my destination with my bags. There, accommodations were arranged for me with a black family just south of Wilshire Boulevard on Federal Avenue. The husband had been a building contractor in Hawaii. This was during the '60s when Hawaii was growing by leaps and bounds. The lady of the house was very courteous and accommodating.

I had been admitted to UCLA as a graduate student. Since I arrived on August 15, I had four extra weeks before my classes started, so I decided to look up my friend Ravindra Badkar who was supposed to live on Centinela Avenue and Washington Boulevard in west Los Angeles. The next day I started walking south on Federal Avenue from Wilshire Boulevard. When I inquired about the distance, I was informed that it was no more than 10 minutes away. I did not realize that the people in Los Angeles always talked about travel time by car. So I started walking, but it was a much longer walk than I expected. I also noticed that the blocks in Los Angeles were much longer in distance than in Ann Arbor and Detroit. Luckily while en route I passed a used car lot. There was an old man there and I started chatting with him. I told him I didn't have much money, but I needed a car in LA. He showed me a '48 Dodge, a two-seater with hydromatic transmission. It was beige in color, but in place of the paint it appeared to have been sandblasted so the car had no shine. It also had no front grill, like an old person without teeth. It was one of the ugliest cars I had seen. When I asked how much, the old man said 40 dollars. I said, "Not bad. I can afford that. But is it reliable?" The old man assured me I could drive the car to New York and back but that I needed to keep a gallon of oil in the trunk since the engine burned oil profusely. Driving the Dodge was no problem for me as I'd learned to drive a '48 De Soto, and both Dodge and Desoto were made by Chrysler and had similar designs.

I found Ravi's place eventually. He had two roommates; one was Om Tandan, who was doing his BS at Northrop in aerospace engineering, the other was Arthur Fujimoto, who was half-Japanese from his father's side and half-English from his mother. Ravi's place was a one-bedroom apartment with three mattresses on the floor in the bedroom for sleeping. There was also a pile of clothes in the middle of the room that needed to be washed that they called "Mt. Fuji."

A few days later Ravi and his roommates asked me to move in with them because I was over at their place all the time. In fact I was becoming good friends with Om and Arthur. In the back of my mind I wasn't sure about my UCLA PhD program. I still wanted to go back to India and start a manufacturing business with the help of my family. Industrial experience would be more beneficial to me. So Om and I decided to go to San Francisco. After all, the old man at the used car lot said my '48 Dodge could go to New York and back. I thought San Francisco would be an easy trip. I had been applying for jobs around LA but had been told that there would be no immediate response; I would have to wait for a few weeks. So I lined up an interview with Hewlett Packard in Palo Alto and Om and I set off for northern California.

While in Palo Alto interviewing for Hewlett Packard, we contacted my Poona classmate, Kumar Patel, who was completing his PhD at Stanford. He graciously spent a few hours with us showing us around the Stanford campus. It would be my last contact with him until the '90s. Once we arrived in San Francisco we found that driving the Dodge in the hills of the city was no small chore. We had no problem going down San Francisco's hills. But going up, no matter how hard I tried to accelerate, I could not make the car climb those steep hills. We eventually figured out that if Om got out and moved the traffic away from behind the car, I could slowly back up and get to a flatter crossroad. That's how we saw San Francisco, driving mostly on the flatter roads.

When I returned to LA I was offered a job with a salary of 600 dollars at Hoffman Engineering in El Monte. I accepted the offer, since in those days 600 dollars was considered an excellent salary. They were a pioneering company in semiconductors and this was the start of the semiconductor revolution that had begun when a scientist at Stanford discovered the semiconductor transistor. Thanks to my experience in microwave measurement at Ann Arbor and a class in semiconductor devices, I was hired to measure the high frequency response of transistors and tunnel diodes. Hoffman was also manufacturing solar cells and controlled high-power rectifiers. For the first few weeks at Hoffman, I felt very unproductive. I thought I was paid for nothing since I felt I did not contribute anything. I was about to quit. I expressed my concern about my being so unproductive and that I should resign before they fired me to an older Indian engineer, Suren Upadhyaya. His words, "Don't worry about what you are doing here. Wait until they train you completely. You will feel lot more productive after you are trained." I am glad I took his advice. I also had good training from a Lithuanian engineer in matters of building electronic equipment. We would compare the meaning of words in Lithuanian and Indian languages. Surprisingly we discovered similar sounding words like Mata and Pita having the same meaning. This is because the Lithuanian language is one of the oldest Indo-European languages, and a clos sister to Sanskrit.

With my new job intact, I sold my Dodge for 25 dollars to Om, who wanted to learn to drive. The story of that car culminated when Om sold the car to Ravi for 40 dollars, making a 15 dollar profit. Ravi learned to drive in the same car. Later Ravi got a "fix-it" ticket from a police officer in Playa del Rey who could hear the metallic brake shoes rubbing on the steel! Ravi just abandoned the car after getting the ticket, taking the car's license with him, because he figured it would cost more to fix the brakes than the value of the Dodge. I moved out of Om's apartment and moved in with Harshad Sheth, a friend going to USC. I stayed with Harshad for about three months near the USC campus and decided to move out after our apartment was vandalized. There were probably as many Indian students on the USC campus as on the UCLA campus.

I was invited by Mr. Val (a short form of Valabhdas) Dani to spend the Christmas holidays with his family, who lived in El Centro. El Centro is a town close to the U.S./ Mexico border right across from Mexicali. Mr. Dani was in his sixties when I met him. He was an uncle-in-law of my aunt Lilifai. She had informed me about Mr. Dani who had migrated to America in the '30s. He received an agricultural engineering degree, probably from Chicago, and had married a lady there. I had written a letter introducing myself from Ann Arbor to which he responded. In fact he stopped by and spent a night at our apartment on his way back to California. He and his wife were touring the U.S. in a new airconditioned Buick during the summer of 1959.

Mr. Dani had migrated to California in the '40s, where he fathered three children: a girl who was married to Robert, a Californian, and two boys. That Christmas I took a bus to El Centro instead of driving. I was picked up by Mr. Dani, who later introduced me to all of his family members except one of his sons who had joined the U.S. Army to get away from his father. Robert and I had become good friends; he described the relationship of Mr. Dani with his two sons as harsher with one and softer with the other. It reminded me of similar situations in families of my father's generation; the perception of one of the siblings would be that the father's affection was not equal.

Mr. Dani had a shop that sold seeds and foodstuff along with farming products for local farmers. He took me to his shop and then to his customer's place, which was a big yard surrounded by a few buildings. What I saw was very unique. Mr. Dani's clients were all Punjabi farmers talking to each other in Punjabi, relaxed, smoking and drinking on the one sideof theyard. Their kids were playing baseball in the center, talking to each other in English. The farmers' wives were Mexican ladies talking to each other in Spanish while doing their chores at the opposite side of the yard. All three groups were separate. Mr. Dani took me to the side of the farmers and introduced me to a few of them. It was an unusual experience seeing members of the same immediate family separated into three distinct groups, and communicating in three different languages. The Punjabi men and the Mexican women communicated seldom in broken English with a few Punjabi or Spanish words slipping in. It dawned on me what America is: a country of migrants from the Old World mixing with other migrants, generating a "mixed soup" of Americans. I suspect they did not fight as often as a normal couple would, since if they tried, they would not have been able to communicate what the fight was about.

Then I moved in with an American student, Bob Smith, going to the LA City College. His apartment was located in the Silver Lake area, which was relatively closer to my work in El Monte. Sharing an apartment with Bob, originally from Michigan, was a different learning experience. Bob had to have a convertible car and was hoping to be involved in the Hollywood movie business. He was almost always broke and did not have enough money for food. His appearance reminded me of the movie star Jack Palance. Occasionally we double-dated, of course at my expense.

About this time I made friends with a Jewish girl named Carol. We started dating even though I was planning to go to Bombay in the summer of 1961. She thought I looked like Sal Mineo, who played an important part in the movie *Exodus*, about Jewish migration to Israel. My parents had sent an airline ticket for me from Bombay to

LA and back. They wanted me to get married and they were starting to pressure me. This was part of their reason for me to come home to India where I could meet prospective Indian girls to wed. The airline ticket I received had an around-the-world travel itinerary, with stops in Honolulu, Tokyo, Singapore, and Bombay. During a couple of days in Honolulu, I visited the University of Hawaii. I spent about four days in a prestigious Tokyo hotel, but I was shocked to experience women peddling their services as prostitutes in the hotel. The cost of almost everything, certainly food, was much higher than in Los Angeles. Later on, I gathered that Japanese women in general had difficulties surviving after the Second World War. I recall how fast Japan progressed after the war; Prime Minister Nehru gave the example of Japan as a role model for India to follow in matters of economic development and progress.

The monsoon season had already started when I arrived in Bombay. Jasvantbhai didn't like the idea of my marrying an American girl. However, the more they pressured me, the more I revolted. I started to care for Carol as I was receiving very tender letters from her. I had given my passport to my mother for safekeeping, but Jasvantbhai took it and went to Ahmedabad. The idea was for me to follow him there, since I had to get my passport back and my parents wanted me to see some pretty girls in Gujarat. They also were not keen on my wedding an American girl like Carol. But my mind was made up. Or so I thought. On this visit I didn't make any proposals for marriage, though there were many offers. I did get my passport back from Jasvantbhai and my family even showed me a potential girl at Bhavnager at a wedding! Jasvantbhai smartly convinced the rest of the family that I was fully capable of getting another passport and other necessary documents from my employer, if necessary. Unhappily for them, however, I returned to the U.S. unmarried.

While in India, Hoffman asked me to look at a company named Mundhra, which was involved in manufacturing radios in New Delhi. Since Hoffman manufactured solar cells, they were interested in designing a radio that ran on solar power for villages. Jawaharlal

Nehru was the prime minister of India at this time. The idea was a good one and the goal was to connect Indian villages via radio communications. It did not materialize. Nehru's government was overcautious about colonialism; India didn't want to get involved with another colonial power like the U.S. My brother Jitubhai and I went to New Delhi to meet the Mundhra company executives. It didn't work out since there were things pending with the government. Ultimately Hoffman, being a relatively small company, couldn't keep up with the negotiations and whims of the Indian government.

I knew there was a proposal to build a massive road system in India from Kashmir to Kanyakumari, and also a transcontinental road from Calcutta to Kutch. General Motors had offered to finance both road systems if India gave GM a 10-year exclusive to sell GM cars in India. Nehru's government also turned this down. When I was in Ahmedabad I visited my alma mater, LD Engineering College. I met my old college mate Bhogi, a couple of years senior to me. He was employed at the college as an assistant probably for a few hundred rupees a month. He could not believe what I was making at Hoffman, he being smarter and more experienced than myself. It was the first time I realized that a person could become envious and resentful about my good fortune in America.

By the time I was ready to leave India I was thoroughly depressed. I didn't know what I was doing with regard to getting married; I had always respected my parents' advice. So I was encouraged to speak to one of the elders and a community leader of the Gujarati community, and my maternal uncle Vadilal Gandhi who lived in Gatkopar, a suburb of Bombay. He along with others tried to impress upon me the wisdom of marrying a girl from India. Obviously, I wasn't sold on the idea at the time.

My return flight was from Bombay via Rome and Switzerland. I decided to visit a schoolmate of mine, Nikhil, in Switzerland. I was in a depressed mood, leaving my family and remembering all the good words about marriage I had heard from my experienced elders. In fact I called my mother from Zurich, and informed her thatI would comeback if she wanted me to do so. However, she suggested coming back after a couple of years with additional training and education.

While traveling from Switzerland to Hamburg, I met a fellow from Iraq named Ahmad. I remembered that my old penpal Doris was from Hamburg, so Ahmad and I tried to locate her. We tracked her down from a rough address and met her with her husband and two children. We also met Olga, Jitubhai's old penpal. Doris suggested we see Hamburg and I was very obliged to her for showing us around. I enjoyed the good German vegetarian food of the region, but I was later very surprised when Doris started talking to me privately about her "old" feelings when we were penpals. I made a mistake confirming the same old feelings, instead of forgetting about it. I regret that I was a bit physical due to her encouragement. After all, she was a married woman with two children. During the period of my bachelor life, I was always cautious in matters of relationships with women. I took every precaution to ensure that I did not become a father out of wedlock. Almost all the girls I dated had the same view.

By the time I returned to LA, I received a letter from Doris saying she wanted to divorce her husband and come to LA and bring her kids with her! A German engineer named Gunther, with whom I was working at Hoffman, translated her letters for me. He was as shocked as I was and then began laughingly calling me a "Casanova." I didn't know what to do. Carol wrote a letter for me to Doris about our relationship. That stopped the letters coming from Doris. Carol and I had a bit of a rocky relationship. Carol had given me a book, *The Prophet*, written by Kahlil Gibran. The book helped me a lot to learn about our relationship. This good book came into play in the future at least a couple of times.

After I came back from India I decided I wanted to live on my own, so I moved into a studio apartment in a brick building for 65 dollars a month. The place was near Santa Monica Boulevard and Western Avenue. It had a "Murphy bed," the one you pull out of the wall. A lot of old people also lived in the building. However, in India the Hollywood address was impressive. After I sold my Dodge, I bought a VW for 700 dollars, which I used until the summer of 1961. Then I bought a brand-new maroon-colored 1961 Corvair for 2,600 dollars.

My father visited me in the fall of 1961. I rented an additional apartment for my father and his companion in the same brick building. He had been traveling to Poland with a business associate, Mr. Shamjibhai Parekh. They were buying machinery in Poland to use on waste cotton and turn it into blankets and carpets. I decided to introduce Carol to my father, but it was a short and superficial meeting. Later my father advised me to consider coming back to India for marriage. He also advised me to move out of my place because he said it was a depressing "low standard" building with a lot of old people around. I drove us all over to places like Disneyland in my Corvair. The car was the envy of many of my friends at UCLA. One friend, a PhD student with whom I played table tennis, who was half-Turkish and half-German, said that if I were in Germany I could attract almost any girl with that car.

Hoffman was a wonderful experience. Phillip Musensqui was one of the key executives and he had an affinity for Indians. But ultimately Hoffman had a problem in California getting contracts. They made some business mistakes and I was laid off. Two weeks later I found another job at TRW (Thompson Ramo Wooldridge, Inc) in their semiconductor division. I moved near the UCLA campus in Westwood after I got the TRW job to make my commute more convenient.

During the '60s, there was the Sputnik race with the Russians. Yuri Gagarin was Russia's first man in space. Because the U.S. was desperate to catch up, LA and California became a hub for the aerospace industry. Lots of contracts and subcontracts were given out to LA firms. I had one disadvantage in that I was not a citizen. Security clearance was available only to citizens of the USA.

The driving time from Westwood to TRW in Redondo was less than thirty minutes, and often I would share a ride with a fellow employee. When the Cuban missile crisis hit the news, every morning we would have a sigh of relief that we were alive, and there was no nuclear holocaust. Almost always I would have an egg sandwich from a food truck, coming to the site during lunch hour. I did not have any other choice, being a vegetarian. My fellow engineers would question how could I have the same lunch every day. However there was one engineer, a devout Christian, who appreciated that I was a vegetarian. One day he brought a bible showing me that every Friday, a true Christian is supposed to be a vegetarian. There was one whole issue of Life magazine devoted to the India-China war of 1962. Tom Wolf, a fellow engineer, brought the magazine showing me a photo of an Indian soldier looking like me. I was not quite sure about it. I suppose for Americans, if you see one Indian, you see them all.

During this time my brother Jitubhai visited me as part of a U.S./ India cultural program. He came in the summer of 1962 as one of the cultural delegates of India. So we drove to San Francisco with Ravi. Jitubhai's delegation also met President Kennedy in Washington, D.C. We were heartbroken at Kennedy's (JFK's) assassination a year later.

Jitubhai even sent a letter to me explaining how he had met the president and fondly remembered that moment. I mailed Jitubhai's letter and a few lines of my own to Jackie Kennedy. She responded by mailing a card expressing her appreciation. Later we learned that Jackie had responded to each and every letter of consolation that had been sent.

Mrs. Kennedy is deeply appreciative of

your sympathy and grateful

for your thoughtfulness

Mrs. Kennedy's response to our letter of consolation after JFK's assassination, received in December 1963.

Jitubhai and myself visiting Self Realization Fellowship, 1962.

My father and I standing, Shyamjibhai seated in my first new car Corvair, 1961.

Navin, a Sal Mineo lookalike as per his girlfriend, 1962

The UCLA students, including myself, believed that there had been a conspiracy to kill President Kennedy. There was a large mistrust among students against JFK's successor, President Johnson, and FBI Director J. Edgar Hoover. There were some who believed that the Italian Mafia was involved since they had suffered a big loss when Castro came to power in Cuba. There were some who believed that the Federal Reserve and the bankers were the culprits, since President Kennedy was to take away the power of printing money from the Federal Reserve. Segregationists were openly critical of JFK's sympathy for Martin Luther King Jr., also known as the "American Gandhi."

King initiated his visit to India in 1959 when I had spent my first year in America. He met Prime Minister Nehru and Vinoba Bhave, Gandhi's spiritual torchbearer. King's biggest success was when he emulated Gandhi's successful salt march with his own march to Washington, D.C. in '63, where he made his most memorable speech: "I have a dream." After the march, he was invited to the White House, where JFK greeted him with "I have a dream, too." The Gandhi-King story unfortunately did not end there. Repeating Gandhi's words in essence that he was not afraid to be killed, King was fatally shot on April 4, 1968.

We all had an intuition about John F. Kennedy when he first came on the American political scene. Almost every Indian had favored Kennedy over Nixon. Both men had visited the USC campus. Nixon said that students should study and not get into politics. Kennedy said the opposite, that students should be involved in politics. Kennedy was obviously the more attractive of the two men, but his charisma inspired people unlike anyone we had seen. There was an intuitive good feeling about Kennedy and the opposite about Nixon. Later in '71, it was clear that President Nixon sided against India during the Pakistan/ India war. There were stories that Nixon and Kissinger even encouraged China to invade India to discourage India against Pakistan.

After my brother's visit, I realized I was eager to find a mate and get a green card. Psychologically, I knew now that I was not prepared to marry a Westerner. It reminds me of the statement made by a fellow engineer from Beirut, Lebanon. When asked about his marriage and wife's origin, his response and advice was, "Marrying an American woman is to marry a man; my advice is go back to your country and find one from there." We had many friends who had green card marriages. These marriages invariably had a high rate of divorce. My observation was that Indian men with American wives were less successful than American men with Indian wives. This observation is only for the decade of the '60s. Still, as the possibility of marriage continued to loom over me, I had much confusion about the whole topic.

I started to play cricket in '62 as a member of the UCLA team. The routine was to practice on Saturday mornings and play the match on Sundays from 10 am to 5 pm. I dated quite a few girls. I would like one, but it wouldn't work out. The reasons were never fully discussed. Intuitively it was usually because of the food, culture or even religion, and sometimes it was just the possibility of my going back to India. Carol had even told me she was willing to go to India with me if we were to be married. At this time I was ready to go back to school for the PhD program at UCLA. It was the winter quarter, and I was dating Cheryl Hall, who reminded me of the humor of Carol Burnett and the looks of Julie Andrew. She was quite funny, a nursing student from Florida. However there was a problem of religion. A few times we visited the Self Realization Fellowship (SRF) temple to expose her to Indic traditions. I could never change my religion.

When Jitubhai left me in LA after his visit, he decided to return to India via Germany. I found out later that he spent some time with Olga, his old penpal. Almost a year later I got a letter from Doris saying that Olga had delivered a baby girl and the father was Jitubhai! I never told Jitubhai about this letter. But in 2001 when I was alone with him in Bombay, I asked him about Olga's claim.

He told me, yes, Olga's baby was his and that her daughter had contacted him because she wanted to meet her real father, Jitubhai. Olga's daughter is a linguist with a good position in Germany. When she visited India with her fiancé, it was clear to Jitubhai that she resembled Jagruti, Jitubhai's first daughter. Jitubhai then informed me that he had met them at the Taj Hotel in Bombay, and given her a father's gift of about 15,000 rupees.

I had lost my job thrice, once from Hoffman after two years of service, a second time from TRW semiconductors after 15 months of service, and a third time from Ampex after seven months of service, covering a time frame from September 1960 to September 1964. Ampex was a company that manufactured magnetic devices like magnetic tapes and recorders. I was not happy working at Ampex. I took the job there when I couldn't find a job in the semiconductor industry. I was offered a job in a small company in Chatsworth, which seemed to be too far for me to commute for so small a company. I discovered later that Ampex products were going to be outdated in the coming years. I was confused and looking for direction. I had the company of a few Indian friends as confused as I was.

There was a Bengali student friend who claimed to be a prince from a royal family. In reality he was not. At least one girl fell for it and would do a lot of things for him, including taking him places in her car since he did not have one. Her mother even encouraged her to marry this man. The relationship must have lasted for months. But eventually it did end when she discovered that it was a hoax. Gullible Americans.

I became good friends with Naidu, an Indian Christian from the West Indies whose family had migrated to America. We played cricket and double-dated on occasion. Naidu visited India as one of the UCLA students in a group. He met an Indian Christian girl with whom he fell in love. Though they corresponded for years, ultimately it didn't work out because she didn't want to leave India and Naidu didn't want to settle in India. I remember a girl named

Leslie, a student residing at UCLA's Daykstra Hall. Leslie was a tall blond girl who had fallen in love with Naidu so she would ask me to help her by convincing Naidu to go out with her. Unfortunately Naidu's heart was only for the girl in India. When I last saw him in 1965, he was married to an oriental girl.

Another interesting experience I had while friendly with a visiting French Fulbright scholar Jon, studying at UCLA. He helped me reduce my weight from about 165 to 155 pounds by playing tennis and visiting the sauna regularly. He often came to my apartment. That was when I was looking for a job. I had gone to New York and Washington, D.C. for a few days for a job interview and to visit the World Fair. I wanted to meet the good senator HubertHumphrey to seeif hecould help meto geta green card. His office staff was polite and stated that he could not help me in such matters unless I was a refugee. After I came back to Los Angeles, I saw that my bank account was about 725 dollars less. When I went to my bank and inquired about the reduction, I was informed that a check for 725 dollars had been cashed. I complained that the check was forged. Luckily Jon, who had forged the check, had deposited it in the bank next door. The manager of my bank held a meeting with his bank manager and caught Jon when he was just about to close the account to go back to France. They let him go when he started crying and pleaded for forgiveness. That taught me a second lesson about money, to keep important stuff like checkbooks in a secure and hidden place.

Occasionally I double-dated with Dr. Jitu Bhat, a gynecologist by profession. I had met him one afternoon at the Self Realization Fellowship cafeteria on Sunset Boulevard in Hollywood. He was practicing at the Sunset Kaiser Hospital. Being a Gujarati we had quite a few things in common. He had come to the University of Pennsylvania with a very tight budget in the early '50s. He married a Pennsylvania girl, Donna, joined the Army, and had the Army pay for his medical school. They were residing in a recently purchased house with their three children in the valley.

Ravi and Elaine were also UCLA students residing in a co-op on Landfair Avenue. Elaine, a Jewish girlfriend of Ravi's, wanted to marry him. She too asked for my help to convince Ravi of her affection. I met another Jewish girl named Leslie through Ravi. I soon found out Ravi was not too happy that I was going out with her. Leslie, like many Jewish girls, went to Israel possibly to find romance and a mate. At least two Jewish girls that I knew said they found Israeli men to be too tough to handle. Though I had kept my mind open to find a suitable mate in Los Angeles, it was very hard. Usually the cultural differences would create too much disharmony. We would have a good time for a few weeks and then it would appear that it would work. But in time later on, the relationship would degrade, mainly due to my own mental conflicts.

I was already twenty-seven years of age and my family was quite concerned I wasn't yet married. So this time when I visited India, I would do it with an open mind. My family sent me a ticket via Europe. I left my belongings at Dr. Jitu Bhat's house. During this trip I stopped by in Copenhagen where I met Anna Marie, a Kim Novak lookalike, through an Indian friend of mine in Denmark. I spent about seven days with Anna. She was quite pretty and worked as a clerk. We liked each other, but I had to depart for Bombay. After I arrived there, I tried to contact Anna, but I didn't succeed. I only had her work telephone number; she didn't have a phone at her home. That was November 1964. Now I was in India and my future loomed ahead of me. It was not realistic to think of marrying Anna Marry; we had a language problem to start with. It would have been like the Punjabis of El Centro marrying the Latino women. Then there were so many unanswered questions about her parents' support, immigration status, and cultural differences that I had experienced with girls in Los Angeles, on and on. I was ready to meet girls in Bombay.

CHAPTER 5

THE PROPOSALS

"I have found it a virtue that with few exceptions most Hindu women feel blessed to walk in the footsteps of their husbands."

Mahatma gandhi

My Experiments with the Truth

Once I arrived in Bombay I waited for a week, and then informed my family that I was ready to meet girls. I wanted to conform to the wisdom of my parents that one needs to get married to become complete; our tradition describes men and women individually as being half. One needs to get married to join the other half, to become one. I was now twenty-eight years old, and it was a high time for me to get married, based on the Indian tradition of the time. I had been advised not only by my parents and brothers but also many uncles and well wishers, who also talked about the advantages of being married and having a life partner to share the pain and pleasure of life. My mother would recite mythic stories, like that of Satyawan and Savitri, just to ensure that I would not change my mind.

My father's good friend and business partner Shyamjibhai had put an advertisement for me in a local paper. The response was better than expected. Maybe it was because I was an engineering graduate with a Master's degree from the USA. I was introduced to numerous girls without any positive result. I wanted to avoid any potential trouble after marriage. For example, the girl from a very rich family could demand to go back because she was missing her family. I was looking for a girl reasonably good-looking and who had a good command of English. We had a response from a Punjabi Army General for his daughter from New Delhi. There was another from a very accomplished Gujarati girl living in Madras (now Chennai in South India) who knew how to fly an airplane and spoke many languages, including French! However, I found it quite difficult and time-consuming to meet girls in faraway places like Madras and New Delhi. As the Christmas holidays arrived I informally met a few girls who were on break from local colleges. One of Jitubhai's friends suggested a good-looking girl with a good figure in his Marine Drive neighborhood. I had an opportunity to meet and talk to her. It was very hard for me to be judge and jury and reject her, because she spoke very little English. I tried my best to avoid meeting girls from rich families and not knowing much about them.

In the last week of December 1964, Jitubhai informed me we were to meet a young girl who happened to be the sister-in-law of my cousin Bhopinbhai. My mother and Bhopinbhai's father, Manu-mama, her first cousin, were like a real brother and sister. Rambhaba, my maternal grandmother, had raised not only my mother, but also Rambhaba's sister's three sons, Laloo-mama, Vadi-mama and Manu-mama. This was because their mother had passed away very early. The suffix "mama" coming after a personal name means, in Gujarati, a maternal uncle. Vadi-mama (Vadilal Chatrabhuj Gandhi), the middle of the three, was a well-known businessman, philanthropist, and community leader in Ghatkopar, a suburb of Mumbai. He had donated large sums of money to fund the building of a prominent school, the Gurukul High School, a Jain temple, and a living facility for seniors in that neighborhood.

Manu-mama's oldest son, Bhopinbhai, had come to know that I was what is called "a suitable boy" for his young sister-in-law, Pratibha. He planned a casual meeting between Pratibha and myself at a restaurant called Bombay Lee, close to the ocean in Church Gate, a prestigious location. When I met Pratibha, I was quite impressed with her looks, command of English, and her communication skills. Though she was only nineteen years old, she was in her last year of college. The next day, Sarojbhabhi, my sister-in-law, and I went to Ruia College, a prominent college in Matunga, a suburb of Mumbai, where Pratibha was an undergrad student.

Sarojbhabhi was there with me to communicate that I had honorable intentions and assuring that our meeting had a positive outcome. Pratibha agreed to go out with me so that I would get to know her better. We both agreed to meet without the knowledge of either of our parents. In those days the meeting of a boy and a girl without a chaperone was not socially acceptable.

The next day, I believe it was Saturday, I picked Pratibha up near her residence in Ghatkopar, and we visited my friend Kishore Shroff and his wife Ranjan at Goregaon. We then went to Tansa Lake, a good picnic place. We talked to each other as a way of getting acquainted. While we were walking around Tansa Lake, Pratibha tore one of her sandals and couldn't walk comfortably. Kishore almost immediately offered her a handkerchief from his pocket, kneeling down and tying it around the arch of Pratibha's foot and the sandal. I suppose Pratibha was quite impressed with Kishore's gentlemanly help. Ranjan, Kishore's wife, was amused with Kishore's action, knowing his theatrics. I had brought with me a Polaroid camera, the camera that generates instant photos. Kishore took our "intimate" photographs that would come in very handy to formalize our marriage. Evidently Pratibha felt assured of my developing affection for her. It was a wonderful and romantic day that I will not forget.

We did go out a few more times. I believe Pratibha was quite impressed with me maybe because I made her feel at ease and I was not as demanding as some Indian men would be. The days were going by fast. I had to return to Los Angeles to begin the February 1965 semester at UCLA. My plan was to go back to school for a PhD program. I had secured the admission and assistantship at UCLA before leaving LA for India.

Pratibha's mother Kamalaben was not ready, however, for her daughter to marry me. There were a number of reasons. For one, Pratibha's father was in Aden, a British colony then, now part of Yemen, where she had actually grown up. Because the school system in Bombay was much better, Pratibha and her mother had moved to Bombay. Her older sister Aruna and older brother Sharadbhai, though engaged, were not yet married. During the '60s, there was also a scare that boys from the USA would have a girlfriend or a wife in America and come to India to get married just to satisfy their parent's wishes. Though this was not the norm, just one incident was enough to spread the rumor and fear among many mothers and their daughters in India. One day when Jitubhai asked Bhopinbhai about the status of Pratibha's betrothal with his brother (me), he was informed about the uncertainty of Pratibha's mother. Kamalaben definitely wanted to wait for any approval of our plans until Pratibha's father returned from Aden, which could delay things for months. Jitubhai had to inform him that I was leaving Bombay because my courses at UCLA were about to start. When Jitubhai showed the Polaroid pictures of us together to Bhopinbhai, he realized that Pratibha and I had gone out and that our affair had gone much deeper. He became very concerned, knowing that we liked each other and that our Polaroid photos were floating around, unacceptable in our conservative society.

Bhopinbhai contacted Vadi-mama, who was a community leader and a prominent personality in Ghatkopar. My father was also informed about my fondness for Pratibha. In fact he indirectly encouraged me to get serious. How? When Pratibha called to our house, my father would answer the phone and hearing that it was Pratibha he would say, "Navin, it's for you. It sounds like someone from America." He knew it was she, but he also knew that I was looking for someone who would adjust easily in America.

Sarojbhabhi took Pratibha and myself to the residence of an elderly relative from her maternal side, who was considered an expert in astrology and palmistry. She thought it would be a good idea to see if our astrological charts matched and, if there were any conflicts astrologically speaking, it would allow us to take an action to minimize them. In India, many couples who get their astrological charts done will often go through some rituals if there is conflict in the couple's charts. They might fast or go on a pilgrimage to a certain location to get rid of the negative aspects, depending on what the astrologers advocated. For example, one of the couple might fast on every Saturday to reduce or eliminate the negative influence of the planet Saturn, associated with Saturday. The elder gentleman looked at our astrological charts and palms as he was also an expert in palmistry. All told, he said we would have a good and prosperous future together. However, he also said that Pratibha had a short "fuse" or temper and that she needed to control it. To this day I still tease Pratibha about his insight whenever she gets angry or upset.

Astrology and fortune telling are quite popular in India. There is a theory that the Magi or astrologers in the infancy narratives of Jesus were actually from India as they brought with them items native to Hindustan. For example, frankincense or incense was found in Yemen or India at the time of Jesus.

It reminds me of an incident that took place in Ahmedabad in 1957 when I was at LD Engineering College. I was on my way with some friends to the canteen for tea, when a turban-clad man singled me out declaring that I would go to a foreign country and stay there. This was a shock at first. And I disregarded it, though I did treat him to a cup of tea with potato and onion fries. Now thinking back, how could he have been so accurate? This was over 57 years ago and I'm still in America. This prediction was also made by a fellow that I had never met before and never knew. That was not the only incident that had happened to me in regards to forecasting the future. There were others. I do not know much about astrology or fortune telling other than what I had learnt reading the book on palmistry at the University of Michigan. I was then an agnostic in this matter.

The next dayI had gone out with Jitubhai and his friends for some entertainment, and came back late around 12 o'clock midnight. We were surprised to see our father, Motabhai (we addressed him this way, meaning "big brother"), waiting for us somewhat angry for our being so late. I then found out that he was consulting and requesting Vadi-mama to help confirm my wedding to Pratibha. Motabhai then informed me that I should be at Vadi-mama's residence around 12 noon. Pratibha was also invited to be there.

When I arrived at Vadi-mama's house, I was asked to go immediately to his room, where Pratibha was waiting. Vadi-mama was very stern with us, asking us if we were both willing to get married. I had requested a private but short meeting with Pratibha to inform her about the details of our both coming to California. Ultimately her marriage to me would take her away from her family. I told her that she might not be able to see them for years. In spite of these potential difficulties, and because she had developed an affection for me, Pratibha agreed to the wedding. I must admit that she was quite brave, knowing me for a period of no more than a month. So we both responded affirmatively to Vadi-mama. My mother told me later, that because I had rejected so many marriage proposals in the last couple of months, and when they saw my strong interest to wed Pratibha, my father had called his brother-in-law Vadi-mama and begged him to help confirm our union.

That same day, January 23, 1965, the marriage was registered in the court. This was done so that we could apply immediately for Pratibha's passport and U.S. visa. We got married again by religious ceremony on February 7. Marrying Pratibha was probably the best decision I made in my life. There were immediate multiple rewards, such as making my parents, my grandparents, and the rest of my family very happy.

My father was the happiest man having one of the prettiest daughters-in-law. Several people compared her with movie stars when she was dressed for different occasions. My mother was also very happy. She developed the confidence that Pratibha would take care of me in the good or bad days of my life. Pratibha was able to give that confidence to my mother by showing her skills in communication but also as a cook and seamstress.

The wedding ceremony with all the religious rituals took place right near our house at a Jain Society Hall in Sion, a suburb of Bombay. We were lucky it was available on such short notice. My best man was Kishore Tejura (Teju). My other lifelong friend Kishore and his wife Ranjan Shroff were also present at the ceremony.

I wanted a brief simple ceremony. I agreed to give additional money or dakshina to the priest if he could complete the ceremony in half the time it would take normally. He did the best he could. At most Hindu weddings, there is a blessing by the priest and a gathering around a small fire. The couple circles the fire seven times after they tie a cloth knot to symbolize the journey of their life through marriage as well as their marriage commitment. In the film *Gandhi*, Ben Kingsley (playing the role of Gandhi) explains to Martin Sheen how Gandhi did this ritual with his own wife, Kasturba. Normally the ceremony takes about an hour and a half, but with my additional offering to the priest, we kept it to about 40 minutes.

For me, it was a lot easier to go through our civil marriage registration in the court. There was little thinking involved on my part because it was done so fast. However, I noticed that during the religious marriage ceremony I was quite concerned thinking whether or not I was doing the right thing. Some of the photos of my marriage reveal this pensiveness in my expressions.

Part of the reason for my reservation was that I was twenty-eight, and in India it was rather late to marry. The older you are the more difficult it becomes to give up one's freedom as a man. There is commitment involved in marriage and coexisting with a woman, as every man knows, can be filled with challenges.

Jitubhai was a believer of Sai Baba, a renowned Indian ascetic monk. He had planned for us a visit to Shirdi, the town of Sai Baba, where my marriage was to be concluded. The trip became an event for family and friends. Pratibha and I went to the pilgrimage site of Sai Baba at Shirdi with Jitubhai, Jasvantbhai, and my bhabis, Kishore and other friends and their wives, in a caravan of five cars!

We had two receptions at the Radio Club near the Taj Hotel in Bombay. One reception was for business associates of my father and our friends, the second was for the members of our larger families. My father was in a grand mood because he was quite relieved I had finally married.

I remember a day after my wedding when my father and my brothers got into a terrible row over some business problems. They were yelling at each other and my mother came in and shouted them down, saying they were making an awful impression on Pratibha, a newcomer in the family. It should be said that it is normal in India to argue loudly over business problems and I suppose my father and brothers didn't think it was such a big deal.

The real challenge now was whether or not Pratibha was to come with me immediately to America. I had to get back for school by the third week of February. Some of Pratibha's family thought she should remain behind in India and complete her Bachelor's degree. I was obviously in favor of her coming with me. Later her family agreed with me, feeling it unnecessary to remain in India for the final exam she had to pass for the degree. By leaving with me, Pratibha and I could stop by in Aden on our way to America for the blessings of her father there. So the collective decision was for us both to come to the U.S. together via Aden.

Pratima/ Pratibha during her high school days.

Navin during in his first year of college (1954)

The Polaroid photo that helped expedite our marriage, December 1964.

With Vadimama who expedited our marriage, February 7th 1965.

Navin With Raj Kapoor visiting Los Angeles filming *Around the World in Eight Dollars* in 1965.

The marriage ceremony; Pratima's thought, "Come on, smile; marriage is good for us." She, delightfully, came out to be right.

The families of Pratima's father and her uncle; her father and mother (on right), baby Pratima in her mother's lap, sister Aruna (seated on pillow, at right), sister Tarla (standing at extreme left), and brother Sharadbhai with a book (far right); probable year 1948.

We booked our tickets through a French airline and flew from Bombay to Aden, then continued on to Europe and eventually to Los Angeles.

Before we left Bombay for Aden to visit Pratibha's father, my mother had a premonition that she didn't overtly speak about. While we were in Bombay she opened her safe box and asked Pratibha to take her 5-carat diamond earrings. Patibha was flattered but said she needn't give the gift now, she would be coming back later anyway; however my mother insisted. "No, now I want to give them," as if she knew we wouldn't see her again. Her final words were haunting: "You never know what can happen." She did not tell us she had a premonition that she would not see us again.

It is interesting to note that of four of us, my three friends and myself, all but one of us married girls who had spent their lives in the continents of Africa and the Middle East. Pratibha had grown up in Aden. My friend Teju was single when I got married, but he eventually found a girl, Nipa, who was raised in Portuguese Africa, probably in Mozambique. My other friend, Kishore Shroff, who had tied his handkerchief around Pratibha's foot, dropped out of college but went to England where he learned a lot about chemical engineering and about essential chemicals like fertilizers, thanks to the expertise of his uncle. Kishore's brother Raju accompanied him to England where he married an English girl. Kishore could have married an English girl but he instead married Ranjan, a girl from Zanzibar, Africa. My friend Arvind joined one of the medical schools to please the wishes of his father, but he dropped out since it was not his cup of tea. Then he completed the undergraduate work, getting his Bachelor's degree in science. Arvind then helped his father in the iron business. They were wholesalers and exporters of iron mainly to Germany. He almost married a German girl, but the family pressure not to marry a girl from Germany ended that relationship. He was probably the smartest of his four brothers and eventually he married a girl from Ahmedabad. We four friends thank our lucky stars for having married girls who made us happy and prosperous. Did the wives bring us luck? I believe so.

We left Bombay for Aden on February 13, 1965. In Aden I met my father-in-law, Kantibhai, Pratibha's father. The British were in control of Aden, like the French in Djibouti; both of these colonies were opposite each other, located in the horn of Africa. Kantibhai and his associate met us at the airport. The next evening there was a fairly small reception gathering to celebrate the marriage of his daughter. Men in the party were served scotch and other liquors, which were not available in Bombay because of prohibition.

One of Kantibhai's business associates was a Parsi gentleman. There were many people working under the supervision of Kantibhai with different political views. Aden was a quiet, clean port city compared to the hustle and bustle of Bombay.

I remember one of Kantibhai's associates, a communist who admired the Chinese. This man wanted to see India have closer ties to China and he spoke highly of China, a country that was still going through great turmoil. However, I gave my opinion to the contrary, saying that the Chinese had captured and occupied Indian lands; they were creating difficulties for India by helping Nepalese and Assamese rebels in north and northeast India. "How can we be friends with the Chinese?" I asked. Kantibhai's Parsi associate also complained, saying that it was difficult to convince their communist associate about Chinese hegemonic intentions.

As I left India and the Middle East, I sensed a change was coming over my own country. India after the idealism of Patel, Nehru and Gandhi was becoming another licensed Raj. Corruption was growing everywhere. Sadly, I remember an incident with my old classmate and idealist friend Harshad, who would never take a bribe even if his life depended on it. In the fullness of time, he found he couldn't survive in India as it began to change. I could contrast that with my friend Teju who came as a refugee from Karachi. Teju had to be more street smart to survive rather than be an idealist like Harshad. Teju had received a Bachelor's degree and had joined his brother in business. Later on he did well in the garment export business.

One day Harshad came to Teju, as he had become desperate. He saw that Teju was able to provide more for his family than he was. Harshad out of desperation said, "I'm throwing in the towel. I'll do whatever you think I need to do. Please help." Teju did help him in the best way he could to "get corrupt" by learning the system that was at that time making it impossible to do honest business in India.

Before we reached LA, we decided to change Pratibha's name to Pratima. I thought the name Pratibha was a little old-fashioned. We left Aden for America flying via Copenhagen. Pratima was freezing wearing Indian clothes in Frankfurt. February falls in the winter season. I helped her get a topcoat and stockings from the airport to keep her warm. India's tropical latitudes are dramatically warmer than northern Europe.

When we arrived in LA, I called Dr. Jitu Butt from the airport and informed him, "I have a surprise for you, come and get it." He had a hunch what the surprise was and soon arrived at the airport. I introduced Pratima to him and he couldn't take his eyes off her. We stayed with him for a few days then moved to an apartment in Brentwood.

I realized then as I do now how fortunate I was to be married to Pratima. She basically had to adjust to my way of life in a new country — America. For an Indian woman this can be a great challenge. Also being separated from family so far away can make times very lonely. However, our love and affection grew every day. Remember, we only knew each other for no more than a month before our marriage. But in India there is a common philosophy that a man and wife fall in love after marriage. In America, it is the reverse. The massive divorce rates indicate that perhaps the Indian philosophy may be wiser.

I was a bit insecure in the beginning because so many friends and acquaintances appreciated Pratima's beauty, or compared her to famous Indian movie stars.

Our routine during the day was that I would go to UCLA for class and she would cook, watch TV, and meet her new friends. On weekends I played cricket. Every Saturday my UCLA team practiced for the match on Sunday. Sunday was a family event— the men playing thegameon thefield from roughly 10 am until 5 pm and the women preparing a brunch of sandwiches and other foods. This was a good social event for Pratima and it helped her to catch up on American ways of life. That season I earned a trophy for being the best bowler for the UCLA team in '65. As a first-year married man, life seemed very good. The team had players from all over the world, including Ireland, the West Indies, South Africa, England, India, and Pakistan. We had a good time teasing the English players; one thing common between the Indians and the Irish was a dislike of the English in matters of politics. It was all in good humor.

Pratima spent her time during the day learning to cook some Indian food preparations that she had never tried before. For example, she once tried to make Bengali Rasagullas out of fresh cheese, sugar, and spices. The first time she made them, they came out like smooth hard white balls, hard to bite and very sweet inside, like the marbles kids play with. Rasagullas are supposed to be soft, tender, uniformly sweet balls with texture. I was very appreciative of her making the dish, since I did not want her to get discouraged from trying to cook new dishes. She would take classes in home furnishing in the evening while I was attending classes in engineering.

In the meantime I would get letters from home about how Jasvantbhai and Jitubhai were both at odds with each other and how my father tried to keep the balance in the middle. My father had purchased manufacturing equipment from Poland for waste cotton products. The machines were installed in a factory in Ahmedabad.

Jasvantbhai was managing the factory and the factory was eating up lots of money because of bad government policies in India. Originally the Indian government had restricted licenses for factories for waste cotton products, but later they opened up many licenses to all sorts of people. This caused an over supply of waste cotton products, reducing the product price, which in turn caused much loss in the industry. It was a big concern for my family as the factory was not making a profit. They were rapidly losing the family wealth.

To make matters worse, my mother's premonition came true. She was diabetic and had high blood pressure. One of her feet got infected due to an accidental wound. Being diabetic, obese, and having a weaker heart, things got very complicated. When I came home early from UCLA in July 1965, I noticed Pratima was quiet when she asked me to have dinner. She seemed to be in a serious mood. I did not realize that she was trying very hard not to cry. Once I had finished dinner, she could no longer hold back her tears. Then she gave me the Western Union wire she had received. The telegram informed me of the demise of my mother. I couldn't stop crying. I called my family. I told them I was taking the next plane to India but they said it wasn't necessary. The cremation of my mother's body was planned for the next day. There was no way I could be there in time. This was the biggest shock of my life.

I was told later that my father had been depressed for weeks after my mother passed away. His mistress, who later became his second wife, had little experience in cooking and other matters to take care of him the way my mother had. As a result his health began to deteriorate. Also, in India and specifically in our community, when a man marries his mistress, his status in society drops.

Discontent between my brothers Jasvantbhai and Jitubhai continued over how Jasvantbhai was running the factory in Ahmedabad. Jitubhai was also starting to feel insecure because Jasvantbhai had built a big house for his family in Ahmedabad, adding expenses to the negative cash flow caused by the factory. Jitubhai and his wife, on the other hand, were still living with my father. So when my mother died, Jitubhai felt uncertain. Also, conditions for business were worsening in India. As the family fortune dwindled and the country began to change, my dreams of returning to India and starting a manufacturing business were dashed.

I would get letters from my father that things were not good, and quarreling between my two brothers did not help. In the meantime, Jitubhai planned to move out of the Sion flat, the flat we all grew up in. He put a deposit on a flat in Breach Candy. As they say in the real estate business, location is extremely important to determine the real value. Needless to say, properties closer to the ocean are a lot more valuable. Sion is not only distant from the ocean but also far from the heart of Mumbai. Jitubhai's new flat faced the ocean and was a lot closer to the business and financial activities in Mumbai. That was probably the best thing that happened for him and his family.

I wrote to my father that out of my wages I could easily send about 150 dollars every month, if needed. My father was very happy to read that letter of support. He never forgot those written words to his dying days. We entertained many visitors from Mumbai, family friends, and some associated with my father's business. One afternoon, Pratima received a phone call from one of her family's neighbors from Los Angeles International Airport asking her for help in getting Indian spicy food. The man was travelling with a Bollywood film crew, including mega-star Raj Kapoor, one of the most popular film stars of all time. To some of us, he resembled the Hollywood hero, Clark Gable. They were shooting the movie *Around the World in Eight Dollars,* with a theme parallel to the Hollywood movie *Around the World in Eighty Days.* I recall Bollywood had produced movies in the '50s and '60s stealing stories similar to the stories of successful Hollywood movies. The dollar, tied to the gold standard, was probably the hardest currency in the world. The government of India would allow only eight dollars for travel abroad, which was a farce. That was 1965, when it was difficult to find Indian vegetarian spicy food. Raj Kapoor was literally dying for some Indian food. Pratima promptly made some vegetarian sandwiches with spicy cooked vegetables. I drove to the airport as quickly as I could and delivered them. Raj Kapoor was very happy and thankful to us.

Meanwhile in America, the Vietnam War was in full swing. After Kennedy's assassination, President Johnson expanded the American commitment to nearly 500,000 soldiers and we were hearing about a "gun and butter policy" for America and the war in Southeast Asia. Marty Centala, as a navigator, had completed many assignments along with his fellow pilots, flying over North Vietnam and dropping bombs. I would argue against the war for wasting lives and resources. Little did I know that Southeast Asia would be the key to my own fortune in the not-so-far future.

My family. Back row: Three brothers and our wives, standing. Middle row, from left: My parents, grandfather, and my uncle and aunt. Front row: Cousins Jayshree, Bharati, Nayana, Jagruti, and Daksha, February 2· 1965.

The best UCLA-B team bowler of the year 1965. Marriage helped me to become more confident both in sports and in my profession.

UCLA-B Cricket team, 1965; I am third from the left, seated. Players came from India, Australia, Hong Kong, South Africa, Ireland, England, and the West Indies.

CHAPTER 6

SEARCHING FOR THE HOLY GRAIL

"In business, the whole concept of supply and demand is king."

J. D. Rockefeller

While attending my classes and doing research work at UCLA, in the summer I looked for a job and was able to set up a few interviews. I was fortunate to get a job at Acoustica Associates. I was hired by Dr. Cameron Knox, the vice president, who became a very good friend later on. Dr. Knox was a guru to me, among several others in my life. Acoustica was mainly involved in research and the manufacturing of products associated with a wide spectrum of sound, like ultrasonic cleaners, Atlas rocket fuel quantity sensors, and other acoustic products.

I was hired for a program Acoustica had signed with the Air Force, to develop an instrument to measure liquid fuel in a tank in a zero or very low-gravity environment. The contract budget given to Acoustica was about half a million dollars. The engineer who was responsible for the contract had left Acoustica, and they needed a replacement who would carry on to *develop* the gauge based on a patent owned by Acoustica. When the gravity is zero in space, away from the gravitational pull of Mother Earth, the liquid propellant or the fuel that is needed for rocket propulsion, stored in a tank, assumes unpredictable and changing shapes, depending on the motion of the satellite and other characteristics of the liquid, such as viscosity, surface tension, pressure and temperature. The principle of the patent was based on the thermodynamic laws for gases, applied to inaudible very low-frequency sound.

My basic activities included taking engineering classes at UCLA in the evening, while Pratima took classes in interior decoration. One of the classes I took was in solid-state electronics offered by a young professor, Vishvanathan (Vis). Often Pratima would sit with me in the class after she had finished her class. Vis noticed us because he had an appreciation for good-looking women. In time we became everlasting good friends. Pratima became pregnant around October 1965. Naturally Dr. Jitu Bhat (JB), a gynecologist and a wonderful friend, was gracious enough to take care of Pratima's pregnancy. A small company like Acoustica did not provide health insurance in those days. However, we were fortunate to have a friend like JB, who did not charge us any doctor's fees. We were quite ignorant in matters of the cost of health insurance; I suppose it would have cost us an arm and a leg to obtain insurance.

On July 4, 1966, Pratima had completed about nine months of pregnancy. Pratima was due in a few days as per Dr. JB's calculations. So on the Fourth of July when we visited him at Kaiser Hospital he said, "She's just about ready any day. Would you like to have her deliver today, now?" And I said, "Well, if she isn't in labor, how can she deliver?" Dr. Bhat responded that there is such a thing as "induced delivery," and he had some reasons why he suggested this for delivering the baby on the Fourth of July. Number one: The Fourth of July, being Independence Day in the U.S., would be a good day for the baby to be born, at least a memorable day. Number two: In his estimation Pratima was ready. He also reasoned that lighter babies grew taller statistically. So I agreed to it. In hindsight, he turned out to be right.

To this day I believe agreeing to have an induced delivery was probably one of the worst mistakes I made. I have been a believer in natural processes. I should not have agreed to an induced delivery; it should have been a natural delivery. Rahul was born in the late evening on the Fourth of July. He weighed 5 pounds and 12 ounces, slightly less than 6 pounds. He was indeed on the smaller side. At that time there was a perception among doctors that delivering a smaller baby was also good for mothers, being less painful. As a small-framed woman, Pratima would find it easier to deliver.

After two days I brought Pratima and Rahul, our newborn son, home. The next day I got a call at work from Pratima who was sobbing at home. I quickly went home and discovered Pratima had noticed Rahul was a bit yellowish or anemic. This was a brilliant observation from an inexperienced mother only twenty years of age. We immediately called Dr. JB and took Rahul back to Kaiser's. Rahul, being anemic, was put into an incubator under observation. The next day the doctors suggested that a blood transfusion would be in order. One of Dr. JB's colleagues, a pediatrician, explained to us that the risk factor was less than one passing away in an auto accident, statistically less than 3 percent. So we agreed to have Rahul go through the blood transfusion, which was performed the same day. Fortunately everything worked out well.Rahul started to gain weight rapidly. During this ordeal he had gone from a little less than 6 pounds to about 5 pounds. When he was released, he weighed over 6 pounds.

In looking back, I think 1966 was a key period. First, we became the proud parents of Rahul. I was working very actively, sometimes overtime, for Acoustica. We still did not have a green card, though Acousta had applied on my behalf. So I was on a student visa and Pratima was the spouse of a student. But by having Rahul born in America, the chances of the parents (us) of an American being deported for any reason were diminished. We had a secure future now that we were the parents of an American child born on the Fourth of July. It was a cinch that we would not have difficulties to settle in America for two reasons: one, being parents of an American, and second, due to the need for specialized engineers.

When John F. Kennedy came into power, he wanted to change the immigration laws. While he was president, there was a quota system, mostly assigned to Europeans. It was literally an open border for people from Scandinavia, Germany, England, and France. Quotas for other European countries were huge. Asian and African countries were much lower. India, the second most populated country in the world, had a quota of only 100. But President Kennedy wanted to change from the old quota system based on the ethnicity of the population of the U.S., which was primarily made up of European immigrants, to the basis of the country's needs. The Asian populations in the U.S. were pretty minuscule, plus there was prejudice and all kinds of laws prohibiting or controlling Asians within the country. Kennedy wanted to change the law based on qualifications. That was the time the U.S. was competing with the Soviets in the satellite race. The American government was placing loads of contracts for the space programs. Companies who had aerospace contracts usually needed security clearances for many of their employees. I didn't even have a green card, so it made it difficult to get me a security clearance. Still, Acoustica applied for one for me and they worked on it very hard.

I believe many of us were grateful to President Johnson who carried out Kennedy's agenda, which included immigration and civil right laws. Thankfully Pratima and I got our green cards towards the end of '66. I ended up working at Acoustica for two-and-a-half years while also doing my PhD. Then there was a slowdown at Acoustica. The aerospace program involving me was not yet renewed. The half-a-million-dollar funding for the contract I was working on was finished by September 1967.

We had constructed four prototype gauges. Our gauges were flown in space to be tested. It worked for about an hour or so and then the gauges stopped working, because they were flooded with the test liquid. There was a question mark about the funding needed for my employment. Ultimately by the end of '67, my job was terminated. I was still working on my PhD at UCLA. So I started to look for another employer. Dr. Knox, who had been working at TRW, arranged a number of interviews for me there. In a period of two months I was offered a job in three different places. Two jobs were offered at TRW, and another at a subsidiary of Xerox. Xerox had some aerospace programs, but their plant was in Pasadena and I didn't want such a long commute from west Los Angeles. I accepted the job at TRW in their propulsion lab.

I started working at TRW in January 1968. Back on the subject of immigration, before the immigration law was passed in the congress and the senate, the only way Indians obtained their green cards was through marriage. It was extremely difficult otherwise. There was another avenue I remember. A couple of good friends of ours who came from Africa said they had bought a car wash with a 40,000 dollar investment and got a green card. Later on, those who had an MS degree in engineering found it quite easy to get a green card. At TRW things were very challenging. I worked on two or three different programs. There was a lot of research work plus writing the reports. Basically I was involved with rocketpropulsion systems and sometimes instrumentation needed in the environment of outer space.

About this time I got a call out of the blue from Ravi Badkar. We hadn't seen each other for a while. Ravi was dating a Danish girl. When he found out I was married, he wanted to get in touch with me and I was surprised and happy to hear from him, and glad he'd taken the initiative. We had not been on good terms due to a misunderstanding about dating Leslie, a friend in common. When Ravi and his girlfriend Gunhild came to visit us, Pratima insisted they have dinner with us. Gunhild was very impressed with our hospitality and thought we were a very handsome couple. I would like to claim that we were instrumental for them to get married within a few months.

We paid 120 dollars a month's rent for our apartment in Brentwood. A doctor couple, Munir and Chandra whom we met through UCLA, suggested we move into married student housing, which would be good for baby Rahul as there would be other married couples with children. Munir, a Muslim, had married Chandra, a Hindu woman. When working for the leaders of India during the freedom movement, they had fallen in love. However, after they married, they realized that the idealism of the freedom movement was dissipating very quickly. They had no choice but to leave India to avoid family conflicts. First they migrated to England, and later to America, working at UCLA.

We applied and were fortunate to get into married student housing located at 3170 Sawtell Boulevard. It was larger than our two-bedroom apartment in Brentwood, and the rent was 95 dollars a month, which included utilities. There were shuttles to UCLA if you didn't have transportation. Rahul now had lots of company and babysitting was easy. There were other students, and we could compare notes for classes and life in general. Many of the students were from a number of different countries, not just India; they were from Iran, England, Egypt, Yugoslavia, you name it. There was a babysitting club and occasionally we had events with all the kids getting together. There was a very good nursery school close by sponsored by UCLA.

In December 1968 and January 1969, Pratima went to India with Rahul, now two and a half. She had a good time and was well taken care of in Bombay and Ahmedabad. She made one error though, leaving Rahul's passport at the airport. Luckily it was found and sent to the American Consulate who returned it to her. Pratima returned to the U.S. in February 1969. She became pregnant with Sonya in March 1969. I was studying like crazy and working at TRW. I had finished all my coursework for the PhD, but in '68 and '69 the Vietnam War was in full blast. There was an election in '68 for the U.S. presidency, Richard Nixon versus Hubert Humphrey. Because of the Vietnam War expansion by President Johnson, a democrat, democrat Hubert Humphrey lost the election to the Republican candidate Nixon. Most foreign students, especially among Indians, were for Humphrey, because we had the impression that he was a good statesman and a good human being.

Sonya was born on December 9th 1969 in the late evening. It was touch and go when I took Pratima to St. John hospital in Santa Monica, about five miles away. Luckily Pratima was able to stay in control till we reached the hospital, in spite of my goof up in the directions and driving a very jerky VW bus to the hospital. We were fortunate that Sarojbhabhi had come from Bombay to help us to take care of Rahul. I must add that things were happening against my desire after Sonya's birth, but for the better as you will read in later chapters. It reminds me of the statement made by the father of astronaut Kalpana Chavla. In his words, "Good things happen in families when good people are born." My father, when he was visiting Los Angeles in 1977, would go every morning to Sonya's bedroom to see her face.

President Nixon started to trim the budget starting from 1969 during his first year in office. However he expanded the Vietnam War, invading and bombing Laos and Cambodia. There were student riots in different universities protesting the compulsory military draft. At a protest in Ohio at Kent State University, police killed several protesting students. Draft dodging went on when students did not want to be drafted; many went to Canada to avoid the draft. Boxing champion Muhammad Ali protested the draft based on his religious belief. He was put in jail but won the case in court. However he suffered because he lost his license to fight and his championship title. Marty Centala, my big brother at Ann Arbor, had transferred to California after completing many missions to Vietnam. He had married Evan, a girl from Michigan, and they were the parents of a boy and a girl.

I was fortunate to be married and also to be needed for the government programs to avoid the draft. When I worked at TRW though, I received a draft notice (sent to anyone from ages eighteen to thirty), but was able to get the exemption, thanks to my employer.

President Nixon cut the NASA budget in half to spend more money for the war. When he was elected in November 1968, TRW had about 14,000 employees at the One Space Park location with lots of contracts. But because of budget cuts for the research programs, a lot of companies in California had to scale back. Small companies who were sub-contractors to bigger companies had to close their doors. I remember an advertisement in the *Los Angeles Times* run by a group of smaller companies that said: "We Voted for You, Mr. President, What Have We Done Wrong?"

This also affected the graduate student program at UCLA, where up to this time almost anyone could get a PhD, because the UCLA advisors were lenient and there was sufficient demand for PhD graduates. With the Vietnam War going on, and the cuts in research budgets by the government, I began to realize that universities were affected by the economic environment. There were more unemployed PhD graduates, thanks to the shrinking job opportunities. In such a bad economic environment, the school advisers extended the dissertation time of PhD candidates, asking the students to do more and more work on their dissertations. It reminded me of the experience of roommate Dhorda at the University of Michigan.

By 1970 we were the parents of two children, as Sonya was born on December 9, 1969. I was among five students appearing for the written qualifying exam for an engineering PhD program. Out of five of us, the department failed four. I was the only one who passed the written exam. I felt very fortunate. Then came time for the oral examination. My impression of a professor coming from any Midwestern or Eastern university, based on my experience in Ann Arbor, was not so favorable. I tried to avoid Professor Bauer, who had recently joined UCLA, coming from one of the Eastern universities. But he insisted on being part of the oral exam committee. While taking an oral exam before this committee, I answered most of their questions accurately. Often Dr. Bauer would argue that the answer was not accurate. I would not contest his argument, thinking that I would impress them as being arrogant. We were taught in India to be polite and humble by conforming to the words of our teachers and professors. The oral exam committee failed me because they felt I did not have a strong conviction in my answers. So the committee and I had a different perception of the truth.

It was at this moment that I decided to protect my job at TRW. Employee numbers were going down and down by the day. After the layoffs were completed, there were only 7,500 employees left, about half the peak population. I was fortunate that in the propulsion department lab where I was working, my boss Dick Salvinski, for whom I had a very high regard, found a place for me in part of the instrumentations department. I worked in that department for nearly twelve years, from 1970 to 1982. Marty Centala, who had also moved to LA, was monitoring for the Air Force a contract given to an aerospace company. I introduced Marty to some of my department heads, so that TRW could get contracts through him. We had a good time with him. He had bought a house in El Segundo, but after a couple of years he left Los Angeles because he preferred the East Coast where he was needed the most, being a nuclear engineer.

Back at UCLA, after they failed all of us, we were asked to take some more coursework and then take another exam. I decided to quit the PhD program. That was June 1970. Also, I had an apprehension that I didn't want to see myself following in the footsteps of my friend Dhorda and other PhD students at the University of Michigan. While Dhorda was doing his PhD work, his professor extended his dissertation a number of times and the frustration caused him to have a breakdown. When I first enrolled in the doctoral program, my professor at UCLA assured me I would complete the degree in a period of three to four years working part time for the program. In spite of the fact that I had spent three years on it, and had taken all the required courses, I believe this was one of the best decisions I had made. Many students had completed their PhD's earlier, before the economic slowdown of 1970, but couldn't find work. This was difficult for UCLA because so many had families and UCLA didn't have the money to keep them on the payroll. I also gathered this was happening in other places where degrees were not being given and more requirements were being asked to be completed. One of the PhD students later updated me, saying that none of the remaining four students had received their PhD degrees five years later, in 1975. Students who had passed the written and oral test were still working on their dissertations!

As time went by, a few unemployed TRW engineers still looking for work found lower-paying jobs as teachers in schools, or went to other countries like Canada. Many of the fellows terminated from TRW were PhD's because the companies were saving money by laying off highly paid and highly qualified employees. I remember one friend with a PhD from UCLA who was a software engineer; when he was laid off he found a lower-paid job at one of the junior colleges. As the space research and defense budget was cut, along with an increasing interest rate, the economy went into a recession; many war-based companies that had been doing lots of business during the height of the war also lost contracts.

By '71 the economy was improving, thanks to the upcoming presidential election. In September 1971 the Middle East experienced the Yom Kippur War when Egypt and the other Arab countries invaded Israel. Though Israel was victorious, it was touch and go for a while. An oil embargo during that time caused the price of oil to go up from four dollars a barrel to over 20 dollars a barrel. That was the start of inflation that lasted all the way through the mid-'80s. I would say America received a left hook and a right blow from the

Vietnam War, the Yom Kippur War, and Nixon's Watergate fiasco. All these events also caused economic dislocations.

After Nixon resigned and Gerald Ford became president, the misery index rose awfully high, devised by adding interest rates, inflation rates, and unemployment rates. Even the next president Jimmy Carter, elected in '76, was not able to control the economic downturn. Unemployment was nearly nine percent, the inflation rate was 10 percent, and interest rates were going up and down but the trend was upward during that time and peaked in '81 when Ronald Reagan was newly elected president. As a result the U.S. government bonds and some municipal bonds were yielding as high as 15 percent per year.

My father still wanted me to come back to India and settle down. In August 1971 I took a vacation and leave of absence of two months for a trip to India. My job at TRW was still secure, thanks to my bosses, Mr. Ramsberry and Mr. Marlon Hed. I almost got laid off in the instrumentation department, but my English boss, Mr. Ramsberry, saw my value and protected my job. We understood that it would be a big effort to resettle in India, so Pratima and I packed, preparing to move to India. I had saved about 20,000 dollars at the time.

My father and Jasvantbhai were very enthused I was returning and had offered me a partnership. Jitubhai was a little bit discouraging because he wasn't happy with the economic conditions in India. Another reason could have been that it is certainly not prudent to have more members of the family dependent on only one business. But they were all trying to help us settle if we wanted to. We took the Air India flight from New York to Mumbai via London, to spend a few days there to expose five-year-old Rahul to some of the educational museums. Pratima was carrying all her inherited jewelry from our parents, worth tens of thousands of rupees, in her purse. Next morning after arriving in London and having a late breakfast, we started off to sightsee. Pratima suddenly realized that she had left her purse somewhere, either in the hotel room or in the restaurant. In exasperation, we ran back to the restaurant. Luckily the angelic waitress had kept it for us; we thanked her profusely and our lucky stars for not losing our only valuable possessions at that time.

After arriving in Mumbai, we settled down in my father's top-floor flat. It was quite congested, as it was also occupied by Jitubhai's family of four, therefore having nine occupants in a three-bedroom flat that included the room on the terrace. As time went by, we encountered a few difficulties, including getting Rahul admitted into a good school. My father had set up a meeting for me with one of the biggest industrialists in India, the Mafatlal Group, also because our family business was with them. Jitubhai and I went to Shree Arvindbhai Mafatlal's huge office, located in one of the high risers at Flora-Fountain, and arrived on time.

After we were seated, I asked him a few questions politely on matters of India's economy at the time, and expressed my desire to start a production factory. He inquired about my education and the experience I had acquired in Los Angeles. After a pause, he strongly recommended that I not settle in India at that time. He was having a very bad experience interacting with Indira Gandhi, the prime minister of India. Corruption was rampant in India after she became prime minister. He had wanted to establish some petrochemical factories in Gujarat, but Indira Gandhi would not give the license to establish the plant unless she received 10 percent of the project cost. Back then, the licensed Raj was in full swing, and one had to pay a bribe to get a license. Arvinbhai, a follower of Mahatma Gandhi's philosophy and an idealist, was not happy with Indira Gandhi; she was then known to be collecting bribe money for her future political campaign. We spent a couple of weeks in Ahmadabad with Jasvantbhai's family. I cannot forget their graciousness, making us feel at home. They took care of all four of us when we were suffering from influenza.

So in '71 I took Arvindbhai's advice, and returned to the U.S. Pratima and the kids were still in India. I had only taken eight weeks of vacation and some leave of absence. I went back to work for TRW without a second thought of going back to India. Then the'71 Bangladesh War broke out between India and Pakistan. One of the reasons most Indians didn't like Nixon was that he favored Pakistan over India in almost every dispute India had with Pakistan. India had a big refugee problem coming from East Pakistan (now called Bangladesh). There were over a million refugees. Pakistan generals in East Pakistan were literally butchering people. Prime Minister Indira Gandhi had no choice but to enter the conflict.

I was very worried over this conflict between India and Pakistan because there were stories of bombings all over India that included Bombay. Pratima and the kids had not been able to catch a flight back to LA when the war broke out. Luckily the war didn't last too long; it ended in January '72. When I came back from Bombay to Los Angeles, I had rented a studio apartment, and now all four of us were living a little bit cramped in one large room containing a kitchen. We spent a month looking for another place and found a two-bedroom apartment in west Los Angeles in February 1972. We then made a decision that we would not return to India, and would accept the U.S. as our home for good.

It was so different when I visited Mumbai in '61 compared to the visit in '71, when my mother was alive. We were then one united family. I had brought an expensive stereo sound system with broadband radio and a record player that cost me a fortune, along with so many gifts for each and every one in the family. I believed I would inherit a portion of my father's wealth before my mother passed away in July 1965, just after our marriage. I had saved only 2,000 dollars from the wages I had earned when I came back with Pratima after our marriage; that was February 1965. My father did not feel secured financially in '66 after my mother passed away, when he had written a letter to me about the problems within the family and the loss of the binding force that my mother represented.

Fast forward to '71. Jitubhai told me that I would have to put all of my savings in the business if I decided to migrate to Mumbai. I had only 20,000 dollars saved when we visited Mumbai to investigate settling down in India. It had taken about seven years to save that amount. Considering the friction within the family, and not having the binding force of my mother, I had lost hope of getting any inheritance from my family. My two brothers and my father, who had another family with two children, were tightly holding their own portions of the wealth that included the business, real estate, and the family jewelry. I would like to add that my father and Jasvantbhai, in later years, were quite generous as the business improved; they would give us gifts, including gold jewelry and pure silverware.

In March 1972, we bought our first eight units apartment building for 80,000 dollars. The rent was about 16,000 dollars a year if it was fully occupied, which was one fifth of the price that we paid for the building. The money I needed to buy this building was only 10,000 dollars. We figured if we worked hard and took on the maintenance and painting ourselves, we could have a cash flow of easily 3,000 to 4,000 dollars a year. This would help in case I got laid off again. Thanks to my inexperience, I thought buying a house was not a good thing to do then.

The eight-unit building we bought was relatively inexpensive because it was located on Olin Street near the noisy Freeway 10, just west of La Cienega Boulevard and north of Venice Boulevard. The neighborhood was also changing; more minority renters were moving in replacing more affluent renters. The building was harder to manage because the rent collection was more difficult. We purchased the building from a postman, Mr. Epstein, who was retiring. A postman owning an apartment building indicated the strength of the U.S. economy with a broad middle class. A postman from a lower middle class was able to save enough money from his wages to invest in an apartment building. Mr. and Mrs. Epstein evidently retired quite comfortably.

I had the full support of Pratima. Whenever there was a vacancy, she painted the apartment. I took care of any plumbing problems, because as an engineer I learned the basics of plumbing and found it was not a difficult job. We also bought a house in the same year in Palms. It was a three-bedroom, two-bathroom house for 35,000 dollars. I got it with a five percent down payment and a 95 percent loan. I needed about 5,000 dollars, which included the escrow, title, and other costs. Those were the good old days. The monthly loan payment was 305 dollars, 100 dollars more than the rent we were paying for the two-bedroom apartment.

I would like to say that, in my humble opinion, this decade was also the start of the decline of the U.S. I believe we saw the peak of America in the early '70s, before the expansion of the Vietnam War, the oil embargo, the Yom Kippur War, and the Watergate fiasco. Americans had a very high work ethic before those events. People would tell me it was not just a crime but a sin to not pay taxes. But after Watergate, when people saw the degradation at the highest level of the presidency, I feel this probably created more suspicion, more disbelief, and more dislike of the government. Under Ronald Reagan in the '80s the American standard of living got a boost, but during the '80s it became clear in this country that to maintain the same lifestyle and standard of living, most families needed both the husband and wife working. Before the '70s it was more common for mothers to stay home with their children. With both parents working, America saw a rise in its juvenile delinquency problems, gang problems, and just raising kids. Because both parents weren't around, the school environment became the key environment for kids. As a result, teachers inherited the problems and conflicts of not only families but of the children who were left behind. Such an environment created divorces and more single parents.

Back in India, my father and his second wife from Goa now had two children, Deepak and Jyoti. The eldest of three, a daughter, had died due to an accident in a swimming pool. The remaining two really had no future in India for the simple reason that children born of a non-gujarati much younger second wife, were not socially acceptable. This is why my two brothers were not ready to put Deepak in their business. My feeling was that the children didn't do anything wrong nor should they be blamed for our father's actions. I also needed help, in both the apartment business and the bedspread business. In America, there are no social taboos similar to those in India, so I offered to help. I suggested to my father that Deepak could come to LA and help me in my business part time, and go to school for a degree. My uncles' sons also were ready to come to America. However I could not handle more than one at the time. Later on, we helped to bring in Jagruti in the '80s and Bhavesh in the '90s, Pratima's niece and nephew. Our velvet patchwork fabric business was then on the right track, and the cash flow from the business was invested in buying more apartment buildings.

My niece Bharati in India was also growing up and the family wanted her to get married. She had always been the "apple of our eye" as a young girl. Now she was tall and pretty at 5 feet 8 inches. The waste cotton plant, which was still losing money, was eventually closed by my family. The wholesale fabric agency business of two operations, one in Ahmedabad run by Jasvantbhai, and the other in Bombay being handled by Jitubhai, were now separated. Jitubhai inherited money, making business in Bombay. Jasvantbhai didn't know what to do once the factory was closed. He even worked for another businessman in Ahmedabad, which was a step down in prestige for him. Later on my father helped him to carry on the wholesale textile business in Ahmadabad, which had suffered thanks to the waste cotton plant problems.

Jasvantbhai was concerned about his economic situation and Bharati's height, since he thought there were not many tall boys in Ahmadabad. Eventuallya young man, Amar Patel, was found for Bharti to marry. He was taller than she, with a BS degree. I had suggested to Jasvantbhai that Bharati come to Los Angeles. I offered to take care of her, but the stress of the moment and the idea of coming to America were too much for her family. As a businessman, Jasvantbhai believed he was a better provider of a comfortable life for his daughter than I, an employee working for a company. There was also no visibility about Bharati's future if she were to come to America. Bharati married Amarbhai, but in my opinion, she could have done much better in America, because she was pretty and smart and would have been considered a beautiful catch in the U.S. Jitubhai and his family had already moved from Sion to their newly acquired flat in a prestigious location, Breach Candy, overlooking the Indian Ocean.

Deepak came to Los Angelesin early '73. He was admitted at one of the business schools in Los Angeles downtown called Woodberry University. He was a good help and handyman. My father was very happy that Deepak's fortune would be better in the U.S. A year later, because of the hard work involved in helping me and my businesses, he wrote a letter to my father complaining. As a result we decided that he'd help us as before, but stay with his friends near the school. I was probably a bit harsh, but I was also learning how to help my teenage half-brother. He finished school and received his Bachelor's degree in business management. Our velvet business was going full blast. I was also working at TRW full time. I was able to operate the velvet business with Pratima and Deepak's assistance. They would pick up the goods from the dock and then we initially would store them in our garage. From there we'd distribute them to our clients. I used my hour or hour-and-a-half lunch break and hours after work to interact with clients. It was probably one of the most efficient ways of running our business.

With some capital in '74, we bought an additional 16-unit apartment building. In '76 we added another 10 units. Every year some of the savings from the velvet business was used to buy real estate and high-yielding bonds. I was always scared of the stock market in those days. Some municipal bonds yielded on the order of 15 percent, tax-free, because in the '70s, the rate of inflation rose every year. The reason for the rise was the loss of confidence in the dollar as a world reserve currency. President Nixon had disconnected dollar ties with gold. America was spending money hand over fist for the Vietnam War; add to it the loss of confidence in the government due to the Watergate events that caused President Nixon to resign. The exponential rise in oil prices due to the Yom Kippur War between Egypt and Israel added to the problem of inflation. In hindsight, it all worked out very well for us.

The work at TRW was also rewarding in many ways. The work environment was quite pleasant, similar to the one on the university campus. I was helping many project managers in matters of developing measurement standards. For example, we were required to measure the power of a chemical laser developed at TRW that would generate several kilowatts of power in a beam of one-inch diameter. I was able to devise a method to measure the power traceable to the National Bureau of Standards. There was also camaraderie among fellow engineers and technicians. Occasionally there was a lunch party for a departing or retiring fellow employee. One memorable event was a lunch party given for Smithy, a technician who cleaned and calibrated thelaboratoryfurnaces. He reminded me of President Reagan, having a very pleasant demeanor and ever ready to deliver a joke. There were over one hundred TRW employees present to give Smithy a memorable send-off. I believe one of the reasons Smithy was so popular was because his body language and mannerisms were similar to Reagan's.

TRW management had no problem if the employee had a side business as long as there was no conflict of interest with the business of TRW. When one of the managers of Northrop, Mr. Gandy, contacted me to consult on a NASA project, I asked my manager for permission to work for NASA. I was offered a 5,000-dollar contract for my consultation on the zero gravity volumetric gauging system I had worked on at Acoustica. He advised me not to worry and accept the contract, since the paperwork to get an affirmative answer would take months and the dollar amount was insignificant.

My colleague, engineer Sorokov, had a hobby panning for gold in his spare time. He would melt the panned gold and make it 99 % pure. I would buy his gold at a 10 percent discount over the spot price, after ensuring that it was indeed 99 % pure. I would take the gold to India and exchange it for antique jewelry from a jeweler who had clients from Rajput royalty. Jasvantbhai had the jeweler come to his house with his inventory of old jewelry for transection. The jeweler was happy to get 99 % (24 carat) pure gold, and I was happy to get 92 % pure (22 carat) antique jewelry with no labor cost.

Occasionally, we would go sailing with my immediate boss Jerry Velutini during a long lunch hour. Jerry had his sailboat docked at Redondo Beach pier, about 10 minutes from TRW. One day we were sailing in Jerry's boat in a bit of rough weather. My lunch was deep-fried spinach Bhajias (similar to French fries or onion rings, but green in color) with a green-colored cold milk because it contained green spicy Khas-khas syrup. Frank Halagan, a fellow engineer, was not comfortable seeing me eating and drinking the green stuff. A rough sea did not help either. Frank was getting sick by the minute, holding the boat wall very tight, and looking disgustingly at me. When he started to vomit with half of his body out of the boat, I stopped eating and held him tight because I was afraid that he could fall in the rough sea. We sailed back immediately for Frank's comfort. From then on, we made sure that I did not have a green lunch and that the sea was calm before we decided to go sailing.

Sonya, Rahul and Navin, back yard of UCLA
married student housing 1971

Marty, Evan and their daughter Mary (on right) with Pratima, Rahul, and Sonya, 1971.

Pratima carrying Sonya with UCLA graduate students' wives and their children at the UCLA married students housing.

FIELD OPERATIONS

TRW has conducted extensive surface studies in support of many important ocean spectrographic sensing projects. The photographs shown here include scenes of TRW measurement support activities aboard the R/V Falcon off the coast of San Francisco during NASA's 1972 Ocean Color Expedition. The surface data was correlated with the data from MOCS equipment being flown in a Convair 990 aircraft. Other aircraft used have included C45, Cessna 180, C54, DC-3, Bell Jet Ranger Helicopter, Lockheed P3-V, Grumman Widgeon, Aero Commander, and Piper Apache.

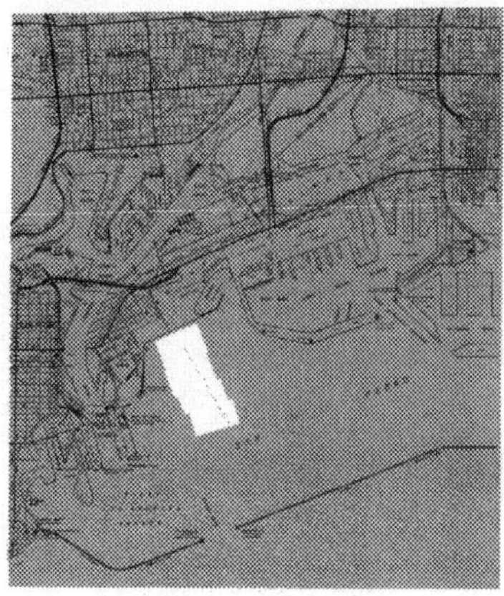

Data collected by TRW remote sensing equipment flown over Los Angeles Harbor was correlated with surface data obtained by ship. Numbered circles indicate positions where water samples were taken. Numbered lines indicate the trace of sensor scans. Sewage outfall of a primary treatment plant, upper right, joining with effluent from a cannery, upper left, is believed to nourish gonyaulax plankton in the bottom frame of the picture.

TRW divers and I plan a test of an ocean device (from a scan of a TRW advertisement pamphlet). The scan also shows a map of Marina Del Ray, 1969.

Sadness on the faces of parents Jasvantbhai and Damubhabhi when their eldest daughter Bharati leaves their house after her marriage, early 1970s.

Bharati at her marriage, with Jasvantbhai.

): Pratima with Rahul, Premkur-kaki (my father's aunt) and my father (front), Nayana, unknown, Narbada-kaki (my father's auant), and Damubhabhi, 1969

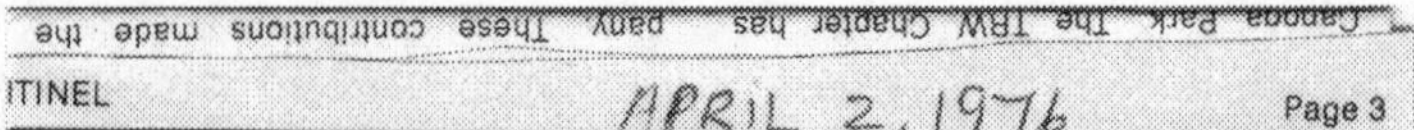

ITINEL APRIL 2, 1976 Page 3

NASA AWARD WINNERS — Fifty-dollar checks are presented to DSSG personnel who have reported innovative technology to NASA. The presentations are made by Dr. Robert Bromberg, vice president for research (second l. back). Winners were (front l.-r.) Navin Doshi, Jorge Decanini, Durk Pearson, Bruce Marcus and (back l.) Richard Salvinski. Also present were Richard Brown, DSSG legal counsel, and Daniel Anderson, patent counsel.

Reporting new technology is important to company growth

(already printed)

): Pratima's visit to India in January 1969, with Rahul, Damubhabhi, Bharati, Jasvantbhai, Nayana, Daksha, MahendraKaka's daughter Harsha, and sons, Rajesh and Piyush.

CHAPTER 7

THE OPPORTUNITY

"A friend to all. An ally to none.""

Andrew Carnegie

One of several things that I attribute to my success is listening to people with experience. For example, the late Dr. Cameron Knox, who had hired me at Acoustica, had vast experience in matters of business in America. He later arranged several interviews for me at TRW when he began working there. TRW (Thompson Ramo Wooldridge) had its beginnings in a garage designing and making microwave systems, including radar guided missiles. Initially it was the Ramo Wooldridge Corporation, established in 1953. Later on, it was acquired by the Thompson Auto Parts Company, and the name was changed to TRW Inc. I remember using a textbook written by Dr. Simon Ramo when I took a class on electromagnetics at Ann Arbor. Dr. Knox and the Acoustica president, Robert Rod, who seemed very temperamental, had disagreements running Acoustica, a small company. Dr. Knox had to leave and was able to find a good position at TRW.

Dr. Knox was in some ways a guru to me. When I was pondering buying a house, I decided to first buy an apartment building as an income-earning property. Dr. Knox convinced me that it was a good thing to buy a house or an apartment building as an investment. He explained to me that the interest paid on the mortgage was totally deductible from the income, reducing the tax burden. When you put everything together — the appreciation, the saving in taxes, and the equity build-up, meaning a portion of your mortgage is used to reduce the debt — and add up all these items, a house actually becomes a good investment. Owning a house also provides comfort, pleasure, and pride of ownership.

In fact, when you really look at it on a long-term basis, a house becomes a substantial component of the owner's net worth. This investment is also influenced by the purchasing power of the currency. Most currencies lose purchasing power significantly over a period of decades, due to the inflation created by increasing the money supply. Central bankers of almost every country prefer to have a slightly increasing money supply to inject a small percentage of inflation. Some currencies have been more stable than others. For example, one rupee in '47 was exchangeable for about one dollar, or a gram of gold. Today in 2014, one needs around 60 rupees to get one dollar, and over 2,600 rupees to get a gram of gold, implying that the inflation in India has been much higher than in USA. Note that even the dollar has depreciated against gold, since 39 dollars are required to buy a gram of gold.

Let us say you're buying a house for 550,000 dollars. You need to borrow 500,000 dollars with 50,000 as a down payment. The average interest rate on the borrowed moneyis about five percent. Normally you would amortize the loan for a period of 30 years. The interest could be higher or lower, but five percent is quite reasonable looking back historically. For the 500,000-dollar loan, the monthly payment would be about 2,685 dollars. If you multiply that number (2,685) by 360 months (30 years), you will come up with approximately 967,000 dollars. This means that for a period of 30 years, you'll pay about 76 percent more for the house. However, when you look at all the different advantages of buying the house, you will see that you still come out ahead by buying it. Why? Let us say we take the inflation rate of about three percent, the average of the last 30 years. Every year, because of inflation, your house is going up in value by the rate of inflation. This needs to be compounded, by multiplying 1.03 thirty times. The house after 30 years should have a value of 2.427 times 550,000 dollars, resulting in 1,335, 000 dollars. The investment of 50,000 dollars (the down payment) has gone up by a factor of 26.7 times. The net return on investment comes out to be about 11.6 percent per year. There are other advantages, like having the deduction of interest payment and taxes that reduces the taxes paid to the government. Owning a house, usually with a backyard, is a big advantage for raising children. In essence, it is a substantial giveaway by the government to an American family.

I initially learned many of these principles of real estate investment from listening to Dr. Knox. However, I also tried to use my own logic and belief system. One needs to be open-minded with regard to investing. For example, there were friends who argued against investing in the apartment rental business because there was a stigma attached to it, often teasing me as a "slum lord." There were also some failures in the business that I knew about. An Indian investor had invested in an apartment building near USC in the '60s. The property values in areas surrounding USC unfortunately dropped like a rock because of a change in demographics. It was originally a predominantly high-wage-earning neighborhood that became a neighborhood of low-wage earners and nearby slums. As a result he suffered a big loss by not keeping it for a much longer period. Today the same property is worth much more. There were racial concerns among those involved in real estate, with code words for African Americans: "basketball players"; Latino tenants: "soccer players"; and white tenants: "tennis players." Our experience was that the buildings with diverse tenants operated with less trouble.

In lower-income neighborhoods, like northwest Inglewood where we first started investing, the cash flow was better because the property values were down, thanks to the poorly administered public schools. An important lesson learnt from this experience was that the first investment for anyone with a steady job that generates reasonable savings should be always a house in a growing area and a good location having good public schools. As explained earlier, this is a government giveaway due to government-created inflation, low real-estate interest rate loans, and the tax laws.

I was also looking for a second income. Our first and mainstream income was working at TRW. There were even seminars at TRW to help employees get second-stream incomes. Some of these seminars were on investing in apartments. The late Dr. Jerry Buss, the owner of the LA Lakers, was one of these fellows working at TRW who gave seminars. Even before Pratima and I started to invest in apartments, I had investigated considering a second income in the restaurant business. If you recall, when I came to Los Angeles in '60, I stayed with Ravi and his roommate Om. Om had a part-time job working at a Mexican restaurant owned by Joe Martinez. Joe, an immigrant from Spain, was married to a pretty lady named Yolanda from Mexico. The two of them ran Casa Martinez, serving full-scale Mexican food. The restaurant was close to where Ravi and Om used to live in Mar Vista. We visited Joe's restaurant all the time. Joe was getting old and wanted to retire, so he suggested selling his restaurant to us. A friend of mine, Suresh Lal, was also interested in investing in the restaurant business. His brother-in-law Mano, who had just finished his education in food technology, was looking to participate in and manage the business.

So we informed Joe that we were interested in buying the restaurant for about 50,000 dollars. Joe also had a liquor license, and explained how he made out very well because the most money you make in a restaurant is in selling liquor and wine. It seemed to be quite a good opportunity. Suresh and I decided that we would have Mano run the business, since we were working full time as engineers.

About this time, I had made friends with a prominent, highly respected Jewish lawyer, Mr. Stein, whose office was located near Fairfax on Wilshire. Mr. Stein and his family had invited us to a Thanksgiving dinner, arranged through UCLA. Their house was located in Pacific Palisades, a very prestigious area. He was an older gentleman, quite unassuming, and very helpful. Mr. Stein was a big fan of Mahatma Gandhi and had corresponded with him. He actually had a handwritten letter from Gandhiji that he proudly showed us when we visited his home the first time. So we had something in common, coming from peoples persecuted by Europeans in India and Germany. We would occasionally visit him with year-old Rahul. Their daughter, also a UCLA student, had fun playing with him.

Mr. Stein represented a number of clients in the restaurant business. Suresh and I decided to meet Mr. Stein for his experienced counsel before we made any commitment to buy Joe Martinez's restaurant. Mr. Stein's secretary, upon my request, gave us the time and the day to meet Mr. Stein. He was gracious enough to meet us at his office on the tenth floor, located at the Wilshire and Fairfax crossing. While we were waiting, we saw that his accountant was entering checks of tens of thousands of dollars received from his clients. We knew this man was prestigious and a successful lawyer. Once in his office, I introduced Suresh, and said that we wanted to buy a restaurant for 50,000 dollars and needed his counsel. Mr. Stein literally stopped us giving him more details. He asked me, "What are you? What is your profession?"

I said, "I am an engineer." He asked Suresh the same question. Then he said, "Why would you want to have a restaurant business?" I responded, "To generate a second stream of income." "Do you know the failure rate of restaurants?" he asked. He started educating us about the restaurant business. Every year three out of four restaurants go out of business. "It has one of the worst records. Not only that you work like a slave from noon to midnight, add to it the pilferage, and the human problem of dealing with workers and customers at the restaurant!" With a negative shake of his head, Mr. Stein strongly discouraged us by telling us we would do much better by just concentrating on being engineers. He also felt that running a restaurant could negatively affect our own profession and family life by diverting time and resources.

In retrospect I'm glad I listened to him, a generous human being. And it became a policy that I would always take another's advice by knowing the right people at the right time, with some luck. I recall Suresh and his brother-in-law going into the restaurant business afterwards and failing. To get an additional stream of income, we looked in all different directions. There was a Mormon engineer at TRW who was selling small flour mills to families; these mills were manufactured in Utah. Many people, and a good number of Mormons, had the perception in the '70s that we were coming to the end of the world. They believed that inflation was going to eat us all up. We were advised that cooking at home was less expensive. Their prediction was accurate, since we had terrible inflation in most of the '70s. So we bought a small flour mill that helped us save money.

I remember Ravi's wife Gunhid, Pratima, and Rajni, Nanoo Patel's wife (good friends of ours from the '60s) even dabbled in a second stream of income by selling custom-fitted bras designed by a helicopter engineer. As in the Avon perfume business, three ladies would have friends invite their friends in the evening for a get-together and demonstration of how well their bras provided needed support. We men were not allowed to participate for obvious reasons. But unfortunately this did not work out well.

In short, our search for a steady second stream of income took a while. But like most things, perseverance paid off. The average aerospace project lifespan was about 18 months, so most engineers were afraid of being laid off when a contract was about to end. Maintaining a house and a family of four, the feeling of being insecure was very strong, because we had no safety net in America.

Typically, in the United States, this was provided by parents or a family fortune. Those who got laid off usually had to stand in line to receive an unemployment check from the government, which was humiliating. I am a firm believer in diversification. And one of the reasons I was later able to weather a bearish stock market in early 2000 and the California real estate crash of the '90s was because of "diversification," a philosophy echoed by a Nobel laureate economist Harry Markowitz in his insightful essays on portfolio selection. In simple terms, diversification means not putting all your eggs in one basket with regards to investments available in different markets. The most important thesis Markowitz presented was that diversification is central to reduce risks. Being flexible and versatile as an entrepreneur can have long-term rewards and create financial stability. A corollary to this rule applies to eating food. My father believed strongly in eating from different food groups to get needed nutrients.

As I was periodically laid off at work, I needed another source of income to cushion these downtimes of employment. The steady second income arrived one day from India in the form of Mr. Shamjibhai Parekh, a family friend and my father's partner in the waste cotton businesses in India. His main business was in manufacturing rayon velvet fabric. When my father was trying to get me married, Mr. Parekh was the one who put the advertisement in the newspaper and got quite a few responses for me. He was also a man I admired and listened to, like Dr. Cameron Knox.

Mr. Parekh informed me that he was planning to visit LA with his wife to explore the possibility of setting up a business to export his fabric from India to America. It didn't sound like a bonanza to me, I must say. This was in March 1972. He stayed with us for a couple of weeks in our two-bedroom apartment before we bought our first house. As I mentioned earlier, the first apartment building we bought was in March 1972. Pratima arrived from Bombay with the children after the Bangladesh War, in January 1972. It had already been quite an eventful year. Once Mr. Parekh arrived, I took him to the LA garment district downtown and showed him around the various textile businesses, garment makers, and the like. We also met a handbag manufacturer. After two weeks he departed for India, leaving a few sets of samples with us.

I visited various places to show the fabric samples. We weren't even sure of our clients because many of them had offbeat names like Funky Chunk, Any Man Designers, and Day Dream Design. The first place we visited was run by a young Jewish man, Bill Forman. From his attire, he had the appearance of a hippy. Tall and heavy-set, Bill had his girlfriend helping him design handbags. She resembled Cher, the singer and ex-wife of Sonny Bono. Bill was actually a college dropout, and the son of a wealthy father involved in a furniture manufacturing business. He was reasonably successful as a handbag manufacturer. Certainly his father's connections helped him too. He was actually our first client and a shrewd businessman. He tried to squeeze us for the lowest price as best as he could. Still, he placed several orders with me. His first order was for the manufacturing of his handbags.

There was also a big fabric house called The House of Fabric. I met the main buyer, who asked me to show him the samples. He appreciated that he and I had the same dentist, Dr. Marwah, a Sikh gentleman, who was also a community leader of Indo-Americans. I was so happy to receive a big order from him. It was wonderful, getting an order worth about 30,000 dollars, considered big money in the '70s. Unfortunately The House of Fabric gave us no more than two orders later on. Evidently they weren't happy with the quality of the fabric. But they were very good paymasters and didn't cause any problems, even though they had a few complaints.

Around this time I became friendly with Rudy, a manufacturer of bedspreads. Ruddy Menon (the lookalike of Hollywood funny actor Danny Kay) was actually raised Catholic during the Second World War, though he was Jewish by birth. He had been adopted by a French Catholic family. He even raised his own family Catholic. Rudy was one of my first clients to buy the velvet patchwork for bedspreads. He also introduced me to other clients like Bedspreads by Shelly, Day Dream Design, Any Man Designers, and others. One very interesting client, Jerry Sokolow, was actually a very good friend of Bill Forman and was a bedspread manufacturer. When Bill ordered the fabric for his bags, he would also order some for Jerry. I could say Jerry was the initiator of bedspreads made of velvet patchwork. His sales were comparatively small but we had a good business relationship. Jerry, a Russian Jew who looked like Joseph Stalin with a good sense of humor, and I became good friends over the years. He would say in fun, "We Russian Jews are considered shrewd business people among all Jews; but you, East Indian Gujju (good Jew), beat us all." Please note that Gujaratis and Panjabis were also known as Gujjus, and Panjjus.

The reason why Mr. Parekh had shown the samples of velvet patchwork and wanted me to sell them was because India had problems manufacturing flawless fabric. The fabric was made 40 inches wide and about 30 yards long. But even in that moderate length and width, the Indian exporters were not able to manufacture it without flaws. A flawed fabric creates unacceptable wastage if it is used to make almost any product. One of the ideas of Mr. Parekh was to cut and sew the patchwork fabric by removing the flawed parts. This would certainly give added value to the fabric. I started selling the patchwork fabric to these clients; Mr. Parekh would ship the fabric to me from India on a 90-day draft. Wishing me and my career well, Mr. Parekh understood that I didn't have the risk capital to pay for this fabric, so we set up a 90-day draft for me to sell the fabric on credit to Los Angeles clients. I would pay back to the bank 90 days later after receiving the shipment.

One of the first consignments Mr. Parekh sent me was for about 6,000 dollars worth of fabric. He shipped the fabric to me by ocean and occasionally by air. Pratima or I would personally pick up Mr. Parekh's imports in a rented U-Haul truck and then store the goods in our own garage, where we warehoused them to cut expenses. Pratima took our handyman Joe Frelot to put the bales in the truck. Pratima's good looks and politeness also helped to get the total cooperation and help from dock workers. I put together an information flyer for my clients explaining why Velvet Patchwork Quilts were good products and why they were so popular. Using the initials H-E-A-R-T, the flyer contained the following statements to increase sales:

Heritage, an American patchwork quilt,
Everlasting value of a patchwork quilt,
Attractive appearance,
Repose from the comfort of a quilt,
Treasure of owning a patchwork quilt.

In America the patchwork quilt is an old tradition that goes back to the early settlers, so the concept was ideal for sentimental Americans. It caught on like wildfire. My first year sales in '72 were around 60 or 70,000 dollars. That was a very good start from nothing. The next year in '73 it went to 150,000 dollars. In '74 it went to 250,000 dollars. In '75 it went to 750,000 dollars. In '76 it went to one million and over. I believe I never exceeded a million and a half. It lasted from '72 to probably the mid-'80s when our sales were around a million to a million and a quarter. Note that a sale of a million in the '70s is equivalent to the sale of over 12 million in 2013 dollars. Then it started to decline from the '80s. I was out of the business by early '90. A conservative mindset in fashions developed among Americans after the election of President Reagan.

From left: Our salesman, Pratima and myself, Sarojbhabhi and Jitubhai at the 1980 Las Vegas Waterbed/Bedspread trade show.

From left: Mrs. and Mr. Parekh, Marty's mom, and Pratima. Seated on the floor, Rahul, Marty with Mary, and Sonya, 1972.

The lawyer Mr. Stein, Pratima, and Rahul, 1967.

The hardest part of becoming rich is to acquire the initial capital. It took me about twelve years to save the first 20,000 dollars (1960 to 1972). My net worth was over a million at the end of '77. I multiplied my net worth over 50 ($20,000 x 50 = $1,000,000) times only in five years, thanks to the Vietnam War. It appears to me that the common denominator for Doshis of three generations acquiring wealth is war and textiles. My grandfather became wealthy in his own right during the First World War, my father during the Second World War, and I during the Vietnam War, all in the textile business. My father was the happiest man when he came to know that I had become a millionaire. He would boast to his friends about my successful business, and claim that he was now a "Crore-Pati," meaning that the family's net worth, when converted in rupees, was over twenty million rupees (crore in Gujarati is ten million). Our net worth kept on increasing through '85 at a very decent rate, about five times by '85, thanks to the bedspread business, and the appreciation of the real estate value. As explained earlier, there are more millionaires made by investing in real estate than any other investment I know. Historically, the rulers of yesteryears and the bankers of recent times prefer an inflationary economy and the business of renting more than anything else. In the U.S., renting implies not only renting real estate but also loaning (renting) money like the mortgage on a house or treasury bonds. Real estate investors, employing leverage, do very well in an inflationary economy. Patience, deep pockets, and endurance are also important attributes to be successful.

Timing is key in any market and believe it or not the time for velvet patchwork had arrived. It was '72 and Vietnam veterans were coming home to America after having exposure to an Eastern culture. India had been introduced to the mainstream U.S. by the Beatles' visit to Maharishi Mahesh Yogi, who later could be seen on the Johnny Carson Show by millions of Americans. Ravi Shankar was playing concerts with Zubin Mehta and violinist Yehudi Menuhin. For the plethora of Vietnam veterans returning from a stressful enlistment fighting a war in Indochina, peace and tranquility were found in lying on a waterbed, with incense burning nearby, the soothing sounds of Ravi Shankar's music, maybe a joint of marijuana, and a beautiful woman at their side. Add a little beer or wine, plus the slow wavy motion of the waterbed, and the newly returned GI had found "nirvana."

Nannoo Patel, my old friend, who had cultivated a business selling incense at that time, also made out extremely well. Incense was something people associated with the East and it also fit with the growing market of Ravi Shankar's music and waterbed bedspreads. While the velvet patchwork business was going full steam, we were living in our first house, about 1,500 square feet, in Palms. The money I was making in real estate and other investments had helped us add a few more apartment buildings in northwest Inglewood. This area was between Palms and Redondo Beach, where I worked at TRW. Pratima and I discovered an area called Ladera Heights close to Inglewood, where we added a few more apartment buildings. One of our clients, Harvey Cole, invited us to his house in Ladera. We had sold some fabric to him; he was experimenting with handloom silk fabric imported from India. Harvey Cole looked in appearance and mannerism like Walter Matthau in the movie *The Odd Couple*. We were quite impressed with the area and decided to move there.

A 3,000 to 4,000-square-foot house went for around the 125,000 to 175,000 dollars range. I consulted Harvey Cole about the prices. "Why are the prices relatively low?" I asked him. He said that the schooling system was one of the reasons. The schooling system was attached to the Inglewood school district. That meant that the students from Ladera would go to Inglewood high school. Inglewood schools had students from lower-earning minority families. He added that the baseball player, Jackie Robinson (recall the movie *42*, the black baseball player who broke the color barrier in baseball) used to live in Ladera, but moved out because of the schooling problems associated with Inglewood school. Though we bought the house in Ladera Heights, we planned to put our kids into a private school.

One of the great things about living in Ladera Heights was that it was quite convenient to go to places of our interest. It took me much less time to go to TRW. For Pratima, who was managing our income properties, it took only minutes to visit them. Later we acquired an office building in Inglewood only a few blocks away from our house. I have always been in favor of keeping travel time short. It is important to me how I spend my precious time. Spending too much time traveling is wasteful and not my cup of tea. I would ask a question of whoever listens to me. What is given to us humans as an asset when we are born? Very few will answer that it is a lifetime. It depends on us how we utilize our assets to achieve our desired goals in our lifetime.

There were reasons to move out of Palms other than the long driving distance to work and to our apartment buildings. Our neighbor did not like visitors parking on a common drive way and complained constantly. My attitude has been to move away rather then confront. I did not confront when they failed me in the Ph.D. oral examination. I did not confront when TRW laid me off in 1982 (chapter 8). The attribute of moving away and not confronting, to find another opportunity also belongs to Russians, described by scholars of Russian history. I have been fortunate that I have always found a better replacement. I am glad that they failed me in the Ph.D oral examination. I believe starting a business and getting richer is a better outcome than working for a corporation or an institution. The house in Ladera has been certainly a better replacement for so many different reasons. We have lived in the same house since 1977.

With the success of the patchwork velvet I had competition from other importers. There were two very large importers of fabric, Chadwick in New York, and Dorel right in Los Angeles. They went to India when they saw the potential of importing patchwork fabric. However Chadwick, run by an Irish businessman, became one of my main competitors; he called me a "pimple on his butt" because he thought I was too small. He failed miserably to squeeze me out of the patchwork business. Initially there were three of us, Dorel, Chadwick and us, Doshi and Associates (D&A), importing the fabric.

For the next 15 years while I imported Mr. Parekh's fabric from Bombay, it would cover tens of thousands of waterbeds in America and be sold nationally in many department stores, from Broadway and Macy's to Gemco and JC Penney. We would also supply matching pillows with bedspreads made of velvet patchwork. I had in fact devised a pillow filling contraption in our back yard to stuff pillows with foam scrap employing a blower powered by an electric motor.

Tempo was a home furniture manufacturer. The owners, Joe Apel and his partner Steve Goodman, started buying fabric in large quantities when they saw the potential of the velvet patchwork bedspread. Another manufacturer in San Jose, named Gary Morse, asked me to supply samples to him for his trade shows. Gary was also a friend of Rudy. Every year I would go to India to get new samples at least once and sometimes twice. During '74 and '75 I had just received new samples that no one else had seen. Gary Morse requested me to give him a few samples to display in a trade show. I trusted him and gave him a few samples, per his request.

A few weeks later, I got a call from India from Mr. Parekh's associate explaining to me that the samples that I had received from Bharat Velvet (Mr. Parekh's company) were being shown by someone named Gary to all local manufacturers of velvet. It was apparent that Gary was creating competition against Bharat and me. I was shocked and angry, so I stopped selling to Gary. He even owed me money for the goods he had bought earlier. He refused to pay when the payment was due. Finally Bharat Velvet intervened and said they would sell to Gary Morse provided he paid up his receivables to D&A. Usually manufacturers want more clients. I didn't mind that. What I didn't like though was that Gary Morse had received fabric through me. Since I was not getting all the fabric I needed, I started to buy from Ashok Mills owned by my uncle Vadi-mama who had passed away a few years back; the factory was run by his son Harish.

It was not a buyers' market, it was an Indian manufacturers' market. And they were still king. Bharat didn't mind me buying the fabric from Ashok, but they didn't want me to buy from anyone else. I had no other choice but to start another company that no one else knew about. The name of that company was Core of Convenience or COC. So I started to get fabric from a third supplier, Thakkar Velvet. It was not the best material, but I got it at a reasonable price. At least I was able to increase the sales of the fabric supplied by three different suppliers from India.

I faced another problem from Tempo. As their need for the fabric grew, they made an effort to monopolize the supply of the fabric. Originally they were buying from all three of us in large quantities. They approached me about supplying only to Tempo. This was the only way they would buy and they said they would pay me 10 percent over the cost. I refused. I could not drop my other clients of the bedspreads in favor of Tempo; up to that time Tempo was buying goods from Chadwick, Dorrel, and me. Finally Tempo decided to go directlyto Mr. Parekh. We complained. Mr. Parekh initially said no to Tempo, saying they would have to buy either from

Dorrel or D&A. Tempo finally gave an ultimatum that they would not pay receivables unless they could import the fabric directly from the manufacturers. We had no choice but to accept that. So Bharat agreed to supply to Tempo. Now there were five of us importing the patchwork fabric.

Gary Morse didn't get a lot of fabric, because he wasn't a really big importer, so he had a supplier in Ahmedabad. As you can see, there was quite a bit of competition even among manufacturers. But as long as the demand was there, we were all doing well. Bruce Brownfield of Any Man Designers was the most ambitious one. He started to cut the cost of bedspreads for his clients. He approached me one day and said, "Look Navin, we can beat all of them." He would manufacture the bedspreads; I would supply the fabric to his clients at a cost. There would be a fixed cost to the retailers. As a result of our efforts, we would then have the least expensive bedspread for our retailers and it would be difficult for others to compete with us. Now I would have to sell the fabric directly to the retailers.

Bruce was a jet setter and had expensive hobbies like driving fast cars and skiing in the Colorado Mountains. He was also in the Ferrari import business. In the '80s after Reagan got elected, there was a change of direction. The "hippie culture" was going down. Conservatism was coming in. As a result, the multicolored bedspreads were too gaudy for clients and consumers, so the demand of the fabric began to subside. When the demand went down, the pricing power went down. Competition became harsher. There were a lot more people not buying, so the retail base went down. The waterbed business was the key reason the velvet bedspread business had flourished. At the peak of the waterbed sales in the early '80s, the business was three to three-and-a-half billion dollars. This business was subsiding. The housing market had crashed because of exorbitant interest rates. The general economy was flattening out. All of these reasons went into lower profits and demand.

Bruce Brownfield's manufacturing area, for example, had gone from 5,000 square feet to 40,000 during the business boom. Now he couldn't pay his bills. He was having the rising pressure of capital shortage. The way he did business was by using the supplier's money. As the market was going down it was getting harder and harder for him to pay money to the suppliers. In short, Bruce was in trouble. Of course it wasn't just hard for Bruce; it was hard for all of us in the business. Bruce Brownfield owed me at one point over 200,000 dollars. Tempo owed me 150,000 dollars. I had big accounts receivable. It was certainly a nightmarish time period since they were delaying their payments to me. Fortunately, because I was handling the business very conservatively, after everything was counted, I lost probably no more than 20,000 dollars in unpaid receivables in all the years I did business. Bruce Brownfield, in spite of his problem plus his good business ethics, actually paid off most of the money he owed me. His outstanding balance dropped to about 25,000 dollars. At that point he said he was having trouble paying his remaining balance. I suggested we work out some deal. Bruce agreed.

"I have Ferraris," he said cheerfully. "Okay," I said, "I'll take one of your Ferraris." It seemed like a fair trade. I didn't know much about Ferraris. My colleague, Ed Burchman at TRW, was an antique car expert. Bruce had about six Ferrari Daytonas. He suggested that I take possession of a black Ferrari he had with an excellent paint job, many electronic gadgets, and in good running condition. So Ed, his friend and I came over to his garage where six or seven Ferraris were sitting. Bruce gave us a ride in his black Ferrari so we could take delivery of that. But my friend Ed was not quite sure. He looked at every car in the garage; he looked at them as if they were being examined with a microscope. Ed's friend was also doing the same, and it was quite a bizarre examination. It was as if they were feeling the skin, as if they were making love to each of the cars. They were going all around the body of each car, touching it, checking it, examining it. In reality they were looking for flaws in the body of the car. In the antique car business, the most important thing in the car is the outside body, not the engine, and not the interior.

So what Ed was trying to find was the car with the best body with the least amount of corrosion. He decided the red Ferrari had the best body. It was actually disassembled and in pieces in the garage. Still, Ed recommended I should take that car. Bruce was hesitant at first, but he agreed. Evidently when Bruce knew we were visiting, he had the red Ferrari dismantled to give an impression it was not in the best shape. It took a week to assemble the red Ferrari and then I got delivery of it. This was a used '72 model Ferrari Daytona with a 12-cylinder engine that could be driven at around 200 miles per hour. But driving a Ferrari with the small 18-inch steering wheel was the hardest thing to maneuver, and I just could not appreciate the car. It ultimately sat in my garage for about six months and remember, my cost for it was about 25,000 dollars. So I decided it was time to get rid of it. Rahul, our son, was against selling it because some of his friends at college were telling him Ferraris were in great demand. I put an ad in the paper to sell it for 40,000 dollars and got several calls. I eventually sold it for 39,000 dollars. I thought I had made good money. In just six months after spending 25,000 dollars, I received 39,000 dollars for my investment. However, within a year Ferrari's were so much in demand that their value had gone up to over 100,000 dollars. Some people would regret selling early and not realizing a bigger profit. But that is in hindsight. I believe as long as I make a profit, I should be happy and let other people make more money. It reminds me of the story of Thomas Edison who sold his patent for 5,000 dollars. After the deal was signed, the buyer said, "Thomas, I was ready to pay 10,000 dollars!" Edison had replied, "Do you know that I was ready to accept 3,000?"

During the same time period, I had started to buy collectable automobiles. I had bought a convertible 1965 Pontiac Firebird. Rahul loved the car and suggested I keep it for him. I had also acquired a 1949 tomato red Dodge in its original shape from a San Bernardino county supervisor. He had kept it in its original shape including the guide book that came with the car. My father, during his visit to Los Angeles in 1977, enjoyed the ride in the car since he had owned a very similar 1949 Desoto in 1950s. In fact, I had learnt driving in my father's Desoto. I also satisfied Pratima's wish to own a sport car by buying a 1969 Jaguar XKE. She originally wanted to buy a Chevrolet Corvette. I was afraid to buy Corvette, a very fast car, for fear of a potentially disastrous accident. I would never want to lose Pratima in an accident with a Corvette. Earlier a Bombay astrologer had warned us that Pratima could suffer a severe health problem at the age of 40. I had also bought a 190SL Mercedes manufactured in 1960. Realizing it was a very time consuming hobby, I sold all of them making some profit.

Losing our market for the velvet fabric was just one of the problems I had to face in that business, but there were others. The velvet business in and of itself was not a business without flaws, particularly working with India. We experienced quite a few problems doing business there. For example, there were strikes either at the factory or at the docks, so the goods could be sitting in India for days and weeks and sometimes months. When this happened we did not get the delivery, and the clients or manufacturers were waiting for the goods to arrive. Many times we had no choice but to get the goods by air freight because the market was so hot. The other problem was the flaws in the fabric dimension. The required width for bedspreads was 45 inches, however occasionally it would be 44 or less. Ashok Mill had sold a large consignment of the velvet patchwork to Tempo. Tempo, being a big user, was getting the material not only from Bharat Velvet but also from Ashok Velvet Mill, which was the second largest exporter of velvet patchwork fabric in India. The third one that I imported from was Thakar Velvet, with whom I did lots of business because I couldn't get enough fabric from the other two.

My first choice for material was always Bharat. My second choice was Ashok Velvet Mill. My third choice was Thakar. I cultivated a very good friendship with Thakar. In any case, Tempo had ordered a very large consignment of patchwork velvet fabric from Ashok. Unfortunately the market slowed down, so Ashok's fabric was sitting at the dock in LA. Tempo was telling the banks they were not taking delivery because the material in the last shipment was not satisfactory. Ashok was in dire need of the money. We're talking about 40,000 or 50,000 dollars worth of goods sitting at the dock. The cost was also increasing because the shipping company, the American President Line, added storage charges for the material sitting there. So months and months passed. My cousin, Vadimama's son Harish, called me and told me that they were stuck. They asked for my help. I took delivery of the goods, paying the freight and storage charges to help them out. I measured the dimensions, then figured what I could sell the goods for. I was able to sell them in bits and pieces to my clients at a discounted price. Harish was happy and thankful for solving their problem.

One of the unfortunate things in India is that Indians compete among themselves so hard that they do not compare their notes as to who is a good client or who is a good importer and who is a con artist. As a result, a crooked importer would buy goods from many suppliers making all of them suffer time and time again. Evidently, at least in the '70s, Indians did not mind that their competition suffered. Later, I believe, exporters formed an association to avoid such problems.

I often had to visit Mumbai to resolve problems associated with U.S. buyers and suppliers in Mumbai. I would use my vacation days from TRW to travel to India. Planned trips would also include attending special events, such as weddings in the family. In fact I attended the weddings of Jagruti in '76 and Nayana in '77. Often we would visit countries in Europe on our way to Mumbai.

Going back to other problems that we encountered in the velvet business, besides strikes or short dimension deliveries, a third problem was when we got the goods with holes from bugs. This created all sorts of problems. First of all, the U.S. Customs Department would not release the goods if there were bugs. Fumigation was first required, which incurred more expense. There were not only fumigation charges, but there were transportation charges to have the goods moved from the dock to the fumigation houses and then back to the warehouses. These extra charges importers had to pay. Then you would have the cost of delayed delivery to the customer's cost that would eat up whatever profit they had. The problem associated with holes due to bugs was probably the hardest to solve. Then they'd cut and remove the patch and replace it wherever therewere holes. Of course that was extra labor expense.

One of the most helpful things for me was the skill of collecting the receivables, the money that your client or customer owes you. Almost always, our clients wanted a credit for 30 or 60 days. There was a client, a lady who used to work for Bruce. She was very shrewd and had some wonderful designs. But when the market shrank we had to take some of the items back. It's amazing how somctimes entrepreneurs overdo it. She grew her business very fast,but had to suffer the pain of expansion, including the shortage of capital. Her extravagant habits, like having a chauffeur-driven limo to take her to work, did not help. This was completely the opposite philosophy that I had. I was always very frugal. I was aware of the fact that every business in the U.S. has a finite life. The U.S. economy, a capitalist system, has an attribute called "creative destruction." The horse buggy went out of business because of the automobile. Creativity destroys the old industries and brings in the new one.

The "black hole" exists in every field and business we know of. We see it represented in overindulgence or overextension of resources or capital. In matters of health, we see it in obesity and in bulimia. In the economy, we have inflation and deflation. Too much of anything can be damaging. Sahadeva, the youngest of the five Pandavas, had the boon (or was it a curse) of possessing the faculty of "Ati-jnana," "excessive or extreme knowledge," with an ability to see clearly into the future. The story of Casandra in Greek mythology comes to mind. In Indian mythology, in the Mahabharata story, Sahadeva suffered great misery due to this ability to see the future. At a crucial juncture of his own life and the life of the Pandava family, when the eldest brother Yudhishthira accepted an invitation to gamble, the youngest brother Sahadeva knew what a disastrous ending this would lead to, even before it all began. Sahadeva knew that Yudhihthira would lose the kingdom and all their wealth, and eventually Draupadi, the wife of all five Pandava brothers, would be humiliated. His ability to know the future had one condition: unless asked to opine and advise, Sahadeva was not allowed to reveal what he knew. He suffered so much due to the extreme knowledge that he acquired the habit of getting drunk. So basically extremism exists in every field. Moderation or the middle path was an important message of Buddha. This way you are able to keep the balance in a dynamic system, with a reduced probability of hitting the barrier. I was always watchful of the expansion of the business and incurred expenses.

My philosophy is to never increase your expenses beyond your means so that when the need arises you have accumulated sufficient wealth to survive for rainy days and months. That also brings in the idea of diversification so that you have multiple streams of income coming in to manage downturns. In essence it also means keeping a balance between two opposite forces. This occurs in any dynamic system like stars, where the force of expansion due to nuclear reaction is in balance against the gravitational pull. I had income from TRW, income from the velvet business, and income from real estate; three income streams. My fourth stream was the interest received from bond investments — corporate and municipal bonds, debt instruments, where you loan money to corporations or municipalities or state or federal governments. The capital from my velvet business was invested in Muni and Treasury bonds, which in the early '80s were paying over a 15 percent return. Was this good timing? Yes. It was just the perfect time to invest in a bond market. Lucky me!

In retrospect I would also call myself an "all trade" jack as opposed to a "jack of all trades." Diversification implies knowing other businesses. I did my graduate and undergraduate work in engineering. At work I was not at one place. Initially I learned about semiconductors, for example, at Hoffman Engineering and TRW semiconductors. When I joined Acoustica and later at TRW I learned about acoustic engineering. Then at TRW I learned more about the assortment of measurement techniques to measure all kinds of things, including the power of a high-power chemical laser beam, and the temperature of a cathode of a microwave tube sealed in a very unique environment. I learned and devised different ways to measure the temperature of a cathode by pyrometry, by calculations, and by photometry. I had correlated results so that we had sufficient confidence in our measurements — not just one but many fields of engineering, including electro-optics, laser technology, acoustics, heat transfer, photometry, pyrometry, and so on.

I learned about the real estate and import business to add additional streams of income. In the '90s, rocket scientists were employed by various financial institutions. What they were trying to do was to use the analogues of science or engineering for financial systems. Some of these rocket scientists were very successful. Remember Neel Kashkary, assistant to the Treasury Secretary Henry Paulson, who had also worked at TRW. I essentially would do the same thing using engineering and science analogues. I was able to compare the laws of demand and supply to the simple Ohms law in electrical engineering, as well as the theory of chaos. And of course, then you add to that the linear systems, the Newtonian systems to known linear systems, the laws of evolution, deterministic chaos, and so on. I believe all of that helped in my understanding of the financial system and coming up with better ideas of investing.

Of course one way of making big money is by employing leverage, as explained earlier. When you're buying an apartment building you're buying with a portion of it as down payment, and a big portion as a loan. For example, we bought apartments with no more than 20 or 25 percent down payment. So for a million dollar property that we buy, we need only 200,000 to 250,000 dollars. The rest would be a loan from a mortgage company. When you buy with 25 percent down and borrow 75 percent, the leverage is 4 to 1. Your investment is only one quarter of the total price. But leverage is a double-edged sword. In good times, it makes money. In bad times, one could lose 250,000 dollars, the whole investment. Some examples of negative leverage I found among a few of my friends, because they kept on over-leveraging in real estate investment. In the end some of them suffered very heavily because of the downturn that happened in the late '80s and early '90s when there was a real estate crash in southern California. The American economy is addicted to OPEOM, meaning employing "Other People's Money." Leverage implies borrowing money from the bank that is the money of the people who deposit in the bank.

I was fortunate that I did not suffer too badly because I was sufficiently diversified, and I did not overindulge. My leverage was reduced from 4 to 1 to probably 2 to 1. Even after the burst of the stock market in the years 1987, 2000, and 2008, I would like to claim that I didn't suffer too much because of diversification. This was because I had good holdings in real estate that did not go down much. Our velvet business disappeared, like the Vietnam War.

The bottom line to succeed, in any endeavor, is to discover a niche and apply an original creative idea employing all or a portion of one's God-given human equipment. The human equipment is onion-like, with layered somatic and psychological selves, with sub-layers of genetics, a gross body with senses, pre-psychology, and layers of an intuitive and intellectual mind. A creative idea in nuclear physics or molecular biology, I suppose, falls in the layer of an intellectual mind. A restaurant or retail business needs a strong body to endure working long hours. One successful business I can think of is Dabbawalla in Mumbai, which picks up hot lunch boxes from the residence of workers and delivers them to their offices just in time, employing a good memory, strong body, and the most convenient mode of transportation. One can learn a whole lot about this successful business by googling the name "Dabbawalla."

Other very successful businesses in America are FedEx and Amazon.com. FedEx uses a simple wheel, hub and spoke concept to deliver packages by picking up a package from any location on a "wheel," flying it to the hub (Atlanta), then flying it out to the destination, also on the wheel. Flying paths from the periphery of the wheel to the hub and back to the wheel represent spokes. Locations on the wheel include all the major cities in America. Amazon employs a sophisticated software technology and a central warehouse to retail merchandise.

The simplest business that succeeded in the '70s for a short duration was the Pet Rock business. In April 1975, Dary Dahl from Los Gatos, California was in a bar listening to his friends complain about their pets. This gave him the idea for the perfect "pet," a rock. A rock would not need to be fed, walked, bathed, groomed and would not die, become sick, or be disobedient. He said they were to be the perfect pets, and joked about it with his friends. However, he eventually took the idea seriously, and drafted an "instruction manual" for a pet rock. It was full of puns, gags and plays on words that referred to the rock as an actual pet. The originals had no eyes.

The first Pet Rocks were ordinary gray stones bought at a builder's supply store. They were marketed like live pets, in custom cardboard boxes, complete with straw and breathing holes for the "animal." The fad lasted about six months, ending after a short increase in sales during the Christmas season of December 1975. Although by February 1976 they were discounted due to lower sales, Dahl sold 1.5 million Pet Rocks and became a millionaire. I am sure that there are many successful businesses at the middle and high level of the intellectual ladder, where a new technology is applied creating a reasonable demand for the product.

Today, in developed world, there are very few opportunities, thanks to little or no growth in economy. I recall a story I had heard when I was studying at University of Michigan. Professor Carry was teaching electrical engineering when I was a student in 1958. He would recite his experience about workers in Bengal when he was stationed in Calcutta during the Second World War. He felt that British were taking advantage of workers, paying them much less. So he would compete with the British and pay the workers more thinking they would be more motivated. The result was the opposite; workers would put in fewer hours, providing them more leisure time for the same pay the British gave them.The moral of the story here is that there was no motivation to work hard as long as they were able to sustain their livelihood. Perhaps the sense of contentment based upon tradition, inherited habits, and British colonial rule are the cause of poverty in India. We can compare that with what is happening now in America.

Over a period of two centuries, the U.S. GDP went up from below one percent to over 26 % in 1960s and now it is below 19 %. Americans have done much better than people almost anywhere else because waves of motivated immigrants worked hard with good work ethics. Successful people like Nelson Rockefeller who came from a rich family, also served as a Governor of New York and U.S. Vice President informed the television audience, sometime in 1960s, how his parents gave importance to hard work. He had earned money selling newspapers while going to school. Immigrants, like Indo-Americans, are successful because we know the value of hard work.

If America is going to dig its way out of what lies ahead, the country needs people who can work hard and can start and operate new businesses. Simply put, job growth is not keeping pace with population growth--specifically, the growth of the labor force which is generally defined as the population between the ages of 18 and 64. So what happens to the economy as millions of people never acquire the habits of hard work or lose them due to chronic joblessness? This is not about employed people already working very hard. The federal government estimates that about 95 million people are *not in the labor force.* To get some sense of what this means, let us look at segments of U.S. population.

The population in America is about 322 million. About 74 million are under the age of 18, and about 42 million are retired (i.e. receiving Social Security benefits) and almost 11 million receive Social Security disability benefits. About 2.4 million people are in prison. Roughly 1.4 million are in active duty in the U.S. Armed Forces. That totals about 130 million people who are not in the civilian labor force.

The balance is about 192 million people is a base labor force. Out of this total, we need to subtract mentally disabled people who are not institutionalized or drawing Social Security disability benefits. Unfortunately many are homeless or in prison. We also need to subtract those who are earning money in the cash economy but not reporting their income--i.e. those who are employed but not showing up as employed in the data. Then there are people who are raising children, home-schooling their children, etc. as fulltime work force. Others are providing care to elderly parents or relatives without compensation.

It is difficult to estimate the people who are performing work but are not counted as employed because they're not being paid. According to the BLS (Bureau of Labor Statistics), about 146 million people have some kind of paid job in the U.S. This could be anywhere from a $100 million hedge fund manager to someone with $100 per year in self-employed eBay-sales income. Roughly 24 million are in part time jobs, and 122 million have full-time jobs.

Our focus needs be on the millions who are not working in unpaid positions in home or at paid positions. Those who fall out of the work force (or never join it in the first place) may lose, or never develop the habits of hard work and cooperating with others; habits that are necessary to be productive.

The earlier one acquires the habits of hard work, the more likely it is that those habits will last a lifetime. We encourage *studying hard* and *playing hard*, but how many programs in our educational system give young people an opportunity to learn how to *work hard*, especially for themselves as entrepreneurs and self-employed? All too often it's assumed that *studying hard* and *playing hard* teach people to work hard. That is not necessarily the case, as work requires another set of attributes and habits. Some of these overlap with study and athletics, but not all.

Today we live in an environment where good jobs are hard to find. One way to overcome this difficulty is to train high school and college students to learn becoming an entrepreneur. The course work would include determination of demand of product and services. Teachers should have the experience of starting their own successful business. Rather than a teaching credential, the qualification should be limited to the instructor who has launched and operated enterprises in the real world. The largest providers of jobs in America during most of the 20th century were small businesses. Small businesses during the last few decades are evaporating along with job growth, thanks to the new technology and big corporations like Walmart.

If we're going to dig our way out of what lies ahead, we need people who can work hard and start and operate new businesses. Entrepreneurship is not for slackers or those who give up as soon as the going gets difficult. It takes creative and imaginative mind and good work habits to persevere and keep learning from others and from one's own mistakes. It reminds me of the history of Gujaraties recited in chapter one. One needs to go where opportunities of growth arise and provide product and services are in demand.

Five generations (G) of Doshis: Back row: Jasvantbhai (3rd G), my father (2nd G), Bharati (4th G) with Anand (5th G), and Kailaskaki. Seated: Nayana (4th G), my paternal grandmother Muliba (1st G), and Mahendra kaka (2nd G), taken in the year 1973

Four nieces, Jagruti, Daksha, Nayana, and Bharati during Nayana's wedding, 1977.

`Rahul, uncle Babufua, 92 year my grandfather's elder brother Ratilal Dada, myself, Shamjibhai, and Dada's son Balubhai, Gene Hackman look alike (1977).

Nayana's wedding with Anangbhai (seated); Bharati, myself, Daksha, her cousin, Sanjaybhai in the back, and Anand, left of Nayana, 1977.

Jagruti's wedding with Premalbhai; Manoj and myself are on the left, 1976. Bottom left

Pratima and myself in Yellowstone National Park, 1977.

CHAPTER 8

THE CHANGING RIVER

"Everything changes and nothing stands still. You could not step twice into the same river. All entities move and nothing remains still."

Plato in Cratylus

If you recall, the late '70s was a period with a very high inflation rate. The interest rate had gone over 15 percent for treasury bonds. Some municipal bonds, like Washington power bond coupons, yielded 15 percent. Paul Volcker at that time was determined to squeeze the excess liquidity by raising the interest rate so that inflation would come under control. Gold was at 800 dollars an ounce and the Dow was around 800. The ratio of Dow to gold was around 1. Compare that ratio to what we saw in the year 2000 with gold around 300 dollars an ounce and the Dow around 12,000. The ratio had gone up over 40. Later on, the ratio went down to below 13 and decreasing, indicating the cyclic nature of markets.

Usually we know that gold rises in value when there are uncertainties in the economy and when there is a negative interest rate, meaning the rate of inflation is higher than the prevailing interest rate. The misery index, defined by then President Carter, is the sum of interestrates, theinflation rate, and the unemployment rate. The misery index in the Great

Depression, for instance, must have been terrible because unemployment alone was over 25 percent. The misery index sometime during the '70s probably exceeded 30 percent. Interest rates had gone up over 15 percent. Unemployment was around 7-1/2 percent. The inflation rate was around anywhere from 7 to 10 percent. Jimmy Carter was elected when the three numbers of the misery index were pretty high. We were going through stagflation after Nixon resigned and when Gerald Ford became president. Carter, after winning the election in '76, was unable to control the economy and the misery index in fact rose during his presidency.

Under Reagan, in the first couple of years, '81 and '82, the misery index rose even higher, but after the midterm elections, it was stabilizing. Things were pretty tight and uncertain. At TRW we were going through a metamorphosis that included many changes. The company was becoming more conservative with more emphasis on productivity and gain and less emphasis on research. Even the philosophy and character of TRW was changing. The main difference that I noticed before the '80s was that corporations looked after the wellbeing of their employees along with the corporate profit. However, in the '80s, corporate profit became the ultimate goal. Corporations were now only concerned with productivity gains and higher efficiency from their employees. Employee benefits started to decline. The bottom line was that we were seeing a new trend toward uplifting the wellbeing of the corporation and investors, with a lesser emphasis on the wellbeing of employees. Corporations started to outsource work to China and Asian countries. I would argue that this was the start of economic polarization, meaning the rich getting richer and the middle class contracting.

Immediately after Reagan was elected there was a strike by the air traffic controllers. The Reagan administration fired all the air traffic controllers who were on strike. The union was destroyed. There were lots of horror stories. This incident showed how the business mood in America was changing. Reagan seemed to be imitating Britain's Margaret Thatcher, who had similar labor problems in England.

Meanwhile, at TRW we were given less money for research because attention was focused on increasing productivity. The U.S. as a world power apparently had declined in the '70s during the Nixon, Ford, and Carter presidencies. America's economy seemed to improve reasonably well in the '80s, especially in matters of corporate profit. From '82 to '99, a period of over 17 years, U.S. stocks rose substantially in valuation. However, the average American family suffered because both husband and wife had to work to support the family; two wage earners were needed to maintain the same lifestyle. Raising children by one of the parents became less important. The responsibility to educate children and grown-up kids fell on their teachers in totality. The outcome, a couple of decades later, was disastrous; the quality of education had suffered tremendously.

President Carter during his four years as president, though a good human being, seemed to be faulted for his attempt to micromanage the U.S. economy. He was defeated after one term by Reagan. America's downturn after the '70s cannot be totally blamed on any one person. Perhaps it was fate. America is still at the top of the world as an economic power. However we are seeing a gradual slide in the standard of living even today in 2014.

As TRW became more productivity oriented with a reduction in research projects, this caused problems for me. Though I worked for the metrology lab at TRW, I was involved mostly in research in matters of high-technology measurements. The department heads at TRW became, shall I say, "slave drivers." Many department heads got promoted for their "efficiency" but not necessarily for their compassion for the employees working under them. I asked for and was offered a position in another research lab because the metrology lab where I worked had changed its philosophy and was moving away from research in measurement and instrumentations to more productivity and more computerization. At that time I wasn't much of a computer man.

Another department that I was helping while still part of the metrology lab asked me to work for them. The metrology lab had a new manager who came from Ford research lab. Evidently he did not like the idea of employees like me who were financially independent. He felt those who had become financially independent would not be motivated to work hard, compared to those who needed a weekly paycheck for their survival.

Chronologically, I started working at TRW from '68. I moved to metrology in '70 and stayed there until '82. Because of my circumstances, I was asked to leave and work for a research lab. While I was in metrology, 30 percent of the time I worked for another research lab that had an arrangement with metrology. This research lab was involved in laser instrumentations. The head of thelab was Dr. Bhuta, a versatile lab manager who directly reported to the vice president of TRW. TRW had a very tall hierarchy. At the top was the president, then the vice president, and below them were the lab managers, department managers, and section heads. The technical staff, like myself, reported to the section heads and department managers. Below us were technicians, secretaries, clerks, and others. The salary and wage difference between a senior member and a regular member of the technical staff was not really that much. However, sometimes a section head was junior to a senior member of the technical staff. Or you could have a section head who was junior to the senior scientist. It was quite possible that the senior scientist could be making even more money than the section head. These levels could also be crowded, meaning there was very little difference in the wages of engineers, section heads, and department heads.

Dr. Bhuta was both hated and admired for being highly aggressive in marketing. He had developed and established important links and contacts in different government agencies involved in developing high-level technology all around the country. Dr. Bhuta even had contacts with four-star generals in defense establishments. When

I said he was "hated and admired," I mean that the people who worked for him admired him and were grateful for the work he brought to them. Research scientists and engineers needed outside funding so they could keep working, and Dr. Bhuta achieved this through his persistent ability to get contracts. But at the same time he was hated or perhaps envied by other managers at his level because of his successes. The TRW management was so structured that each lab was a profit center unto itself, a kind of small independent company. Each lab had to be able to stand on its own two feet. They had to get contracts and used the TRW facilities to support the contract. Certainly there was competition going on between different laboratories within TRW.

One day Dr. Bhuta asked to see me in his office. He informed me that TRW was changing. He himself was being transferred to another department, choosing among a few offered to him. He chose one based on job security, since he was to retire in just a few more years. He advised me to watch my back because my boss at the metrology lab had contacted Dr. Bhuta and asked if he could absorb me in his lab. "It's evident that the metrology lab doesn't want you," he said. I was of course quite surprised and concerned. This was the summer of 1982. Pratima was visiting Bombay at the time, and she called me from India and told me I'd better get on a plane because my 75-year-old father had contracted cancer of the stomach and did not have much time to live.

I immediately talked to my boss in metrology. Remember, this is a boss who has asked Dr. Bhuta for my transfer. Still I asked the metrology lab for eight weeks of leave that included an accumulated five weeks of vacation and an additional three weeks leave of absence, to give me a total of eight weeks. Thankfully they granted me the eight weeks of leave, and I left Los Angeles for Mumbai.

While I was in India for the first five to six weeks, Jitubhai and I saw our father Motabhai every day. He would initiate hugging, and we would comply. Motabhai was a slim man already, but he had lost a lot of weight, probably weighing less than 100 pounds. Deepak and his mother, along with my aunt and uncle, took care of his regular needs. We hired a "hospice" nurse who camefrom eight in the morning until five in the evening to take care of his medical needs. After my father had chemotherapy, the nurse would stay with him at his house through the night. Jitubhai came with me to visit him regularly to ensure that he was being taken care of in every matter.

I also looked into various possibilities back in the U.S. to see if there were things that could be done for my father's cancer. In India we have two ways of curing illness. There is the Western, more costly way of medicine, and the second way is the ayurvedic or more natural and traditional way of healing. After his chemotherapy, my father's health declined even more. The cancer was slowly spreading. I thought perhaps an ayurvedic approach could help to slow down the spread of the cancer. My father had a very high regard for an ayurvedic doctor in Bombay by the name of Dr. Chandra Shekhar Thakoor. He was also a professor in Bombay's Ayurvedic Medical School. It was very hard to get an appointment with him due to his popularity. I called his office and told him I was from the U.S. and that I'd like to see him. When I arrived at his office I only waited for fifteen minutes before his secretary asked me to go in. There was quite a long line of patients waiting to see him. But there is an advantage for those coming from America when one is dealing with people in India. Even today Indians believe that Indo-Americans are wealthier and can afford to spend almost any amount of money.

Dr. Thakoor was an astrologer and palmist besides being an ayurvedic doctor, who wrote a column for *The Times of India*, a widely circulated newspaper. He examined my horoscope and after seeing my planets and stars, he concluded that I was the right man to become friends with. He also discovered that I was successful and would behelpful to him during his planned U.S. visit. I mentioned to him about my father. He said, "If you want the honest truth, no ayurvedic medicine can help your father." But I was persistent and requested that in spite of his busy schedule, could he please visit my father. With a smile and a sigh, he agreed.

When Dr. Thakoor arrived at my father's house, my father was very happy and thankful that I was able to bring such a reputable ayurvedic doctor to visit him. Dr. Thakoor was very frank with my father. He spoke to him gently but firmly. "Look, Haribhai, curing cancer through ayurvedic means is not very likely," he told my father. But my father was quite grateful for the time Dr. Thakoor spent with him. In the meantime I had to get back to Los Angeles. My date was not fixed, and I had only three weeks left of my eight weeks of leave.

Around this time Pratima called me from Los Angeles saying TRW had called and were concerned because it appeared the metrology lab now needed me back at TRW, otherwise I might lose my job. I quickly planned my return trip with the blessings of my father. I felt assured he was being well taken care of. My brothers Jitubhai and Deepak were there to look after my father. Deepak had come back from LA to take care of him. Because of his high regard for me, my father advised Deepak to do exactly what I said in matters of the divorce Deepak was going through. Deepak had married a pretty girl Gita, apparently accustomed to a much higher lifestyle than ours. She left Deepak and went to Canada and did not come back. I advised Deepak to divorce her as fast as he could, since I thought she had married Deepak for only one reason, to get a green card. Deepak, after the divorce, informed me that she had married an American, and was probably living "high-on-the-hog" as they say, from paycheck to paycheck. Kapi, Deepak's second wife, would later tease Deepak that if he had stayed married to Gita, he would be broke and have a fat wife. Gita, I was informed, had gotten fat on her style of living.

When I returned to TRW I was shocked because the metrology lab had sent me a termination notice. This was in spite of the fact that I had spent over thirteen years of my life in the lab and that they knew I was visiting my dying father. It was clear the term "slave driver" was correct for many of the new department heads, who were only interested in productivity, with little compassion for their employees.

I talked to Ed Burchman at TRW, who had helped me select my classic auto, a Ferrari acquired from Bruce Brownfield. Ed spoke with his boss and I was able to start working for Ed at the research lab he was heading. The only condition was that I could not work full time; I could work 20 to 30hours a week. I had been offered a full-time research job in a lab, but I didn't want to work full time because of my commitments to my two other businesses. Because I had been helping in Ed Burchman's lab for the last eight years, which had been Dr. Bhuta's lab before that, it was a great psychological boost to work there. They also agreed that I work only 20 to 30 hours a week. I had a parting shot at my metrology lab boss. "Wendell, I am surprised you let me go with all the experience I have accumulated in the last thirteen-year period for the company. I would have been ready to work 20 hours or even 12 hours a week, if you'd had the budget to support me," implying it was utter stupidity to let an experienced engineer go, since there was no one capable of doing the work I was doing at the time.

One of the other problems working full time was that it was clearly understood without any documentation that department heads could ask you to work more than 40 hours a week. I did not want to do that, since I was always short of time with my involvement in my own investments and businesses. After spending all those years at TRW, it had become a habit and it was difficult to stop working there, even part time. The psychological impact of an immediate termination was not good for me. Working at TRW, and interacting with other employees who were more like a family, was like a security blanket. I do not think that I needed the money, but relationships we establish in our business and work are often beyond any price.

For the next two years I experienced a transition period, getting out of TRW and being on my own. I could have left TRW, perhaps in the late '70s, because I already had two or three other strong income streams coming in from the velvet business, the real estate business, and from stocks and bonds. Working part time in Burchman's lab was more of a psychological boost.

I disconnected with TRW in the middle of '84. By then I was feeling reasonably secure, also more of my old-time associates were leaving the department voluntarily or otherwise; my "TRW family" was contracting. I had received a couple of patents through working part time on my acoustic gauge system for propellants under no-gravity conditions. I had started on this project when I worked for Acoustica Associates. By '84 I had fine-tuned the technique and made it simpler and more functional. Around this time I contacted NASA and tried to get a contract from them or from other government agencies. When I later consulted Dr. Bhuta, who was near retirement, he advised me that unless I was affiliated with a large corporation or some large organization with big facilities, it would be near impossible to get a contract from NASA. However I had no desire to work for any big corporation.

As my years ended as an engineer, I spent more time in liquid financial vehicles like stocks and bonds. If you remember, '82 was the year where interest rates peaked. They started to recede after that. Then the stock market took off in a falling interest environment. As I educated myself about financial investments, I realized that it was the right time to get into the stock market. In '82, the bottom of the Dow Jones index was established at around 850 or so. By '84 the market had gone up 30 or 40 percent to near 1,200. It was a good time to ride the wave. Bull and bear markets come in long waves; this was the beginning of a long bull market. I started to invest in liquid investments, mostly in bonds because I was still feeling cautious. I didn't want to invest too much in stocks because I felt they could fluctuate much more than bonds. I also invested in tax-free quality municipal bonds.

As I was investing, I developed "a line of defense." The first line of defense was cash municipal and U.S. Treasury bonds. The second line of defense was corporate and convertible bonds. Then I had divided the investment capital further, in precious metals, different stocks, and real estate investment. Stocks and real estate would provide growth and capital gain, precious metals and real estate would provide protection from inflation, and bonds would provide interest income.

From '82 my net worth was 55 percent invested in real estate, with approximately less than 10 percent invested in my velvet business. The rest of my assets were in stocks and mostly bonds. Slowly my real estate investment percentage began to go down to below50 percentbecausethestocks and bonds were rising so rapidly. My velvet business percentage was also slowly going down. During the peak time for my velvet business in the late '70s, I had 40 percent of my money invested in my business for fabric and other items. As the velvet business began to recede, my investment in my business slowlywentdown to less than 5 percentby'85. Itwas certainly an indication that the velvet business was shrinking. I was totally out of the velvet business by the early '90s.

My stock market experience was very pleasant until '87. Many people have not forgotten the '87 market crash. At that time I was leveraged in bonds at around 2 to 1. Luckily it was in bonds and not stocks. The Dow dropped 30 to 35 percent in a week. It went below 1,500 from 2,700. It was the biggest drop in history. I lost sleep, because I must have lost about half-a-million dollars, roughly 25 percent of my liquid assets. When the market bubble burst in 2000, I probably lost a lot more than half a million. But the '87 crash was a much bigger shock because it was the first time I had experienced such a large loss.

I remember after the Monday crash in '87 how it was big news all over the country. In just one day the market had dropped 500 points. On that day, Rahul, our son who was in medical school at

Stanford, called me inquiring if I was okay. "Are you able to handle this, dad?" Luckily, a few days later, I was able to come out of it.

Fortunately the market only took a year to recover and we were back on the bullish trend, which I rode till the late '90s. This time I made sure I was sufficiently diversified. By '96 my real estate holdings were about a quarter of my total assets. Seventy-five percent of my investments were still in liquid assets.

The small business owners were audited the most in 1970s and 1980s by IRS. The first audit occurred in 1974 since my young and not so experienced accountant depreciated the land of our first apartment building. The auditor spent no more than an hour with us asking us to pay a little more to the IRS. The second and the last audit was in 1980. It was an exhaustive audit due to our velvet fabric import business. I was quite nervous during the process. The auditor was a lady who was checking the cost of goods on her calculator. Numbers did not match. I became even more nervous, any one could see that. Pratima added the numbers and came out with the right number. She was cool as an ice cube. I could not resist to say, "What will I do without you, Pratima?" The lady auditor, quite impressed with my comment, responded with a smile, "that is very sweet of you to say that," and completed the audit within half an hour. In our later years in 1990s and in new millennium, Pratima has been handling all legal matters, including landlord tenant issues, since she is lot tougher than I am.

The '80s were also the decade of junk bonds, with an exorbitant yield on bond investments. The originator of junk bonds was Michael Milken, who later was prosecuted and found guilty of breaking the SEC laws. One of the junk bonds that I invested in was Trans World Airline (TWA) when Carl Icahn bought it by issuing junk bonds. Along with the junk bonds came airline coupons giving a great discount to fly on TWA. I gave away these coupons to four friends, so six of us flew to the Bahamas. One afternoon, four of us decided to go swimming on a private beach where the rich tourists were having fun riding dune buggies; we'd had enough of the protected beach of our hotel. We hardly saw anyoneswimming, so two of us men wentin thewater. When I was swimming about 400 feet away from the shoreline, a man was yelling and waving his hands to come back to shore. Without any hesitation, I swam as fast as I could. As I came close to knee-deep water, we saw a 12-foot-long shark right behind me. I was profusely thankful to the man who had given me the signal. In fact I lost some sleep for a couple of nights, thinking that I could have been dead or paralyzed if the shark had attacked me. This was the third incident where I could have lost my life. I suppose the Divine Being wanted me to be alive so that I could write books, including this one.

Pratima and Sonya with Damubhabhi, Sarojbhabhi, Nayana, and Bharati in 1981.

My uncle (aunt's husband) Babuphua, my father, Jitubhai, and Sarojbhabhi, July 1982. My father passed away in December 1982 at the age of seventy-five.

Ayurvedic doctor Chandra Shekhar Thakur with my friend Kishore Shroff, July 1982.

Rupa (Jayshree's daughter) and Sonya feeding pigeons, Trafalgar Square, London in the early '80s.

I had put some money in London to follow the rule of diversification. We would often visit London and stay with my cousin Jayshree. Arvindbhai, her husband and I got along very well. I remember travelling with them visiting Portugal and Spain. It was fun for me to drive at a very high speed since the high speed driving, I believe, was allowed or tolerated. Well, I got in a terrible accident when I took a left turn, without seeing a car coming from the opposite direction, hitting the back side of our car. Both cars were unrepairable and total loss. Arvindbhai rightfully was concerned about an accidentin a foreign country. Luckily no one was injured and we were insured; my American Express card saved us from any trouble. I suspect America's power and prestige was probably at the highest level in 1980s. I recall our Indian friends saying that the best of the best was their choice of having an American passport, American Express platinum credit card, Japanese wife, French wine, and Mercedes automobile.

After the stock market bubble burst in 2000, I was back with maybe 35 to 40 percent of my investments in real estate. I had been involved with real estate for some time. Most of it was in southern California, but I also got involved in some real estate in Texas. Nanoo Patel, who did well in the incense business during the '70s, had been a friend of mine for a long time. He was part of a very large family that had settled in the U.S.; one of four brothers, he had invited two to come to America. They had all lived in Africa. Nanoo tried to help his brothers and family, but his incense business was too small for him to help them all. One of the brothers in fact became an even bigger problem for Nanoo; as a result he had to sell his incense business. He probably would have done better on his own if he had kept the business for himself. In hindsight, I am glad I took the advice of Arvindbhai Mafatlal in '71 not to join my brothers in Mumbai.

Nanoo was a good human being. He and his wife moved to Dallas after he got out of the incense business. Dallas was a hub of merchandising, so Nanoo started a real estate partnership in the late '70s and early '80s. Basically he would get capital and buy properties for others. Real estate was pretty good there. Unfortunately bad luck struck again. In the late '80s, Dallas real estate crashed because of a combination of high interest rates and a poor oil market. Texas was chiefly a state of big oil business, and as inflation came into control and all prices (oil included) started to decline, the Texas economy was badly hurt.

Nanoo was in bad shape and had no choice but to come to LA. Being experienced in apartment management, he decided to work for a man named Sashi Jogani who owned thousands of apartment units. Working in LA for Sashi, Nanoo was separated from his family; his kids were going to school in Dallas. His wife Rajni was trying to raise them alone. One day when she was visiting Los Angeles, Rajni asked me to invest in Dallas. She was working as a real estate agent generating a second income. But the market was so depressed in Dallas, Rajni wasn't doing a lot of business. I asked her, "Who would manage my property if I invest?"She didn't have an answer but she wanted her husband Nanoo to come back to Dallas. After some thought I suggested to Rajni, "Look, if Nanoo goes back to Dallas to be with you and if he manages my investment, I will consider investing." Of course Rajni liked this idea.

I had several things in mind. Number one, as a true contrarian, I figured that if the Dallas real estate market was so depressed, there would be less risk for a further decline in the market. When the market did pick up, there would be good rewards. Number two, investing in Dallas real estate would be a geographical diversification in real estate for me. Number 3, Nanoo had helped me in my velvet business by providing good consultation. He being an honest man, but a victim of circumstances, my investment in Dallas would also mean Nanoo would be together with his family in Texas. Of course, managing my building alone would not bring the livelihood Nanoo needed, but it would be a step in the right direction.

So I invested in Dallas real estate and bought six duplexes and six four-plexes, a total of 36 apartment units. The LA market had peaked in the '90s. I had sold a 10-unit Inglewood building at an excellent price and used the proceeds to buy these 36 units. It was a wise investment. I was quite fortunate, thanks to Nanoo's excellent management, that it all worked out. The Dallas properties gave me a reasonable cash flow and a good appreciation. Most importantly I was able to help a good friend. I was proud that I had accomplished all the objectives that I sought when Rajni first suggested investing in Dallas. I consider myself very fortunate to have good friends like Nanoo and Rajni Patel.

I had also invested in different movie projects, none of them panned out, and were total loss. I suppose both my father and I did not have enough luck to make money in the movie business. My father had invested in a Bollywood movie studio that resulted in a total loss. Krishna Shah who was hired by Japanese entrepreneur, was looking for capital to upgrade a Japanese made animated film of the Indian epic Ramayana. Many of us invested in the project, but the project was a total loss. Babu Subramanium convinced me to fund the writing of a script for the Bhopal project. It was again a total loss.

Coming back to more recent times, after the 2008–09 market crash, the Western economy was in uncharted territory. I have never before experienced what we are going through in the last five years (2009–2014). Private and public debt keeps rising, and the velocity of money is either stagnant or falling. Markets are manipulated by bankers with deep pockets. Banks can borrow money with close to a zero percent (ZERP) interest rate, and get involved in any industry of their choosing. This is not free enterprise or a free market, where price is discovered based on the supreme law of demand and supply. Senator Dick Durbin from Illinois stated that the U.S. Congress is essentially in the pocket of the bankers. Too big to fail (TBTF) banks, with the blessings of the Plunge Protection Team, control the markets by trading major market indices. The Plunge Protection Team, constituted of the secretary of the treasury, the presidents of stock exchanges, and a Federal Reserve (the Fed) chairperson, was created after the '87 market crash. The elected president, democrat or republican, will choose his secretary of the treasury almost always from one of the big New York banks.

The only way I see to get out of the jaws of TBTF banks is to first nationalize them, then break them down to smaller sizes. The failure of a small bank does not affect the economy significantly. Ever since the history of money began, kings and rulers have had the power to create or print money. Today the Federal Reserve has the power to create money. The Fed does not report to the congress or the president but to the big banks.There is a very interesting book about how the Fed was created in 1913, *The Creature from Jekyll Island*, authored by G. E. Griffin.

Here is a joke quite appropriate for recent times. Stockbroker John, a father of two boys, decides to teach simple economics to his nine-year-old son James during dinner. He explains, "Jim, you know I go to the office to work every day and bring money home and give it to your mom for her to spend. Think of me as a capitalist, and your mom as government. Maria, our maid, works for us; think of her as workers." Jim asks, "What about me and little Bobby?" "Think of yourself as people and Bobby as the future. I want you to remember and understand these participants; we will talk more about it in the morning," the father replies quickly in order to catch his favorite TV show. They all go to bed. Around midnight, Jim smells something bad and realizes that the infant Bobby has done double in his diaper. He goes to his parents' bedroom and sees his mother fast asleep, thanks to her valium addiction. So he goes to the maid's room, where the door is locked but the light is on. He looks through the keyhole and sees his father having intercourse with Maria. He gives up and goes to bed. Next morning Jim, in a serious mood, comes for breakfast. John, already sitting at the table, asks, "Jim, did you think about what I said last night?" "Dad, the people are totally confused!" The father asks, "Why so, Jim?" Jim responds, "While the capitalists are screwing workers, the government is fast asleep, and the future happens to be in deep shit!"

The bottom line here is that wage earners and retirees are suffering the most due to the ZERP policy of the government, while bankers are making a killing. Latest data given in the *Economist* magazine dated November 8, 2014 shows that the wealth held by the bottom 90 percent peaked around '85 and has been falling ever since. However the wealth of the top half percent has been rising continuously since '78. The economy is on the right track when the GDP is growing. Two sure ways to grow the GDP are by increasing productivity through creativity and innovation, and by increasing employment. None of the two is increasing significantly. In fact the full-time manufacturing workforce with higher wages is receding, while the part-time workforce with lower wages is rising, thanks to Obama Care.

The hope to save the Western economies, I believe, lies in the wisdom of our collective memory represented by the morphic field named by scientist Rupert Sheldrake. In the chaos theory, the *butterfly effect* is the sensitive dependence on initial conditions in which a small change in one state of a nonlinear system can result in large differences in a later state. The name of the effect, coined by Edward Lorenz, is derived from the metaphorical example of the details of a hurricane being influenced by minor perturbations such as the flapping of the wings of a distant butterfly several weeks earlier. The probability of markets falling into the butterfly vortex keeps rising as the leverage and therefore the systemic risk rise. Market bubbles, or any bubble, do not have a state of equilibrium. As they expand, the probability by the day increases for them to burst, as happened in 2000 and 2008/9.

In family matters, my father, at the age of seventy-five, passed away in the month of December 1982. I had called Mumbai and talked to him several times. The last time I talked to him was the first week of December, when he was hardly able to speak. One of my very big regrets is that I did not convey my love and affection for him and gratitude for what he had done for me. I had done that to my mother just before I left India in February 1965, immediately after our wedding. In fact I kissed her on her cheek, being influenced by Western culture. However she did not appreciate it saying, "We do not do such things in India."

My father was a very religious man, and he passed away chanting Lord Shiva's name and associated slokas. He was an ardent disciple of Swami Nityananda of Ganeshpuri. I give him, and certainly my late mother, the credit for putting me on the path of transcendence. One of Jitubhai's business partners, Batukbhai, said that considering what my father had done for Jasvantbhai, not being reasonably successful at the time and financially the weakest of the three brothers in my father's opinion, he should wash our father's feet and drink that water. I would modify that statement, and say that all four of us including Deepak should have done the same. He helped us all to the best of his capability. It is unfortunate that both Jasvantbhai and Jitubhai often complained about his shortcomings and did not appreciate our father's help to us. The difference in my opinion may be due to the different paths we chose individually. I believe it is always harder to start a fresh enterprise of any kind from nothing as opposed to joining a profit-making running business.

Jasvantbhai had found suitable boys, Sanjay and Anang, from good families for his daughters, Daksha and Nayana, and got them married off. Bharati, the eldest daughter, had already married Amar in the late '60s. Pratima, with Rahul and Sonya, attended Daksha's wedding in '75 and visited her family in Indore. I attended Nayana's wedding in '77. My visit in '77 was a bit exhausting, since at my arrival to Mumbai, I had to leave the same day in a car with my father to Ahmedabad without resting from jetlag. However it was a memorable and good eight-day visit, since I had an opportunity to spend more time with my larger family and specifically with my father.

One incident I distinctly remember, when a well-educated member of the family challenged me that I could not sustain myself without a cup of coffee during my stay for Nayana's wedding. Evidently he had read about Americans being hooked on coffee. When I accepted the wager of about 1,000 rupees, my father had the biggest laugh, since he thought and commented on "Navin" trapping the gentlemen who had wagered with me. It was another example of my father having a very high regard for me in matters of self-control, and my cleverness and capabilities. The marriage was held out in the open in Jasvantbhai's bungalow with so many guests sleeping and eating at the same place. I was able to adjust to using the same bathroom and toilet along with so many guests. The marriage ceremony went well, except later in the evening when the rain created a bit of inconvenience.

Jasvantbhai unfortunately was like our mother in matters of health, suffering from obesity, diabetes, and a weak heart. He suffered a heart attack and passed away in '84. Damubhabhi informed me later, in her words, "During his last days in the hospital, whenever he saw the young doctor who was taking care of him, he would compare and think of his youngest brother, Navin." The day he passed away, it was around 12 midnight in Los Angeles. I got up about the same time to go to the bathroom. While walking towards the bathroom, I felt dizzy and fainted, falling down. My two upper central teeth were broken. As I am aging, I have become a strong believer in the existence of the morphic field and resonance, based on multiple experiences I have gone through. I suppose there was some "quantum" connection with my brother Jasvantbhai, who had great affection for his youngest brother. I regret that I did not express my love and affection as much as I should have. I had learnt a lot from his street smartness, and his disciplining me during my growing-up period. He was well connected in Ahmedabad during his later years due to his interest in art, poetry, and entertaining guests. He had friends in Bollywood and in politics. Prime Minister Atal Bihari Vajpayee, before he became prime minister in the mid-'90s, stayed with my brother during his visit to Ahmedabad, since both enjoyed Scotch whisky, which was difficult to get due to prohibition in Gujarat. The prime minister never forgot his friendship with my brother after his death, and would make a point to meet Damubhabhi during his visits to Ahmedabad. Damubhabhi was a compassionate lady who helped my brother's mistress Harina and her son after his death.

The story of Harina is quite interesting. She was one of many wives of an old royal family, and she was treated terribly by the whole family. Jasvantbhai was a regular visitor to Rajasthan where he had cultivated many friends. Jasvantbhai would inform me that he saved her from misery by bringing her and her son to Ahmadabad.

The story was similar about my father's mistress. Young girls in many places in India would be given away to temples because the families could not support them. These girls were also known as devdasi, meaning a servant of the temple god. The story is similar to the story in the movie, "Water" produced and directed by Deepa Mehta. The head of the temple would encourage wealthy men to have relationships with these girls for money. My father met this young girl in her twenties. He was probably in his middle 40s when he was visiting a newly acquired manganese mine in a southern state of India. The brighter side that I see here is that my father and my brother gave better lives to these two young ladies. Yes, they also suffered in social circles and created terrible problems within families. It is unfortunate, even today, that women in India are not treated as well as in western countries.

Jitubhai's daughter Jagruti was married in '76 to Premal Parikh, who was in the diamond business. I remember attending her wedding in Mumbai. I was a guide to many international business associates who came from Europe and America. Premal's family were in the diamond export business. Jitubhai's son Manoj, a lot younger than Jagruti, got married in '87. Manoj and his wife Radha came to settle in Los Angeles in '88, but it did not work out since Radha was a lot closer to her family. However Radha delivered a baby girl, Sharmi, in '88 and the young family went back to India.

We also sponsored Jagruti, Pratima's niece, for higher education and to help Pratima in the business. She finished her B.A. and found a boy, Kamal Mehta, to marry. Sharadbhai, Pratima's brother and Jagruti's father and mother also attended Jagruti's wedding in '88; the parents were very thankful to us for seeing Jagruti settled in Los Angeles. That was our first experience of having a marriage in the family in Los Angeles.

There was much to cheer about the '90s, because our family of four was getting larger and larger every few years. After Jagruti's wedding, two years later in '90, Rahul and Manda informed us that they would like to get married, and the wedding day that they planned was June 30, 1990. Manda's father Kantibhai Patel and I gave them first a budget of about 70,000 dollars. With Rahul's high taste, the budget went up to around 100,000 dollars. The marriage was held in the famous Biltmore Hotel with about 600 invited guests. The guest list was divided in three equal parts: 200 guests each for the Doshis, Patels, and friends of Rahul and Manda.

We had my aunt Ramuphai, Damubhabhi, Jitubhai, and Sarojbhabhi come from India. We even had friends from my high school days attending the wedding. Some uninvited guests made the total over 650. We were later informed by some of the guests that the wedding was the best that they had ever attended. That was 1990. Lately we have heard that there have been weddings in the Indo-American community costing over half-a-million dollars. After the wedding, Rahul would say, "Dad, I wish we had taken the 100,000 dollars for ourselves, instead of spending it for the marriage." Well, it was too late.

We celebrated Sonya's wedding with Kevin at Dr. Marwah's ranch in Malibu on August 13, 1994, the same day I had left India in '58. Dr. Marwah, a dentist, is a very influential community leader and was a good friend of the Los Angeles mayor Tom Bradley in the '70s and '80s. He is even now, in his late eighties, wonderfully helpful to those Indo-Americans needing support. Our friendship has been for the last five decades and is still going. Sonya's wedding was much smaller, with fewer than 300 guests. Sonya and Kevin married twice, the first ceremony in a church in the morning, and the second, a Hindu ceremony in the afternoon in Malibu. I enjoyed Sonya's wedding for several reasons: a smaller number of guests, less involvement, less stress, and less costly. We did not have to be concerned about too many guests coming from out of town. The day initially was a bit warm, but later in the early afternoon Dr. Marwah's ranch was a wonderful and very pleasant location with the view of the Pacific Ocean. Sonya was somewhat stressed after the Indian wedding, because of some goof-up by the food caterer.

We had a wonderful time travelling with Sonya and Kevin to India. First, we had a wedding celebration in Mumbai, inviting members of the family and friends, since they were not present at the Los Angeles wedding. We went to Ajanta and Elora, planned by Jitubhai, via Aurangabad during their summer vacation. Kevin was quite adventurous, eating whatever we ate, including paan with betel nut. He stood in a long line with us, the men folks, with no shirt, for the "Darshana" (glimse) of Tryambakaswar Jyotirlinga (a temple of Shiva). There are twelve Jyotirlingas in the whole country; these have been held in great esteem since ancient prehistoric times. The Puranas talk in many sections as well as in detail about the glory of these abodes. Devotees have been pulled towards these kshetras (fields, locations) due to the highly benevolent divine presence in there since ancient times.

The line of devotees for the Darshana was like a long organism, more like a segmented earthworm, moving slowly but continuously without stopping, going around the Shiva linga and exiting the temple. Devotees of Lord Shiva must have wondered why a tall European or American with a snow-white upper body was in the line. He was an odd white segment in the brown matrix. The comparison with an earthworm is quite appropriate, because each segment, like a person, is autonomous. The experience of going back to Mumbai in an extremely crowded train was also a new experience for Sonya and Kevin.

Kevin got terribly sick for few days. Then we flew to New Delhi, and spent a few days visiting the Taj Mahal in Agra. We rented a car with a driver and headed north to visit Haridwar, Rishikesh, and Badrinath. Unfortunately, the roads were washed out to Badrinath, so we settled for Mussoorie and Dehradoon. Sonya wanted to visit Kullu Manali in Himchal Pradesh, but they settled for naming their first child Manali, born in '96. This was a wonderful experience for both of us, travelling India with our grown-up adult kids. We have travelled with our whole family, that is, with the families of Sonya and Rahul, but mostly in America. We are hoping one of these days that our whole family will travel to India, to have them discover their deep roots there. I certainly would like to be their guide.

We became grandparents for the first time in '94, when Manda delivered Anjali, and then the second time when she delivered Natasha in '97. Sonya delivered Manali in '96, and Kieran in '99. So just in one decade, we became a family of ten members. Krisan and Kailesh were added to the family by the year 2005. We are very proud of Rahul who became a prominent and successful electro-physiology cardiologist, and Sonya who was a financial executive at Wells Fargo.

Deepak came back to Los Angeles in early '83, after my father passed away. Later on he remarried to Kapila in '83, and fathered two pretty girls, Priyanka and Namrata. My citizenship became instrumental in bringing Deepak's mother, sister and her husband as part of my family. Deepak started his own textile and home-furnishing business, while I eased out in the early '90s. Deepak and Kapi are currently running the same business. Priyanka graduated from my old alma matter UCLA, and now is a successful pharmacist. Namrata is currently studying to major in psychology. Priyanka has found a young man of her liking and will probably get married within a year. Angali is at UC Berkeley, Manali is at UCLA, and Tashu is at USC with her dad, Rahul, also teaching there.

When Deepak turned fifty in 2005, I was asked to say a few words. The speech is reproduced below, revealing our connectedness after he came to Los Angeles in '73. FRIENDS, GOOD EVENING.

FIRST I WOULD LIKE TO THANK GOPICA AND RAJIVE (Deepak's friends) FOR BEING GOOD FRIENDS OF DEEPAK AND HOSTING THIS EVENT.

I AM GOING BACK TO ONE COLD NIGHT IN JANUARY 1973. WE HEAR A KNOCK ON THE DOOR OF OUR MODEST HOUSE IN THE PALMS AREA. PRATIMA AND I ARE WONDERING WHO COULD IT BE AT THIS HOUR

OF THE NIGHT. GUESS WHAT? WHEN WE OPENED THE DOOR, WE SEE A SKINNY, LANKY INDIAN KID, DEEPAK. DEEPAK IS MY HALF-BROTHER, AND WE HAD MET HIM ONLY ONCE BEFORE IN A WRINKLED LENGHA AND KHAMIS IN 1972.

WE WERE TO RECEIVE HIM THE NEXT DAY AS PER THE TELEGRAM. THE CONFUSION WAS PROBABLY DUE TO THE TIME DIFFERENCE. YOU SEE, I HAD LEFT HOME IN 1955, JUST ABOUT 50 YRS AGO, TO STUDY ENGINEERING IN PUNE AND THEN HAD LEFT INDIA TO COME TO THE USA IN 1958 FOR FURTHER STUDIES.

DURING MY VISIT TO MUMBAI IN 1972, OUR FATHER EXPRESSED HIS CONCERN ABOUT DEEPAK'S FUTURE. HE WAS NOT QUITE SURE OF HIS FUTURE IN MUMBAI. HE ASKED ME IF DEEPAK COULD BE OF HELP TO ME, SINCE WE HAD JUST STARTED THE BUSINESS OF IMPORTING VELVET PATCHWORK. AFTER GOING THRU THE DIFFERENT FORMALITIES OF IMMIGRATION (INS), DEEPAK WAS TO COMPLETE STUDIES FROM WOODBURY UNIVERSITY AND HELP ME PART TIME. PRATIMA AND DEEPAK GOT ALONG VERY WELL. PRATIMA WAS VERY HAPPY TO HAVE AN INHOUSE BABYSITTER WHENEVER SHE NEEDED ONE, AND DEEPAK LOVED KIDS AND PLAYING WITH THEIR TOYS. AT THE SAME TIME, WE WERE LEARNING TO BE THE PARENTS OF AN 18 YEAR OLD. HE WAS TRYING HARD TO LEARN AMERICAN WAYS THAT INCLUDED HARD WORK, THE LANGUAGE, AND CULTURE.

THE TEXTILE BUSINESS WAS EXPLODING DUE TO THE VIETNAM VETS COMING HOME. FOR THEM NIRVANA WAS TO LAY ON A WATERBED COVERED WITH A VELVET PATCHWORK BEDSPREAD, LISTEN

TO RAVI SHANKAR'S MUSIC, AND BURN INCENSE IN THE BACKGROUND. EVIDENTLY NOW AND ALSO THEN, DEEPAK HAS THE STRONG INFLUENCE OF BOLLYWOOD. HE KEPT HIS SHIRT UNBUTTONED SHOWING OFF HIS BARE SKINNY CHEST DECORATED WITH A HEAVY GOLD CHAIN, AND STYLING HIS HAIR WITH FUGGA (Remember Elvis Presley!). HE THOUGHT HE WAS AN AMITABH BACHAN LOOKALIKE, BEING TALL AND SKINNY. AS TIME PASSED, HE DID LEARN TO WORK HARD AND COMLETED HIS STUDIES. TO HIS GOOD FORTUNE, HE FOUND A GOOD-LOOKING MATE, A LOOKALIKE OF BOLLYWOOD STAR HEMA MALINI.

I WOULD LIKE TO ADD THAT BOTH OF US ARE VERY FORTUNATE TO HAVE A GOOD FATHER. OUR FATHER DID HIS BEST TO TAKE CARE OF HIS KIDS. MAY GOD BLESS HIS SOUL.

DEEPAK, MY HEARTFELT CONGRATULATIONS ON YOUR FIFTIETH; YOU HAVE FULFILLED THE WISHES OF OUR FATHER. YOU NOT ONLY HAVE LEARNT TO TAKE CARE OF YOURSELF BUT ALSO OF YOUR FAMILY, INCLUDING YOUR MOTHER, AND THAT HAS A LOT TO DO WITH YOU MARRYING A CONSIDERATE, FAMILY-ORIENTED WIFE WHO IS BEHIND YOU ALL (MOST?) OF THE TIME.

Rahul wedding Manda with Pratima and myself, June 30, 1990. Pratima looks more like Rahul's sister than a mother. A friend had difficulties distinguishing Pratima and Vaishali, her sister's daughter.

At Sonya's wedding; from left Pratima, Dr. Marwah, Sonya, Kevin, Mrs. Marwah and myself. The wedding was performed at Dr. Marwah's ranch on August 13, 1994.

Family photo, Diwali, 2005. Back row, from left: Manda, Pratima, Kapi, and Sonya; Middle row: Deepak, Rahul, Kevin, and myself; Front row: Tashu, Angali, Manali, and Kieran.

Kevin, Pratima without her chunni, and Sonya on a bridge in Hardware (1995). Pratima could not hide her compassion; so she wrapped her Chunni (shawl), on a shivering disabled woman.

CHAPTER 9

RAISING OUR CHILDREN

"Your children are not your children. They come through you but not from you. Though they are with you, yet they belong not to you."

Khalil gibran, from The Prophet

Some Pain but Mostly Pleasure!

Our second child, Sonya, was born on December 9, 1969, a Sagittarian girl. Rahul was born on July 4, 1966, a moonchild. So out of the four of us, three are Sagittarians, and we hold our bows and arrows ready and have good aim! The common attributes I find in us three include being thrifty, idealistic, adventurous, and loving Nature. We are often blunt and tactless in the search for the truth. Moonchildren are very quick to learn, hardworking, faithful, but also enjoy the material aspects of life. All this is stated in Sydney Omarr's book on horoscopes. Both my wife and I feel very fortunate that we have two great kids who have grown up to have successful careers and wonderful families of their own. We are also fortunate in having wonderful sons and daughters-in-law, and to top it off, we have six grandchildren evenly divided; three granddaughters and three grandsons.

But it is not easy raising kids. Rahul was always outgoing with lots of friends. But those "lots of friends" also got us into a few problems. Rahul has a very expressive face; whenever he made a mistake or was naughty, you could easily catch him by his facial expression. One day while playing basketball at our Bentley house, Rahul broke the glass of one of the windows. After I sat him down and asked him if he had broken the glass, he plainly said, "No." When I kept looking at him seriously, without uttering a word for a few minutes, his expression would give him away, and later on he would confess.

Almost all parents find that kids are angels when they are babies. As children grow up and get more involved in life matters, you could say that their cherubic innocence begins to diminish through influences from far and near; the philosopher Krishnamurti describes this process as conditioning. Both of our children went to a private school because we had moved to Ladera Heights and were told that public schools in that area were not quite up to the mark. Rahul and Sonya went to St. Bernard High School, a parochial school. Though our children were raised in a Hindu family, we didn't mind them taking theology classes where they learned about the Christian religion.

While Sonya and Rahul were growing up, Pratima and some of the other Indian mothers would teach their kids over the weekends about Indic traditions. The lessons included Sanskrit slokas, Indian dance for girls, and other cultural activities that related to India. We enrolled Sonya in Bharatnatyam (classical) Indian dance. This is traditional among Indian families. Sonya was a natural dancer and did quite well, learning for a number of years. I have one regret about not exposing Rahul and Sonya to deeper education of Indian traditions including the Gujarati language, since I am a strong believer in cultivating stronger and deeper roots in every generation. We had a disadvantage not having our parents and their grandparents in close proximity, as some of our friends did. Sonya has some grasp of the Gujarati language, but Rahul has much less. I spent a lot of good time with Rahul before he went off to college. I taught him table tennis, which we'd often play together as well as regular tennis. With regard to diet, Sonya by her own conviction and desire remained a vegetarian. Rahul to this day is not a vegetarian, finding it difficult to remain so because he spent so much time with friends eating hamburgers.

Rahul excelled in his studies, and so did Sonya. Both were on an average "A" graders. Rahul's friends though got him into trouble occasionally. I remember one weekend, Rahul was spending time with other teenage friends using our Buick station wagon; around 11 pm we received a phone call from a policeman, saying they had a station wagon full of teens down at the police station. Evidently they had experimented with drinking beer and got caught by the local police, as they were under the legal drinking age in California. Rahul asked us to come and pick them up. When Pratima went to the station, it turned out not to be such a big deal, except for going to the police station at midnight.

Almost all parents go through difficult times with their teenage kids. Rahul had difficulties holding money in his possession. He always seemed to want more and more money to spend. He wanted a better car and a newer car. Part of the problem was that Rahul had friends whose parents gave their kids everything they wanted, like flashy cars and expensive stereo systems, you name it. We being frugal ourselves, not having had a safety net like supportive parents, wanted our kids to be frugal and self-sufficient. Thinking this through, I decided that if Rahul needed money the only way he could get money would be to work. At first he wasn't thrilled with my logic. But while he was going to high school and later at UCLA, Rahul spent time helping us with our businesses. It was really a blessing. Rahul was very good with an Apple computer when it came out, I believe in the early '80s. He could do things for us either in accounting or whatever I needed. He was also very good with his hands. He liked repairing things, and he was happy receiving money to spend.

I came up with another idea to help Rahul improve his cash flow while at the same time improving his studies. He was actually very quick with his studies and with anything else he wanted to learn particularly in the field of science, which is what I wanted him to know. I told Rahul that if he studied science and mathematics, above and beyond his homework, I would give him five dollars an hour. Note that was in the late '70s, when five dollars an hour was quite reasonable; the minimum wage was around three dollars. So there was always an incentive for him to work and study. With Sonya we didn't have that difficulty. She was always highly motivated with her schoolwork. But with Rahul we did. Still, though Rahul became more motivated, he suffered from the peer pressure of wanting more material things from his parents. How vividly I remember Rahul complaining to me saying, "Dad, you are not the best dad, there are better dads. I wish I had another dad (like the dad who gave a BMW to his friend)!" His disillusionment with me stemmed from the fact that I wouldn't buy him a BMW like the parents of several of his friends. I still don't think parents should spoil their kids like that. Later on when they were raising Anjali and Tashu, Rahul's tune was very different. He would say, "I am going to raise them just the way you raised us." That of course is a great compliment. It reminds of my late friend, Arvind in Bombay, who gave his only son a fast BMW. Sadly, his son, while attending a prestigious Eastern university, died in a car crash.

To protect Rahul while he was driving, we initially gave him a bigger car, a Buick station wagon. It was really a safety issue. For the most part it was a cinch raising Rahul, but every time we gave him a car, he'd wreck it. These wrecks were not always his fault. One day we sent him to fetch some food for a party we were giving. En route to the store, Rahul got hit on the side of the car by an old driver. Luckily he wasn't hurt.

Rahul graduated with flying colors from St. Bernard's High School. He was admitted to UCLA because of his high GPA and the fact he'd been involved in various school sports and other activities. He was also the recipient of the science award. Sonya also graduated with excellent grades, in addition to being elected president of the students' organization and homecoming queen. She thus became both president and queen! She had no difficulties being admitted to UCLA. I understand it's getting harder to be admitted to UCLA and to all the UC schools. It was a wonderful experience seeing our kids excel in their school activities and studies.

Now, in 2014, our three granddaughters go to UC Berkley, UCLA, and USC. The credit certainly goes to their parents but also, I suppose, they share some credit with us as their grandparents.

Sonya seemed to want to grow up a lot faster than Rahul. Some parents say girls mature more quickly than boys. Sonya wanted to date when she was around fifteen, but coming from a conservative Indian family, we were reluctant. But later, like many other Indian transplanted families in America, we agreed. Because Sonya was a girl, we were understandably more conservative. Kids in America are often raised to be aggressive with the opposite sex. Films and television seem to promote unacceptable interactions between boys and girls. The epidemic of sexually transmitted diseases, rising cases of AIDS among teens, or teens' attitudes about sex becoming more liberal than during the '50s and early '60s, are evidence of changes in values over time. Pratima and I tried to be protective with our kids, but we didn't completely stop them from dating. We did encourage them to be selective. Between the two of us, the father was thought to be tougher than the mother, as was the case when I was growing up. It seems to me that the mother's infinite love for children compliments perfectly the father's desire to discipline them. Occasionally we had different perspectives in raising children; however we never exposed our differing views to our children. Often

Pratima was able to convince me, employing different sources of wisdom.

In Sonya's case we arranged for her to date a few Indian boys. Evidently things just didn't click. In matters of transportation, we bought Sonya a more expensive car than her brother's; a three-year-old Saab, thanks to Pratima's influence. It was smaller and safer. We convinced her it was a good car to have and she liked it. After Rahul's station wagon accident, we got him a Ford van, which was updated, repainted, withall sorts of goodies. I'm not sure that was the best idea, because Rahul ended up using the van for all sorts of parties with his friends. One evening when Rahul was in college, he planned a big beer party. The boys got a keg of beer and there were lots of Indian and American boys and girls. They had very loud heavy metal and rap music with all sorts of depressing lyrics blaring out in the neighborhood. I heard words like "killing" and "drugs" and other profanities. It was a far cry from the music we used to listen to in our college days. As parents we tried to discourage our kids from listening to that sort of music. Needless to say, those were quite difficult years. After Rahul graduated from the Ford van, wegave him a three-year-old Audi, a luxury car, because he was doing so well at UCLA. He wrecked that car within a year. The only car he did not wreck was a Toyota Supra, which he took to Stanford Medical School. That could be because of Manda's influence, the girl he later married.

When Rahul graduated from UCLA with distinction, he was admitted to three or four medical schools. There were two reasons he was able to maintain his good GPA. One, he was very selective with his classes, and chose professors who were known as excellent teachers. The second reason, looking back in time, Rahul was certainly smarter and more successful than his father. After Rahul graduated from UCLA in '87, he had two girlfriends. One was Indian and one was American. One day he asked me which girl he should chose to go steady with. I'm not sure I gave the right advice but I said that the choice was his. "If you like the Indian girl, you have more in common with her culturally than the non-Indian girl," I said. He must have liked the Indian girl. When Rahul chose Stanford Medical School, his Indian girlfriend Manda went to Berkeley, making it convenient for them to meet in the Bay Area. Later on, Pratima and I found out they were actually living together. Three years later, in June 1990, they married. They have been married for about twenty-four years and have three kids: Anjali, the oldest, goes to UC Berkeley, Natasha went to USC in 2014, and Krisan is in elementary school. Rahul received his Doctor of Medicine degree from Stanford, and was trained at Cedars-Sinai in the field of E.P. Cardiology; he currently holds a position at USC Medical School as head of the E.P. Cardiology department.

Sonya finished her Bachelor's degree in both English and Psychology at UCLA, then continued on to get her Masters in English Literature. After getting her Bachelor's, Sonya decided to return to her alma mater high school, St. Bernard, and work as a teacher. It was there that she met her future husband Kevin McCarthy, who was then a math teacher, like his father. After going together for nearly three years, they married and have three children. Sonya later joined Paine Webber stockbrokerage firm, after passing several exams and receiving a brokerage license. Currently, she is an advisor at Wells Fargo. Apparently she has been quite successful, not just as a financial advisor, but often as a voluntary but practical psychologist (without a degree) to her clients. Rahul has been a speaker in demand in his field, and has shared the platform with celebrities like First Lady Laura Bush and President Clinton. We are very proud of both Rahul and Sonya for their accomplishments.

In looking back at my years as a parent, I learned some key things based on my experience. With the reader's permission, I would like to call them "Doshi's Laws for Raising Children." Of course, the name "Doshi" could well be replaced by many other names! But

I have derived these rules from my own and Pratima's pains and pleasures of parenting.

Rule # 1: Parents will never be able to give their kids all they want to give them.

Why? Most probably kids do not want all you want to give them. You are probably not able to give all you want to give anyway. And/or you may not be able to give kids what they want from you. The reason for this may be because the parents were raised in different environments than their children. The generational gap may be attributable to some degree to the changes that occur in time. Recall that Nature is always changing. When children are little babies, they are influenced by you. But when they grow up and go to school, the environment is different. Peer pressure is different, and peers have a huge influence on kids.

Rule #2: Parents will always give something to their children even if they don't plan to give or don't want to give. This is genetic, of course. You do not want to give your advice, knowing that they do not agree with you because you do not see eye to eye. So you decide not to give your advice. Perhaps you feel it won't be appreciated. Perhaps you believe your children need to be self-sufficient or they might do everything the opposite of what you ask them to do. For that reason you may not want to give them something that is precious to you. But you still will give or may have already given to them sometime during their upbringing because of the love and affection and that genetic connection you have with them. Recall the statement, "Blood is thicker than water." I refer to the book published in '76, *The Selfish Gene*, written by Richard Dawkins. "The gene-centered view follows that the more two individuals are genetically related, the more sense (at the level of the genes) it makes for them to behave selflessly with each other."

Rule #3: Avoid "reinventing the wheel," whenever it is applicable.

Kids should avoid the tendency to reinvent the wheel when having a common interest in the parents' fields of endeavor. One of the biggest problems in the USA, probably in many other countries, is that children do not accept or carry on their parents' business. As a result, the business dies or ends up being sold. Sometimes children want to "reinvent the wheel" or change the family business, which is fine as long as there is continuity and it is on the path of growth. There is an opportunity for kids to enlarge their parents' fortune and make it grow even larger. One of the few but quite important prerequisites for the son or daughter to take over the family business is to have reasonable experience working for another employer. The intention is to ensure that kids appreciate the father's success in developing the business right from the start.

Matters of money often create friction between a father and son, or between two brothers. I saw the friction between my two brothers, and occasionally my brothers were critical of my father. Earlier, I had tried to go back to India, hoping to take advantage of my father's established business. However, I saw too many difficulties and friction among the participants, and problems associated with the Indian government.

One good example I can cite within my oldest brother Jasvantbhai's family. His grandson and Nayana's son Aniket came to America for higher education. After receiving his Master's degree, he was offered a job working for the MicrosoftCorporation and heaccepted it. As years passed, he had a girlfriend, and he thought of settling down in America. As I heard from his father Anangbhai, who had established a thriving business in chemicals, he offered Aniket to either join him and make the business grow, or go back to America. If he settled in America, Anangbhai said, he would only help him buy a house, no more no less. Aniket smartly chose to join his father, and as I understand, he has been successfully developing and growing his father's business.

Rule #4: A father and mother should never ever take sides, or disagree in matters of raising children or making decisions about children, in their presence.

Parents should always be in unison when conveying a message to the kids. If the parents are in disagreement, the kids will take advantage and even help to divide you more. This is not good for the marriage and not good for the kids. Kids are very smart. We may not think they are, but they are very observant and will know your weaknesses. If parents have differences of opinion in matters related to the kids, they should discuss their disagreements in the absence of the children and then come up with one decision and implement it. This is very important in the children's growing-up period. I have seen firsthand how a family can fall apart. Akbar, a real estate broker friend, who had sold me our first apartment building in 1972, was married and fathered two children. A tall handsome man from the Hyderabad royal family, and his Audrey Hepburn look-alike wife (half Indian and half European) did not see eye to eye in raising children. Akbar enjoyed the good life, fast cars and the company of the rich and famous. However they would fight in the matter of raising children. The daughter had some mental problems that became further aggravated with the medication prescribed by a psychiatrist from UCLA. Often the parents did not agree on how to resolve the problem. Akbar wanted to file a suit against the doctor and UCLA. I advised him not to because, having deep pockets and a battery of big lawyers on the pay roll, it was almost impossible to win against an adversary like UCLA.

The marriage ultimately resulted in a divorce favored by their children. The wife and children had hired a lawyer for the divorce. Akbar was able to convince his wife to talk to me as a mediator. As a neutral party, I informed them that if they could settle the issue of dividing the wealth fairly, then they will save a lot by not spending on legal costs. After all, most of the wealth would go to their children after their demise. I reminded them that they loved each other for several decades and raised two children. If they wished now to part company they could do so in a friendly manner. They took my advice and the matter of sharing the wealth was resolved amicably.

Rule #5: Never ever stop communicating. Maintain a strong link between you and your children to establish strong roots.

The roots should go as deep as they can. If the grandparents are alive, make sure they are strongly connected. I am reminded of one particular story about my good late friend from high school years, Arvind, who excelled in the iron business in India. After his marriage he fathered two kids, a boy and a girl. Of course in India the boys are more spoiled than the girls. The male child in India is more valued, which I totally disagree with. We need to change that. Arvind's son came to America for higher education. Arvind bought him an expensive BMW, and one day received a phone call that informed him that his son was killed in an accident because he was driving at a very high speed. Arvind was devastated losing a precious son. Arvind's daughter did her Master's and married a young man, a college dropout. Unfortunately, she fell in love with a boy that Arvind did not approve of. They were both Gujuratis so there was no caste problem. The boy was involved with his parent's business of precious stones and diamonds. Still Arvind did not approve of him. The boy's father had also divorced his first wife at a very young age. Personally I didn't understand why Arvind had problems with this boy. Arvind disagreed and didn't want her to marry this young man. The daughter being in love and being accepted by the boy's parents decided to marry him. Arvind did not even attend the marriage. His main objection was that the boy's parents were divorced, and the boy did not have a degree from a reputable university.

While I was visiting Arvind in Bombay I asked him, "Why are you doing this?" I even gave him Khalil Gibran's book. Arvind would say, "Maybe you are more philosophical, Navin. But in India, it is different. We have to think in terms of the society. What would society think?" So evidently in his mind, society was a lot more important than his own daughter. I tried to convince him not to ever lose communication with her. He did not like the boy but even if she'd made a mistake,

I challenged him as to how he could disconnect totally. Later on, he did maintain some communication with his daughter, but not the son-in-law. Arvind passed away without knowing his son-in-law. I still believe that he could have done much better with his kids if he had maintained discipline in matters of his son, and communication with the daughter. In India, when the father is busy and often so caught up in business, fathers do not have a strong link with their children. That was my own experience in India and that was why my link with my father was much weaker than with my brothers and my mother.

Rule #6: Look for the positive and discard the negative in kids. Always encourage the positive and discourage the negative.

This is the Vedantic philosophy. Even in the best of human beings there is some bad. Even in the worst of human beings there is some good. In the worst of human beings the good can outgrow and even change a person. Sometimes all it takes is a little encouragement from parents. In Khalil Gibran's book *The Prophet*, he speaks of the gift of children. And they are a gift, a joy. I received that book from Carol in '61, one of my first girlfriends. I still cherish it. One time when I was with Rahul and the grandkids at a bookstore, I spotted the book. I gave it to Rahul and his wife Manda to read and contemplate. My intention was for them to appreciate Gibran's inspired words about raising children.

Rule #7: Make sure that kids are always busy, either in studies, or in games, or mutually agreed extra work, so that they do not fall into anything undesirable—undesirable activities, friends, company, and so on.

There is a much higher probability of kids getting into trouble during a period of boredom than otherwise. There is another message to implement this rule; never ever lose the line of communication. The problem I had with Rahul could have been due to not expressing enough love and affection. So it is very important that parents create an environment so that kids will never forget that their best caretakers are their loving parents.

Rule # 8: This rule is about autonomy and detachment, also to have children develop their own creativity.

First, let me quote (to parents) from Khalil Gibran's book *The Prophet*.

"Your children are not your children, they belong to Life's longing for itself. They come through you, and yet do not belong to you. You may house their bodies, but not their soul. Their souls dwell in the house of tomorrow, which you cannot visit, not even in your dreams."

Now, may I refer to a line or two from my own book, as those words float up in my mind at this juncture, and might clarify a few things relevant here. A line from *Transcendence, Saving Us from Ourselves* reads as follows: "Autonomy is the prerequisite to detachment. Detachment is the prerequisite to sub-ration, and sub-ration to transcendence." Human beings need to experience both transcendence and immanence, as explained in the non-dual traditions of Vedanta and Buddhism. Autonomy implies, after a certain age, that growing children should gradually be given the freedom to choose, particularly when they insist they are ready to do so. Parents need to be sufficiently detached to follow the wisdom of Khalil Gibran. For kids it is very natural to sub-rate. An example of detachment and sub-ration is when a teenager detaches from a bicycle by sub-rating the bicycle to obtain an automobile.

Rule # 9: Every wrongdoing must be criticized, and if necessary there should be an appropriate punishment.

I have observed during my lifetime that there are parents who do not want to criticize any wrongdoing of their kids specifically in public. Often they try to minimize the wrongdoing. I believe it is very important for kids to learn and admit when they have done something wrong to others. An apology also has to go along with the admission of guilt. Often self-respect is confused with the boosting of the ego. I would make every effort to side with the truth than worry about hurting kids' feelings.

Among books written about raising children, one particular book I have read the reviews of is *The Battle Hymn of the Tiger Mother,*written by Amy Chua. The belief, I gather, is that the Chinese believe their children can be "the best" students, that "academic achievement reflects successful parenting," and that if children did not excel at school then there was "a problem" and parents "were not doing their job." Chua contrasts them with the view she labels "Western" —that a child's self-esteem is paramount. Isabel Berwick of the *Financial Times* called the "tiger mother" approach to parenting "the exact opposite of everything that the Western liberal holds dear." However one poll of readers compared Eastern and Western methods, and two-thirds agreed that the "demanding Eastern" parenting model is better than the "permissive Western" model. I would argue that demanding and permissive parents are in all cultures. The story of educating deaf and blind Helen Keller is about employing "tough love." In the film *The Miracle Worker*, starring Anne Bancroft as the teacher Anne Sullivan, the impulses and reflexes of the pre-psychic self, with little light within the somatic self, are trained and cultured. Samskara is brought in to uplift first the body, then the mind, as described in my book, *Transcendence, Saving Us from Ourselves.*

A balance of discipline and loving parents are very important in my mind to have a child develop control over the pre-psychic urges, releasing creativity through a quantum connection with the divine. I believe creativity is spontaneous, and appears when the Rutta and Samskara are in sync. Pratima and I wish we had had the opportunity to have our children schooled at the Krishnamurti Foundation or the Maharishi School in Fairfield, Iowa. Children in these schools receive the broadest education based on Eastern traditions. The Maharishi and Krishnamurti schools, in the West and in India, provide high-quality academic education along with learning the arts of looking, listening, and learning; compassion, integrity, psychological freedom, living meditatively, broad awareness, and the dangers of competition, fear, ambition, and conflict are all explored.

Sonya with Vikram and Anjana's daughter Niyati and son Nirav, to compete for Home coming queen.

Four lifelong friends; myself, Arvind, Kishore Shroff, and Kishore Tejura (Teju) 1989. Comare this photo with the one chapter 2. Arvind passed away during his mid-sixties, Kishore and Teju passed away in their mid-seventies around 2010.

Sonya is crowned Homecoming Queen of her St. Barnard High school, 1985.

Granddaughters Manali, Anjali, and Natasha in Indian garb, 1998.

Dada (Navin) with his three granddaughters, Anjali, Manali, and Tashu.

First grandson Kieran, sticking with Dada at Kevin's 40th birthday party, 2000.

Two more, Krisan and Kailesh, two late arrivals, 2012.

Discovering a Path of Transcendence from a Tragic Event

Tragic events occur naturally and often they are also due to human mistakes. I have come across three different families, where two of them raised a mentally or physically handicapped child, while the third couple raised mentally impaired twin daughters. My friend Mark Lee, a former director of the Krishnamurti Foundation of America, and his wife Asha, a saintly couple, became parents of twin daughters. In Mark's own words, "The twins were born quite normal in 1970, but at the age of six months contracted viral encephalitis from mosquito bites in South India. We had unknowingly entered an epidemic area near Pondicherry, India. The girls lived because Asha is a doctor and knew how to save them, but they were rendered permanently brain-damaged. The doctors had told us to let them die but that was advice we could not agree to. Now they are forty-four years old and live very limited lives needing constant care and attention, 24 hours a day. One lives at home with us, and the other in a home in Santa Barbara. Neither speaks but both are happy and healthy otherwise. Asha gave up her medical career to care for the girls and has been amply rewarded with the great love and affection they have for her." Mark and Asha later became parents of a third baby girl, Nandini, who is currently a practicing medical doctor.

Another couple within my own family, my half-sister Jyoty and her husband Deepak Lakhani, became parents of a healthy baby boy, Milan. About a year or so later, they were informed that the child was autistic. Later on they became parents of another baby boy, Sagar. The parents raised them as best they could until Milan grew up to be a teenager. Then it became very difficult for the mother to handle a strong, often out-of-control son while the father was at work. Later they found an institution providing home-like care for Milan. He died at the age of about thirty almost immediately after his grandmother passed away.

The storyof thethird family is interesting and inspiring. My good friend Sitanshu Mehta was a recipient of many honors, including India's highly acclaimed honor, Padma Shree; Anjani, his wife, was a university professor herself, the chair of psychology at a college in the women's university, SNDT, in Mumbai. They came for graduate studies to one of the universities in America. In the meantime, they became parents of a baby girl. Unfortunately, the baby Vipasha suffered from cerebral palsy (CP). CP is a condition that includes not having control over physical movement, and speech difficulties. The parents decided to go back to India after Sitanshu finished his PhD, since it was easier for them to take care of Vipasha in India. As I have observed in so many families, there is a very special bond between father and daughter. That includes me too. A daughter is always a princess in the eyes of the father.

In spite of Sitanshu having a very busy schedule, occupying different positions such as vice chancellor (VC) of one of the Gujarat universities, he always found time to educate Vipasha. Note that the position of VC is the highest in all the universities in India; the state governor occupies the position of chancellor, based on the Indian laws. Anjani, the mother, gave up her full-time teaching position at the university and took up a part-time position in a college closer to home. She saw Vipasha through her early schooling and college graduation. The father then took over and assisted Vipasha through post-graduation and a doctorate. Parents, working as a team, are the best help for a disabled child. I cannot imagine how Vipasha, suffering from CP, could graduate, not just from high school, but receive a PhD degree. The father was determined, and he succeeded, employing any and every technology that he could find to help Vipasha communicate with the world. She used a head stick tied to her chin to type on the computer keyboard. Vipasha, now in her thirties, has been settled in one of the Independent Living Housing apartments of her own. Vipasha is now a published and much anthologized author and a shining example among the physically challenged sorority and fraternity.

A fourth story is about a nephew, Mantu Joshi, of our longtime friends, Bimal and Sulebha Masih. Mantu graduated majoring in biology, then received a Master's degree in divinity. When he started ministering, he married his college mate who was blind. In spite of her handicap, she graduated and received a doctorate in psychology. After their marriage, they adopted handicapped children one after the other. Mantu then published a book titled, *The Resilient Parent: Everyday Wisdom for Life with Your Exceptional Child.* If there are angels in this world, they would have to be them.

I would certainly suggest to anyone to buy this book, just to discover that there are truly wonderful and selfless people living in this world of ours. As we learned in our Indic tradition, Dayaa (compassion) makes us human, Daan (charity) makes us angels, and Daman (control over our senses) makes us selfless. Mantu, based on what I have heard and read about him, has truly achieved all three precious attributes.

We have been reasonably successful, I believe, raising Rahul and Sonya. We are also very happy to see Deepak and Jagruti (Pratima's niece) doing well. Most of the credit for their success goes to their parents. But, as we all know, pain is as much a part of human life as is pleasure, a pair of opposites among multitudes of pairs created by Nature. Parenting involves pain, sometimes deep pain for the entire family, the entire extended family in Indian society. I cite a happening in my own extended family to express a deep pain that we felt and which I share even today. I narrate this not in any way to criticize but simply to express sorrow and to try to learn from our collective pain. We experienced a tragedy with Manoj's daughter, Sharmi, though we were not involved in raising her.

Manoj, my brother Jitubhai's son, was an adorable baby born in 1964. He was the first baby boy in the Doshi family after four daughters. Manoj was certainly a pleasure for my mother. That year I visited Bombay in November, hoping to find a suitable mate. Damubhabhi, my brother Jasvantbhai's wife, in Ahmedabad requested that I fly to Ahmedabad with Manoj, so we did. Damubhabhi and their three daughters had a wonderful time playing with baby Manoj. Later on, Manoj's mother Sarojbhabhi joined us in Ahmedabad. After my marriage in January 1965, there was not much interaction with Manoj, other than meeting him occasionally during my visits either for marriages or for the business. After completing his high school education, he decided to specialize in textile technology, and enrolled in one of the textile technology schools in Philadelphia.

I visited once to help out in different matters including finding an automobile for him. That was probably in the early '80s. Earlier, I had helped Jitubhai, Sarojbhabhi, and Manoj get their green cards. They all came to Los Angeles and stayed with us to see if they could adjust to living in the USA. Jitubhai was then in his late fifties, and it could be difficult adjusting to the American lifestyle after a certain age. He was running a successful business established by my father, and had a comfortable living in a prestigious location overlooking the Arabian Sea, with helpers to take care of routine work at home and in the business. So they decided to go back to Mumbai, and gave up their green cards.

Years later, in '86, I attended the wedding of Manoj with Radha, who came from a wealthy family. A month or so later, Jitubhai called me to see if I could help Manoj and Radha come to Los Angeles and possibly settle there. I agreed. They also informed us that Radha was pregnant with Sharmi. The objective, I believe, was to give Sharmi a choice to be a citizen of either India or the USA. A child born in the USA is a citizen by law, and she would be a citizen of India because of her parents' citizenship there. After a few months, they decided to go back to Mumbai after Radha delivered Sharmi in '87, because Radha was missing her family.

Then again, in 2005, when she had completed high school, they asked us if we could help Sharmi go to college in Los Angeles for her higher education. Pratima and I agreed. Radha, Manoj, and Sharmi flew to Los Angeles and stayed with us. Manoj left for Mumbai early, but Radha remained for three months until Sharmi was settled and attending Santa Monica City College. Sharmi two years later enrolled in UC Berkeley, and received her B.A. two years later. I helped Manoj financially with Sharmi's education costs. Sharmi was a smart girl who excelled in collage debates, and was chosen to represent her university. She was able to get both a scholarship and a loan to complete her education. In the meantime she had fallen in love with her debate partner, Ryan. So they planned to get married, hoping that her parents would approve. That did not happen. They both were asked to visit Mumbai to meet Sharmi's family in 2009 or 2010. Ryan came back to America, anticipating that Sharmi would join him later. That did not happen. We were told that they were able to convince her to marry an Indian boy. Evidently Ryan was heartbroken.

In November 2011 we received a call informing us of Sharmi's accidental death. We were told that around 4 am, while talking to someone in America, she accidently fell from the 11th floor of a building. Her parents and grandparents came to know only after the person who had been talking to Sharmi called their home informing them that something must have happened, since he heard a loud sound after a pause, and could not reconnect to her cell phone.

Sharmi's death at such a young age was both a deep pain and a baffling enigma for us all. In Mumbai, they said that it was an accident, and being a tall girl she lost her balance. However her friends in America believe that she committed suicide. It reminded me of the story of the brilliant Indian Rajput student who committed suicide because of terrible loneliness. It also reminded me of my own experience, how my family tried hard to get me to marry an Indian girl and so took away my passport during my trip to India in '61. It is also true that her parents and grandparents wanted Sharmi to marry an Indian boy from a rich family and settle down closer to them in Mumbai. Comparing my experience with that of Sharmi's, I was economically independent, while Sharmi was not. Sharmi had wanted to have a law degree in America, and with her debating skills, would surely have been great in that field.

I received a nasty email from Manoj in April 2013 that broke my heart. I prefer not to dwell much on the content, and instead to learn from this experience. As philosophers would say, there are a few things that should be passed over in silence, so that the dignity of a tragedy and of our pain is not sullied. Pain can lead to conflicts within a family or a society, or it can bring them closer together. Let us choose the second option, the pathway to a closer bonding, so far as it is feasible.

My niece Bharati's son Anand invited us for his wedding on November 30, 2013. We had attended the wedding of Daksha's daughter Uttera in Australia. I was honored when Daksha said with a sweet smile that I was filling the void, even partially, created by the absence of my late brother and her father, Jasvantbhai. I felt strongly about attending Anand's wedding, the son of my favorite niece, Bharati. We enjoyed the wedding thoroughly and met friends and the family. Jitubhai did not come to Ahmedabad, but we did meet Jagruti, his daughter. So I called Jitubhai twice and expressed our sorrow as much as I could. I admit to not being a good verbal communicator, so I had prepared an email to fill the gap.

I share the following edited email, composed out of sorrow at the tragic event, and from an unflinching wish to learn from it, so that such tragedies could be avoided in families living and raising their children in India as well as in the USA. The original email, I admit, was harsh and contained a negative and retributive response. I hope the reader finds it mostly positive and nonjudgmental.

> *Dear Daksha, Nayana, Jagruti, Anand, and Piyush: (Today 12/12/2013, my birthday)*
>
> *First, I want to convey to you that the trip we made this time was unique, mostly pleasant, but also saddening, seeing my dear and favorite niece Bharati in such a condition. (Bharati, like her mother, the late Damubhabhi, is suffering from Huntington's Disease.) I have enjoyed very few weddings in my lifetime; this indeed was one of the few. Aniket (Nayana's son) took care of our needs without a flaw. Observing a mature and responsible Anand, some 11 years later, was heartwarming. How can I forget the child Anand playing cricket with me in 1984, and helping me to break the wall of our house based upon his architectural skill and our desire to remodel, during his stay in Los Angeles in 1993! The marriage ceremony under the banyan tree was very creative and classy.*
>
> *We thought we would keep a row of seats under the shade (on the left side) reserved for Bharati and our family. However, the friends and the family invitees of the bride and the bridegroom did not believe in reservations. But my concern was not really justified.*

Our family and friends placed a row of chairs right in front of them, and closest to the stage for Bharati and her helpers. Brilliant!! Our family is also gifted in many ways. Daksha's spoken words, during the wedding ceremony, were as good as those of "culturally superior" Bengalis (I am trying to be funny). But they could not compete with Daksha and Uttara (Daksha's daughter) in matters of Indian classical dancing. Now we have at least two good singers in the family, Antara (Bharati's daughter) and Sonya's Manali. The credit of Samskaric training goes to Damubhabhi. But I have to give credit to Unmeshbhai (Daksha's father-in-law), a Gandhian, giving freedom to their kids to pursue their interests.

Piyush always takes good care of me whenever I am in Ahmedabad, but particularly this time during Pratima's absence while she was visiting Mumbai, and staying with me as my assistant during every occasion including the meeting with the future prime minister, Narendra Modi. Kailaskaki (Piyush's mother) has done an excellent job raising very down-to-earth children, and she has been rewarded in spite of carrying the burden of her mentally impaired husband's care. (My father's youngest brother, Mahendra kaka had become mentally impaired earlier in his middle life.) I must thank Jitubhai for bringing Piyush into my life.

Jagruti, it was gracious of you to greet us. You have also done well for your family, and in the past decades we have been more connected than with my nieces in Ahmedabad. I did call Jitubhai and talked to him for about fifteen minutes, but he could not bear the pain remembering Sharmi.

When we had an opportunity to talk to Jitubhai at length a week or so after Sharmi's demise in 2011, he asked me to talk to Manoj. I talked to him for at least half an hour, and suggested that they adopt a child in memory of Sharmi. They took my advice and later on adopted a very sweet baby girl. Manoj then talked to Pratima asking a question. Was Sharmi happy in the USA? She was doing so well and seemed to be happy. In my view, Sharmi could have been an excellent lawyer or a politician because of her communication and debating skills. She represented her university, and certainly that was a great accomplishment, and was admired by her fellow students and professors. Rahul and Manda planned and implemented a day of "Remembering Sharmi" a week after her demise. Over forty of Sharmi's friends and family visited Rahul's home, in spite of the fact that Rahul resides far away from Los Angeles. Our interaction with Sharmi was very little during her two years stay with us, since she was not available most of the time, being busy in her school activities and debate preparation.

I am a student of Indic traditions (IT) that include Vedanta, Buddhism, and Jainism. Western scholars consider IT very rich in the field of psychology. Two cardinal laws of our traditions are that every human being should have the freedom to choose, and a strong attachment to anything (for example, Manoj's attachment to Sharmi) is a sure path of misery. Detachment is the path of transcendence.

There are few tragic events in our own family, like losing a child or a grown-up daughter. My mother lost a baby, and later, so did Pratima. My father lost a grown-up daughter (Deepak's older sister, and my half-sister) in a swimming pool accident. These are depressing events. But these tragic events did not prompt them to lose dignity either within themselves, or indulge in unseemly behavior, like hurling insults towards others. Words can hurt like no weapons can. This tragedy created a disconnect with my only living brother. I am afraid I may not be able to see him during these few years left in our lives. I do wish and pray that Manoj not only comes out of his depression and regains control over all of his faculties, but seeks the path to transcend to higher levels.

With love and blessings,
Navinkaka

About nine months later, on Diwali 2014, my brother, about eighty-one years old, called to wish me "Salmubarak" (Happy New Year) and all the best for the coming years. We could not talk much because we are both somewhat hearing-impaired.

About eight months later, in June 2015, Manoj called me and asked for some financial help. I suggested that he first write a letter of apology for a nasty insulting email he had sent; then I would consider helping him. He sent the following email:

From: Manoj [mailto:manoj.doshi@hotmail.com]
Sent: Saturday, June 27, 2015 3:25 PM
To: harilal@ca.rr.com
Subject: From Manoj
Dear Navin kaka:

I had raised Sharmi with a lots of love, tenderness and care. She was an exceptional person with a very soft heart. I had sent a piece of my heart in your care with the confidence that you would extend the same love to her.

After she left us I was in a state of shock for a very long time and still am. When I read her old email to

Radha, I reacted very strongly with some very harsh words. Please extend my apologies to you and the entire family, I had just reacted and vented out my anger in that email.

Manoj
Sent from my iPhone=

I responded to my whole family with the following email.

Dear family:

I am delighted to inform you of receiving the email from Manoj, which I am forwarding to you (above). I am very relieved that the wall that was created between my very dear brother Jitubhai and me, has been removed.

Jitubhai and I have been talking by telephone in the recent past, but in a painful state of mind. This will, God willing, give me an opportunity to meet him in the near future. After Manoj taking the initiative to talk to me several times during last week, the cause of an angry email from him, to my understanding, was insignificant; to him it was his depressed state of mind.

My love and affection towards all of you, is and will remain the same as it was given to me by my brothers and Bhabhis during my growing up period. Please email me a line or two whenever you find time; in my old age, it gives me great pleasure to hear from you and remain connected. I do wish all the best in your every endeavor you undertake.

With love and affection,
Navin kaka

Few weeks later he asked me again to help him financially. I asked for more information about household cash flow; I did not receive it, but he suggested helping his sister. I did extend badly needed help to Jitubhai's daughter; she was gracefully grateful for receiving it.

Pratima and I visited first the island of Bali then India during 2015 Christmas holidays and enjoyed meeting our families. I had lunch with Jitubhai twice, concluding that we may not see each other again due to our age and health related problems. I also discovered that Jitubhai and I were far apart in perception and philosophy of life. Even now, keeping up with Jones is more important than going broke by over spending. In Gujarati, an equivalent statement is *to keep cheeks red unnaturally by slapping the face.* Showing of wealth and status is more important than the truth and real values of existence. Jitubhai's view was that I wrote the book for my glory. My view has been to share our experience so that readers may get a sense of history and so that they may learn from our achievements and mistakes, particularly that they may not commit the same mistakes. Common sense tells me that it does not matter to us after we are all dead or being close to death.

I conclude this chapter with a few applicable aphorisms I have learned during my lifetime, also stated in my first book, *Transcendence, Saving Us from Ourselves,* published in 2009 by Ithaca Press, New York.

There is always some good in the worst of us and some bad in the best of us. Forever perfection is nonexistent.

The good and the evil is a pair of opposites among multitudes of such pairs created by Nature, where evil is the ignorance and raw material that can be converted to the good, employing the wisdom obtained from human experience and knowledge.

Samskara, after birth, based upon our Indic tradition, is a positive life-fulfilling spontaneity of the physical body, obtained by culturing and cultivating the bodily urges and feelings. Maya, the opposite of *Samskara*, is the defamed trickster that tries to confuse the body, negating *Samskara*.

A strong will, persistence, endurance, resilience, and intuition are attributes of a *Samskaric* person, acquired through culturing and hard training of the physical body. Note that the mind, with all its constituent components, takes a much longer time to evolve.

Rutta, central in the Indic tradition, is the eternal truth of the ultimate reality, Brahman in its dynamic and temporal material form. Rutta is Nature in its best mood, benevolent, loving, and truthful. It is the first evolute, the first incarnation of Nature.

From left, standing: Kevin, Navin, Mark Lee, and Sonya; Seated: Pratima and Asha Lee.

Anand bowing for blessings from granduncle; Bharati and Nayana (left bottom), December 2013.

Samskara is the energy, the feminine side of Rutta; Rutta can operate only through *Samskara*, and is the cause of the scent of the rose, and the joy of music and the dance. A *Samskaric* person will bring out the best mood, love and truth among people.

Human impulses of sympathy, compassion, and charity are instinctive and spontaneous. They are the signs of being humane and *Samskaric.*

Time heals all wounds, physical and mental. Physical wounds are cured due to the workings of the interior of the body. Mental wounds are cured due to the workings of *Samskara* and the philosophical mind. *Samskara* is the first and foremost instrument for transcendence and immanence.

One needs to put more emphasis on the positive, and not the negative. Free will and the freedom to choose is a gift from Nature to humanity. However it can never be absolute, since Nature assures and imposes limits to all of our endeavors.

I was fortunate to get connected with a child psychiatrist who would give her view on matters of raising children given in this chapter. Diane Powell has long credentials in this matter. I am reproducing her review of this chapter.

Review of Navin Doshi's Memoir
By
Diane Hennacy Powell, MD

It is a great honor to write a review for the memoir of Navin Doshi, a deeply devoted family man, successful entrepreneur and engineer, student of Vedanta, philanthropist, visionary, and bridge builder between East and West. He came to the US in 1958, continuing his Vedanta studies with Swami Chinmayananda and Swami Parthasarathi, and reading books by other scholars and philosophers of Indic traditions, including J. Krishnamurti, Maharishi Mahesh Yogi, Aurobindo Ghosh, and Paramahansa Yogananda. He expresses the wisdom he has gained from these teachings in his personal and professional life, and in his writings. This memoir is no exception. It is his gift to anyone who wants to learn from a life lived well.

As a professional child psychiatrist, I was asked to comment on his Chapter 9 on raising children. Navin's children were blessed to have parents who understood the importance of recognizing them as individuals, each with their own needs. One formula never fits all. His parenting was influenced by Khalil Gibran's The Prophet, which stated, "Your children are not your children, they belong to Life's longing for itself. They come through you, and yet do not belong to you. You may house their bodies, but not their soul. Their souls dwell in the house of tomorrow, which you cannot visit, not even in your dreams."

What exactly does this mean? Parents are like gardeners. The word "kindergarten" is derived from the German for "garden of children." The seed of life germinates in the woman's womb, like a seedling for a tree does in Mother Earth. The gardener has certain expectations for the planted tree. If it is a plum tree, it will have beautiful blossoms that later turn into plums. The gardener does their best to make sure that all of the proper nutrients are in the soil, and that it is planted where it will receive the appropriate amount of sunshine and water. As the branches grow, some may need trimming because they are too numerous, or growing in the wrong direction, for a healthy tree. Done well, the tree thrives and has its own unique shape and beauty, while being true to its own essence as a plum tree.

Unfortunately, some parents are like gardeners who neglect the needs of their tree and still expect it to bear delicious fruit. Topiary gardeners don't recognize the natural beauty of irregularities and try to make the tree conform to an unnatural shape. Gardeners at the other extreme don't understand the need for proper pruning. Navin has come up with what he calls "Doshi's Laws for Raising Children."

The following are his nine basic rules to being a successful gardener for our future generations:

1. Parents will never be able to give their kids all they want to give them.
2. Parents will always give something to their children even if they don't plan to give or don't want to give.
3. Avoid "reinventing the wheel," whenever it is applicable.
4. A father and mother should never ever take sides, or disagree in matters of raising children or making decisions about children, in their presence.
5. Never ever stop communicating. Maintain a strong link between you and your children to establish strong roots.
6. Look for the positive and discard the negative in kids. Always encourage the positive and discourage the negative.
7. Make sure that kids are always busy, either in studies, or in games, or mutually agreed extra work, so that they do not fall into anything undesirable—undesirable activities, friends, company, and so on.
8. Autonomy and detachment are necessary for parents to follow these rules. Children must also develop their own creativity.

9. Every wrongdoing must be criticized, and if necessary there should be an appropriate punishment.

The details of applying these rules will differ from family to family and child to child. Nonetheless they hold the wisdom of universal truths. We live in a particularly challenging time for raising our children who, more than previous generations, have far more distractions, conflicting messages, and non-parental influences. Being a good parent is one of the most challenging and rewarding experiences we can have. It isn't always fun. If we follow these rules and provide our children with unconditional love, Navin Doshi's memoir is proof that it all works out in the end.

CHAPTER 10

ON HORSES, ENERGY, AND PSYCHOLOGY

From the early days of my childhood I have always had a great affinity toward horses, more so than any other animal I can recall. My grandfather had a horse and a four-wheeled Victoria carriage that was fun to ride in. Later, I rode a horse whenever the opportunity arose, going back to my first visit to Matheran, a hill station resort near Mumbai. We were four — three brothers and Jasvantbhai's friend Jitendra, from the Tarwala family in Matunga. My brother Jasvantbhai and his friend rented the two best horses they could find. The horses, as I recall, seemed like big race horses. I was around seven years old. After riding the horse for a few minutes, Jasvantbhai's friend lost control and fell off. Then Jitubhai was asked to ride the same horse, but he could not keep his balance either. Jasvantbhai was not sure if I could ride that horse, but he allowed me to ride it, with some hesitation, due to my persistence. It was my first experience, and I had a wonderful time riding for about an hour. I visited Matheran many times with a strong desire to ride a galloping horse, and I did, every time enjoying it immensely. I also rode with Rahul and Sonya in Griffith Park in Los Angeles while they were growing up, and during our visit to Hawaii in my later years.

Our son Rahul was born in '66, the Chinese Year of the Horse. What a good-looking baby he was, resembling his pretty mother! In the Chinese zodiac, the horse is one among its twelve animal signs. Here is a description of the attributes of the horse:

"Thank goodness for open spaces, because the Horse needs plenty of room to roam! Energetic, good with money and very fond of travel, Horses are the nomads of the Chinese Zodiac, roaming from one place or project to the next. All of this Sign's incessant activity and searching may be to satisfy a deep-rooted desire to fit in. Paradoxically, Horses feel a simultaneous yearning for independence and freedom. Horses crave love and intimacy, which is a double-edged sword since it often leads them to feel trapped. And often they do get trapped."

It reminds me of the movie *The Misfits*, Clark Gable made with Marilyn Monroe and Montgomery Clift. In the movie, Marilyn, Clark's lover, was able to convince him to let loose the horses he had trapped. Love connections tend to come easily to horses, since they exude the kind of raw sex appeal that is a magnet to others.

"This Sign tends to come on very strong in the beginning of a relationship, having an almost innate sense of romance and seduction. Horses are seducers in general; check out any A-list party and you're bound to find the Horse in attendance. This Sign possesses a sharp wit and a scintillating presence; it really knows how to work a crowd.

Sweet and happy baby Rahul at his first birthday, with his mother Pratima, who made the baby suit.

Riding with Rahul in Griffith Park, 1970.

"Horses are self-reliant and, though they might lose interest fast in a tedious, nine-to-five day job, are willing to do the work necessary to get ahead. This Sign really knows how to motivate others, though, and gets a lot accomplished. Once they find peace within themselves, they can learn to appreciate what's in their own backyard. The spirit of the horse is recognized to be the Chinese people's ethos — making unremitting efforts to improve themselves. It is energetic, bright, warm-hearted, intelligent and able. More recent findings indicate that Horses communicate with each other employing their ears, based on research conducted by Jennifer Wathan of Sussex University. Ancient people liked to designate an able person as "Qianli Ma," a Horse that covers a thousand li a day (one li equals 500 meters)."

Our son is in good company with other "horses," like Sir Isaac Newton, Rembrandt, Sandra Day O'Conner, Teddy Roosevelt, Denzel Washington, Kobe Bryant, Cindy Crawford, and Genghis Khan.

The dance forms of different traditions are another entertaining connection to horses. On my special birthday, 12/12/12, which occurs every hundred years, my family and friends celebrated the evening with the presentation of two interlinked dance forms—Kathak from India and Flamenco from Spain, though gypsies originated in India. The audience experienced the wonderful connections between these two dance forms with visual, rhythmic, and kinesthetic similarities. Some of the dancers rode horses.

Looking into Indian scriptures, we find a description of Brahman as a sacrificial horse in the opening chapter of the Brihadaranyaka Upanishad. Here it is, *translated by Sri Aurobindo.*

1. OM. Dawn is the head of the horse sacrificial. The sun is his eye, his breath is the wind, his wide-open mouth is fire, the master might universal. Time is the self of the horse sacrificial. Heaven is his back and the mid-world his belly, earth is his footing, the regions are his flanks and the lesser

regions their ribs, the seasons his members, the months and the half-months are their joints, the days and nights are of his body. The strands are the food in his belly, the rivers are his veins, his liver and lungs are the mountains, herbs and plants are his hairs, the rising is his front and the setting his hinder portion, when he stretches himself, then it lightens, when he shakes his frame, then it thunders, when he urinates, then it rains. Speech, verily, is the sound of him.

2. Day was the grandeur that was borne before the horse as he galloped, the eastern ocean gave it birth; night was the grandeur that was borne behind him and its birth was from the other waters. These are the grandeurs that came into being on either side of the horse. He became Haya and bore the gods, Vaja and bore the Gandharvas, Arvan and bore the Titans, Ashwa and bore mankind. The sea was his brother and the sea was his birthplace.

Horses are noble herbivorous animals, revered in Hinduism based upon several scriptures, including the Brihadaranyaka Upanishad. Man is Nature's living museum. Not only that, but within him reside attributes of every creature, good and bad, both the successes and failures of Nature. These form the complexity of the human mind where man is a multidimensional adventure of Nature. Ancient Indian sages have made great efforts over centuries to understand this complexity, and the results of their search have dazzled and provided much light to mankind. No wonder that in their search, they saw the noble attributes of horses and compared them with the Divine.

Since part of Chapter 9 has been about the misfortunes of several parents with their children, the question of human psychology and how to deal with these conditions comes up. In this respect, I was particularly interested in Sitanshu's way of dealing with his life situation since, I believe, he is an intellectual and poet residing in the realm of the philosophical self. Professor Houston Smith of the

University of California in Berkeley has observed that three great civilizations of the world have made three significant contributions to mankind. Western civilization provided the knowledge of Nature; Chinese civilization brought about the development of sociology; and Indian civilization produced a profound awareness and understanding of psychology through its scriptures. I expressed how I understand human psychological and philosophical selves, as seen through the eyes of ancient Indian rishis, in my book *Transcendence*. In conversation with my philosopher friend, Professor Debashish Banerji, I have arrived at a further adaptation of this scheme, which I present here.

Ancient Indian psychology presents a profound understanding of the human being, as we find in Vedanta, which could be understood as a concealed treatise on human psychology. According to this, our biological or somatic self (sthula sharira) is combined with a subjective or psychological body (sukshma sharira) to form the "physical being" (annamaya kosha). As a given, when we are born, this psychological self is fused with the somatic self. But with the growth of the mind and the feelings, we realize a degree of separation between these two bodies. Indeed, upon death, it is this psychological body (sometimes called the subtle body or astral body by modern parapsychologists) that separates from the somatic body and continues living. According to Vedanta, this psychological body (the self) contains three other bodies within it. Closer to the somatic self is the body of life-energy (pranamaya sharira) constituted by our desires, drives, impulses and emotions. In Western traditions, this is sometimes referred to as the vital self or body, the recognition of which leads to the branch of philosophy known as vitalism. Even deeper is the mental body (manomaya sharira) constituted by the senses, intelligence, and a mental sense of a separate self (the ego or ahankara). At the deepest level is the awareness of the Divine Being within each entity. This has been called the soul or psyche in Western traditions. In Vedantic traditions, spoken of particularly in the Gita, it is the atman within (antaratman). All these selves are formations of the One Conscious Being, Brahman. Hence, this differentiation of human psychology is based in a philosophical monism. This is why the psychological self can realize psychological monism, which enables it to be free of the suffering of separation from the somatic and from "others."

The different bodies within the psychological or subjective self are involved in each other's activities, but the yogi is asked to separate these selves so that they may each arrive at their highest potential and their union with a corresponding aspect of the spiritual self (Brahman), guided by proper habits (*samskaras*) and the soul within (antaratman). The natural quality of the inmost self or soul (antaratman) is spontaneous love, due to its intrinsic knowledge of the unity of all things. Through love it tries to bridge the separation between the other selves within the human being and between different human beings. This is illustrated in Indian mythology through the figures of Radha and Krishna. They are able to purge their subjective bodies of all bondage through their love for each other. Their total personalities find fullest realization in their mutual love and in the full, pure joy of their souls, which struggle to overcome the primal fear of separation.

Though born out of the physical energies of the somatic self, the different subjective selves, such as the vital and mental selves, each has its own aspirations related to achieving unity. It has glimpses of a heavenly world never seen on earth. The vital body wants to be weightless, soar to any height unchecked, disregarding material things. The mental body wishes to arrive at omniscience, the knowledge by which all things may be known. But the somatic self and the ignorance of separation, which is our normal condition, keep us stuck in grooves of habits that are self-perpetuating and prevent us from achieving our highest aspirations. This could be called psychological gravity, a conservative force of Nature. Moving against gravity is the process of sub-ration and transcendence. Sub-ration implies sub-rating and rejection of lower values, and exploring for the stuff of higher values.

Psychological truth is a perpetual process of harmonizing between pragmatic and intuitive truths. At the pragmatic level, a person and a society adapts to the changing demands of a shifting environment. The objective, if any, is to survive. There is nothing eternal or absolute about this; it comes from the individual's and the society's ability to conform to the supreme law of Darwinian evolution, the survival of the fittest. It can also be seen as a variation of the economic law of supply and demand. The ability to change and a sense of temporality is the power behind this truth. However, the pragmatic truth and associated actions do not have a purpose and a direction, which brings us to a basic problem.

Pragmatic truth could very well be capable of change, but it cannot forever be temporary. It must be conceded that the ever-changing responses of the pragmatic self to the ever-changing demands of a shifting environment is a search for something stable, a march towards the permanent. The subjective selves must mature to a state so that they can be reborn into the spiritual self. The processes of sub-ration and transcendence are not processes of a mixed melting pot—they are processes of *samskara*, hard work and tough love, detachment, gradual transformation, and evolution.

How can this be achieved? My perception is through the loving soul (antaratman), liberator of the subjective selves. It is not the liberator of the somatic self nor of the spiritual self, and the reason is clear: the subjective selves (vital self and mental self) are under the influence of the ego or the sense of a separate self. Pride and its evolutes are the constituent components of the ego. Pride and intellect are the components that bind their self-importance, their feeling of uniqueness. The moment pride is given up, love springs forth. The journey from being self-centered to being selfless is the truest and most worthwhile journey. This is the realm of the philosophical self, an integration of the subjective self under the influence of the soul, at the doorstep of the spiritual self.

Thus, what impels these different selves towards transcendence is the power and influence of the soul, which is also our true individuality or sense of personal self. However, this source of the personal self does not experience its uniqueness through separation but through its recognition of universality. It recognizes all uniqueness as specific appearances of the universal and infinite being, Brahman. The reflection of this true self on the other selves, suffering from separation, is the ego. What I have called psychological gravity is upheld by this false sense of a separate self, the ego. On the other hand, the true self, soul or antaratman, though within each separate being, carries in itself the knowledge of the intrinsic unity of the divine consciousness (Brahman), since it is a projection of that in each being. The strength of the soul is in its vision and detachment from worldly things and its union with the divine consciousness. The influence of the soul on the other selves helps them to develop a higher part, which runs counter to their lower gravitational pull supported by the ego. The self of life has such a higher part. Its vision is noble though perceived unrealistic, and when challenged, it finds difficulty in countering the challenge; it is of the beautiful and good, but is powerless in a material world. It is like an angel flapping its wings joyfully, with all those clever materialists aiming to shoot it down like a game bird.

I see a horse as a symbol of the higher vital self, or the higher being of life energy, under the influence of the soul. Like the life body, it is energetic and expresses the prakritic quality of *rajas*. In Western traditions, we see how the horse has helped in crossing great distances, conquering wars, or achieving difficult feats of energy. It is for this reason that the horse metaphor persists in the transition from a more primitive state to the modern state of technology, when we speak of mechanical, hydraulic or electrical energy in terms of horsepower. The vital being also has lower expressions, when it is under the influence of a selfish separateness or ego (ahankara). Then it expresses selfish traits like anger, violence, jealousy, cowardice, and so on. Under the influence of the soul, it expresses nobility, loyalty, aspiration, and courage. We can see how easy it is to project these higher qualities onto the ideal potential of the horse. We idealize such horses in the form of angels with wings (for example, in the Greek mythical horse-god Pegasus, a symbol of wisdom and fame), running fast and hard, resulting ultimately in flight.

There are comparable attributes between Pegasus and the Hindu monkey god Hanuman, an ardent devotee of Lord Rama, and a central character in the epic Ramayana. A strong flyer, being a son of Vayudeva (the wind god) and also a reflection of Lord Shiva, are also reasons for Hindus to worship Hanuman. The belief that Hanuman's celibacy is the source of his strength became popular among the wrestlers in India.

Yet the vital self as universally present in each one of us is a mixed thing, sometimes under the ego and sometimes under the soul. Religious fanatics have taken advantage of its shattered dreams of beauty and truth by building a religiously sanctioned heaven and asking the masses to submit to their preaching. It is high time in today's world to liberate the psychological self from religious and materialist zealots. Similarly, the mental self, under the influence of the soul, develops the higher qualities of wisdom, aesthetic appreciation, universality, and an impartial seeking for truth. But under the influence of ego, it expresses selfish cunning, diabolic tendencies, and rational justification of desires. Human nature is not just a matter of heredity, but also responsibility and achievement. There are individuals born as human beings who behave worse than animals. On the other hand, Nature looks to human beings for greater possibilities, not to be explored in contradictions and exploitation but in balance and harmony. The great Indian scientist and botanist Jagdishchandra Bose made a lasting contribution to human knowledge and sensibility when he demonstrated through scientific experiments that Nature, including plants and trees, knows and feels.

Spiritualism in Indian tradition has never been despotic; the somatic and psychological selves have never been subjected to the dictates of the spiritual domain in any Indian tradition, be it Vedic, Buddhist or Jain. Monks and sages were free to paint, carve and sing of the somatic and psychological selves. The union of the two was depicted in paintings and sculptures in the caves of Ajanta and Ellora and countless other magnificent places. The poetry and plays of Valmiki and Vyasa, Kalidasa and Bhasa, depicted the somatic and psychological selves as well as the spiritual self, without pontific, eulogistic interference or disapproval. Yet the soul or antaratmanis the integrating or connecting force, a string that keeps connected all that man contains— procreation, self-importance, imagination, virtue, intuition, science and religion, spiritual aspiration, love and the intellect. If the string is broken, the gems fall apart, inviting looters within and without. To be happy is one of the most natural objectives of all of humanity. Surprisingly, most do not know its how, why and what. If pressed to define happiness, most of us would begin to wonder what it is. Mental and vital happiness is relative and momentary under the influence of the ego. A person with a modest existence may be mentally more stable than a person with great wealth. Pain and misery are associated with both extreme poverty and extreme wealth. Rogues and parasites will find a way to be close to extremely wealthy people. The laws of Nature, it should be recognized clearly, also apply to the realm of the mental and vital selves. The psychological or subjective self is as much a part of Nature as the somatic self. In Nature at large, the Newtonian laws of motion apply. In the natural domain of physics, an object accelerates when an external force is applied. The object stops accelerating and moves at a slower speed when the force is removed. Similarly, in the subjective domain of the mental and vital selves, as one's desires are fulfilled, one feels "accelerated," happy, in a state of ecstasy. But that state is not lasting and eventually fades when there is no more "acceleration."

How to deal with these fluctuations? What is true of happiness and success is also true of unhappiness and failure. How then to be happy? What is "happiness"? Happiness is the intrinsic state of the deepest soul or antaratman, because it is the presence of the spiritual self within the individual. Thus to experience a lasting happiness at the level of the psychological (mental and vital selves), these must be yoked to this innermost self. Such a yoking is an aspect of yoga. This requires each of the selves to develop a will for sub-ration and transcendence. These constituents of the psychological self can only transcend by keeping their right proportions and control by the innermost or true self. Man needs to be careful that any one of these components does not enslave his psychological self through subjection to the ego and psychological gravitation. For this, each self needs to be oriented in its own way towards the soul. The first step to get there is the formation of habits of being and response that keep the psychological selves in contact with the soul. Such habits are *samskaras*. I would say that a psychological self, trained through *samskaras*, is able to adjust to both success and failure; the *samskaras* acts as filters moderating the effect of both.

The practice of *samskaras* guides the different selves to transcend their ego tendencies and orient themselves towards the divine consciousness under the influence of the innermost self, the soul. As this orientation matures, the higher aspects of the different selves become expressed and the proper proportion between the different selves is maintained. The expression of a higher functioning of the combined mental and vital selves yields what may be called the philosophical self, full of wisdom and compassion. An even greater expression of the proper combination of these selves is the ideal of the philosopher-king and the realized fullness is the spiritual self. The spiritual self is universal, impartial, and transcendent.

Returning to our image of the horse, we see more references to this noble and powerful animal in both Indian and Greek philosophical traditions, referring to what we have just discussed regarding the different selves, and their integration and utilization in the service of moving to the spiritual self. Both the Katha Upanishad (ratha kalpana) and the Gita use the image of the horse chariot to exemplify this relationship of the selves, the soul, and the spiritual self. Here is a passage from the Katha Upanishad (I.3–3–4) translated by Sri Aurobindo:

3. Know the body for a chariot and the soul for the master of the chariot: know Reason for the charioteer and the mind for the reins only.
4. The senses they speak of as the steeds and the objects of sense as the paths in which they move; and one yoked with Self and the mind and the senses is the enjoyer, say the thinkers.

The integration of mental (reason and mind—charioteer and reins) and vital selves (senses—horses) is achieved here by the soul (the master of the chariot, the enjoyer). Without this integration, the horses run after the objects of sense and the charioteer, unaware of its master or its goal, is caught up in the environment and misdirects the horses. This may be thought of as the vital and mental beings under the influence of the ego as against the influence of the soul. Later, the goal of the journey is described as "the highest seat of Vishnu," which we may think of as Brahman or the spiritual self. The Gita, which undoubtedly got it from the Katha Upanishad, repeats this metaphor in Chapter VI, verse 34. A very similar image appears in Plato's *Phaedrus*. Here the horses are even more accurately mapped onto the vital being with its two potentia, the ego-driven horse of "ill-breed" and the "well-bred" horse under the influence of *samskaras* and easier to direct by the master of the chariot. Here too, this master is shown to be the soul, while the charioteer is the reason (mental being), and the goal of the journey is a higher state of consciousness, which we may call the spiritual self. These two horses or two potentia of the vital being are also spoken of in the Katha Upanishad as shreyas and preyas, or "the proper" and "the pleasurable." "The proper" here refers to the paths that follow *samskaras* and are oriented towards the leading of the soul, while "the pleasurable" are the transient desire-fulfillments belonging to the separative selfishness of the ego self. The properly balanced system of horses, chariot, reins, and charioteer under the control of the master of the chariot may be thought of as the well-developed philosophical self. Yet such a system is very difficult to achieve for human beings and takes much effort and clear discrimination. Moreover, it is subject to fate or circumstance, creating different degrees and kinds of difficulties, often insuperable given the frailties and limitations of human subjectivity.

The field of philosophy encompasses not only mathematics and science but also the fields of the humanities, including morality, human well being, rationality, realism, and idealism. The process of transcendence is one of growth. During the growing-up period, the child learns to walk and talk and play simple games, employing the somatic and pre-psychological selves. As the child grows up, more human faculties are developed. For example, intellect is needed for science and mathematics. Intuition, feelings, and idealism come along with intellect. To be in the realm of the philosophical self, every human faculty has to function. The philosophical self is fully developed when every human faculty is integrated, in balance with its opposites, complementing each other, and each pair is in balance with the other pair. The total human self is at the doorstep of the spiritual domain, when every human faculty is in total harmony with all other faculties. This occurs when the soul sufficiently governs and integrates the vital and mental selves.

Vedic sages wanted psychology to be studied for the removal of dehumanizing power and to free our minds from the momentary pleasures of life. Perpetual regression brings feelings of revenge, exploitation, and therefore bondage. In the realm of the subjective selves, the life forces and mind need to disassociate themselves from historical compulsion and enter into the realm of pure love and freedom. It is difficult to give up the past since it contains our heritage and culture. However we need not forget the past—it is good to learn from history, but we need not dwell on it or allow it to condition us. A philosophy of the universal is needed to pull people out of a negative mindset and teach them about love, truth, and human goodness.

The philosophical self, an integration and refinement of the subjective selves, is not in the realm of the spiritual self of non-evolving permanence; it is associated with Nature and therefore evolving. The philosophy of exception and exclusivity (such as "My God is the only God") cannot meet the challenge of natural evolution. The subject-object relationship is natural and ingrained in the somatic realm. However, as one transcends from the somatic to the subjective realm, it helps to comprehend "becoming," that is, removing the subject-object distinction. When the subjective self is in balance and harmony, it cleanses the mental faculty of the prejudice of skin color and castes. The man who has evolved psychologically derives strength not from the deep historical past, but from the philosophical height. The natural movement is unidirectional towards the proximity of the philosophic mountaintop, based on the natural laws of thermodynamics.

Psychology and philosophy are two different disciplines; the light of philosophy is brighter than that of psychology. The brighter the light, the greater the need for humility; Buddha did not consider his light to be superior to that of the nightingale. He stopped his sermon to let the bird sing the same message of balance and harmony in her melodies. Current problems are due to excessive faith in science and intellectual reasoning, and almost none in other human faculties such as intuition, imagination, devotion and love. Joseph Campbell suggested that we need to give space to myths, fantasies, and other human urges to establish democracy within. Ritam, the truth of Nature in material form, works in concert with all the mental faculties.

For this, we must dive deeper into the innermost self, not merely through the intellectual tools available to Western science but also through the tools available in Eastern and Indian traditions. Though a few words are in order about the Indian tradition. It is very long, extending back many millennia. In the last thousand years of its history, during its "medieval period," people of India allowed their somatic and psychological selves to be shattered in the hope of entering into an immortal spiritual self. This obsession with the spiritual self has been responsible for a terrible history of plunder and slavery that became their lot for nearly a millennium.

Vedic sages, in ancient times dating back perhaps to five millennia before the Christian era began, had become obsessed with the spiritual self, when the psychological self was under the assault of great unhappiness. The somatic and psychological selves are always in flux, either towards or away from happiness. The first layer of the somatic self, which is kaleidoscopic, random, and directionless, must not mix with the psychological or subjective flux, which is directional and has substratum, bedrock moorings. The subjective self is a go-between, a bridge between the two ends of man's total self, the physical and the metaphysical.

The development of *samskaras* acts in different ways on different beings and different parts of each being. Indian mythology describes this process and the differences of action in this way: The God of creation (Brahma) not only created humans, but also demons and angels (gods, devata). Demons lack ethics, compassion, and are totally ruthless and self-centered. A man or an animal in form can be a demon, human, or an angel. His rules of the game were simple. Demons could transform to humans by becoming compassionate (daya). Humans could transform to angels by becoming charitable (dana). Obviously the receiver of dana, who is desperate to receive help, would believe the giver to be an angel. And control (daman) over desires, implying detachment, sub-ration, and transcendence, could bring a person closer to divinity.

The spiritual self is universal and, depending on what one believes, is everywhere (as All-Pervading Brahman) and is associated with all species of living beings — or is nowhere (ultimate nothingness or Sunyata). It was clearly stated that what was knowledge for the spiritual self was ignorance for the other two, namely the somatic and subjective selves, and vice versa. There was no judgment associated with this. This is because the spiritual self (Brahman) is a unity consciousness, where everything is known to be parts or features of the One Being. But in the separated experience of both the somatic and subjective selves, all is experienced as separate, not as united. The knowledge of the spiritual self is knowledge by identity – this means that in spiritual consciousness, one knows something because one is that thing and hence knows it directly, just as we know ourselves. In the separative consciousness, all knowledge is indirect knowledge, knowledge through inference by deduction, induction, analogy or correspondence. The scriptures warn in non-ambiguous language that "those who think that the real is material, are in darkness. But those who think that the real is spiritual, are in greater darkness." One must know both the spiritual and psychological selves. One must transform the psychological selves by the power of the spiritual self.

I must admit that it is difficult for me to discover the line of demarcation between the philosophical self and the spiritual self. Based upon my perception, spiritual selves are existent beyond the boundaries of space and time drawn by Nature. Evolving from the somatic self stuck in material needs, we can rise to the higher functioning, oriented by the *samskaras*, of the vital self, which has emotional maturity, and the philosophical self, which dwells in the realm of profound meanings. Those who make this transcendence are angel-like human beings, able to discover or create *heaven* in a commonly perceived *hell*. Some human beings have highly developed psychic and intellectual selves, which allow him to have deep sympathy and also arrive at a philosophical peace that one comes across in his presence and in talking to him. Yet at a certain level, such peace also involves an acceptance of the world as it is, imperfect in terms of our human wishes, but the only world given to us.

Top, Riding in Hawaii. 1999. Bottom: Kevin, Sonya, and Pratima in Mussoorie, India, 1995.

A war chariot with horses in ancient India. Believe it or not, even now, the width of two horses' behinds has become the standard of all transportation, including automobiles, trains, even rockets (rockets need to be transported in a train or a truck).

CHAPTER 11

THE STATE OF VANAPRASTHA

Vanaprastha is the third stage in the four main stages of life classified in Hinduism: Brahmacharya (student), Grihastha (householder), Vanaprastha (retirement from worldly attachments), and Sanyasa (renunciation). Traditionally old age was a period spent in pursuit of religious activities, reading spiritual literature, accumulating good karma away from the demands of the material world, and transcending personal desires so as to arrive closer to a universal perspective and consciousness. But in today's world, such lifestyles are seldom followed. Many people lead their entire lives caught in the mesh of personal desires. However, among Indians, something of the older philosophical attitude has persisted, with people spending their senior years more detached from their years of striving. Older people can choose to spend time with their grandchildren or watch unlimited hours of soaps, sports or news, among other activities. Outdoor opportunities may become restricted. Confined for the most part within the four walls of their homes, it isn't a surprise that many seniors do not have much to look forward to, specifically those having some physical disability or financial dependence. This attitude, called "ageism," has often been perceived in our collective psyche as our culture.

More specifically, Hinduism classifies four layers of the ageing process, which we can observe in Nature. These layers, created by Nature through evolutionary processes, have been observed in self-similar patterns, formally explained employing fractal mathematics. The Hindu stages of life represent the wisdom of such a fractal observation of Nature. This is also one way of understanding the cyclic sense of time in Hinduism, which the German philosopher Nietzsche endorsed when he acknowledged the "eternal recurrence of the same." Understanding these recurrent patterns in Nature and reflecting on their wisdom in our lives brings us the peace of a life in harmony with Nature.

Of course, this does not mean a slavish repetition of mechanical conventions. Evolution implies changes needed for self-survival, and we need to adjust to today's changing globalized world: feel free to do the things you always wanted to do within reason, not going overboard or breaking social laws. There are always exceptions, as when Gandhiji broke the unjust British laws. Above all, we must accept the responsibility of ageing; exercise regularly, be disciplined in dietary habits, and reach out for those behaviors that reinforce critical requirements in healthy ageing; for example, helping others based on your life experiences. So I was ready to add appropriate activities along with my business activities, since I am a gradualist. I have always been slow in changing direction, and am a believer in slow transition. I was ready to transition from the state of Grihastha to Vanprastha.

Here I need to discuss transcendence as one gets older, moving away from the sensory pleasure associated with the body. As an example, the lowest kundalini chakra is tied to the sexual organs. I believe, because the sexual urges ebb in time, the pleasure cannot be as it was during the younger years. One needs to transcend to a greater and lasting joy, for example, by assisting other human beings who need help. One needs to become a shakshi (witness), avoiding the limelight, which can be dangerous. It reminds me of the movie, *The Fastest Gun Alive*, starring Glenn Ford. The theme was that the hero, formerly known as the "fastest gun alive," emerged from his secluded life in a small town to be challenged to a final deadly match. At the end of the movie, both the hero and the challenger appear to have died, while in fact the townspeople, to protect him, arrange for the hero's coffin to be filled with stones, his gun, and his reputation as "the fastest gun alive," thereby allowing him to resume his peaceful life with his wife, out of the limelight.

Transcendence also implies rising from a very stressful environment to one less stressful. The worst thing that can happen in life, as I have perceived through my experience and observations, is to be born into the highest level of the social strata and then fall down or be thrown out. I think of autocrats like Saddam Hussein and the Shah of Iran, though there are better examples, like Buddha. But it is not easy to choose to give up power and wealth. However, one ought to try to transcend even from a lower level to become selfless, rather than acquire more wealth and power.

The beginning of my exposure to Vedanta studies came from stories and movies heard and seen during my school days in India. Many years later, after coming to the U.S., I was invited to speak about Hinduism to an audience in a Los Angeles church in '65, and to a ladies' organization at TRW in '74. Evidently my presentations went well. I based them on what I had learned from a small paperback book on the Upanishads that I had received from a friend. Pratima and I had attended a course on Vedanta given by Swami Chinmayananda during the '70s at USC. I met Swami Parthasarathi (Swamiji) in '82 when I was visiting my dying father in Mumbai. After returning from India, with the support of a few friends I invited Swamiji to Los Angeles, when he was visiting the U.S. He had authored several books on Vedanta and the Gita, and was a good teacher. We invited him to Los Angeles for at least three successive years, and we learned a good deal about Shankara's Advaita Vedanta from him.

We also formed a study group, meeting almost every Sunday at my house, and studied books written by Swamiji. However, we read one particular book on Advaita Vedanta authored by Professor Eliot Deutsch of the University of Hawaii several times, impressed as we were by the writing and trying to understand the deep meaning articulated by the author. The people in the study group included Ravi and Gunhild Badkar, Pravin and Barbara Dave, and Alicia and Patrick Fletcher. After several years, we decided that it was time for all of us to put into practice what we had learned. We would meet occasionally after that, not to study but to socialize. Still, the lessons of those years didn't vanish from my mind. I'm not sure how much I could recall the details of the text, but certain key ideas have stayed with me. Personally, I have continued to read books by other scholars and philosophers of Indic traditions, including J. Krishnamurti, Maharishi Mahesh Yogi, Aurobindo Ghosh, and Paramahansa Yogananda. To this day, based on these teachings, I try, within my humble means, to express them in my life and writings. I also try to help my family and friends, based on their needs, by sharing my good fortune, just as my parents and grandparents did.

I have been a contrarian by nature in almost every endeavor I have pursued. That includes investment and charity. Some of our friends were donating large sums of money building temples and sending money for much needed help in India. Equally important to us is educating Americans about India. Exposing Americans to education about India would go a long way, basically bridging India with America in every field of endeavor.

One of the fortunate things that happened for us in the year 1998 was that we decided to endow a chair at UCLA. Without knowing what was going to happen in 2000, 2001 and 2002, we used the money I had made in the stock market to make the donation. We were very fortunate because we did not pay capital gain tax when UCLA liquidated some of our stocks. As we know, the stock market had crashed in the year 2000 and the 9/11 event kept the market in bearish territory for another two years. I committed $500,000, giving it to UCLA in three installments for the study of Indian history. It was not known in our Indo-American community that we could afford to endow a chair. That is because our life style is not extravagant. A few of them were critical that we were donating for our own glory and taking away from our children's heritage.

When a person endows a chair, UCLA appoints a professor to occupy the chair. In 1999, this would have cost the university about $100,000 for the professor's salary and would be paid from the UC budget. The return that they normally give out to the professor to spend on research, conferences, or anything pertinent to the area of scholarship is about five percent of the total donation. UCLA would spend five percent of $500,000, that is $125,000, for an endowment of half-a-million dollars, which comes out to about 25 percent of the donation. I consider that to be the return on my investment, since UCLA is spending every year $125,000 to teach the subject of our interest.

If we were to consider the advantage of the tax deduction, then the money invested goes down to about half of the total investment, since about 50 percent comes back from Uncle Sam, assuming we are in a 50-percent tax bracket. We had divided the payment in three installments, about $167,000 each to get the tax benefit. The return is even higher if one considers the estate taxes after death. An additional advantage in endowing the chair in 1999 was the cost then compared to what it is today. The cost to endow a chair at any of the UC campuses in 2014 has gone up to one-and-a-half million, three times the cost of the endowment I paid. The cost of almost anything keeps rising in time due to depreciating currency. An agreement was made that Professor D. R. Sardesai, an emeritus professor of Southeast Asian history, would occupy the chair as long as he wished to hold it, without any additional remuneration.

The first three years with Professor Sardesai went very well. Conferences on interesting subjects, including the Constitution of India, Ayurveda, German Indology, and the Nuclear Issue for India, were held under his leadership. The Indo-American community appreciated and enjoyed these events. Professor Sardesai, however, was not willing to carry on after three years.

Dean Scott Waugh then appointed a search committee to find a replacement to occupy the chair. They were not able to find one out of the many they interviewed, due to disagreements within the search committee. We went through quite a bit of aggravation after establishing the chair, not knowing who the next holder would be. The few members of the search committee, I was informed, wanted to appoint a scholar of the Muslim period of Indian history, which would contradict our wishes. Fortunately there was no unanimity in the search committee required to offer the position. Another candidate of very high caliber was selected and the offer was made. However he did not accept the offer since his current employer matched the UCLA offer. Often universities do not fill a chair for many years after it becomes vacant for one reason or the other.

Big universities occasionally may not conform to a donor's wishes since they do not want to give up their autonomy. My experience has taught me that a donor should have a very clear vision and objective as to what they want when they endow a chair. I recommend that donors have a lawyer and an experienced academic associated with the university as their counselors. It is even better to have an agreement about a candidate who would occupy the chair for a long time when the agreement is signed. Our agreement with UCLA was somewhat loose. We were advised by a few knowledgeable academics never to fight a university on a legal battlefield. Big institutions like UCLA have deep pockets and a battery of lawyers ready to fight.

Fortunately Professor Dan Neuman, a friend of India, became the executive vice chancellor (provost) in 2004. I had complained to him about the chair being vacant for three years. Dan and his wife Arundhati visited India almost every year. I requested him to meet me in New Delhi. I had cultivated a good friendship with Vishal Gujral, son of the late Prime Minister Inder Kumar Gujral, also a personal friend of Professor Sardesai. I had met him for the first time in 2000, when he was invited by Professor Sardesai as a keynote speaker for the first Sardar Patel Award event. The Sardar Patel Award of $10,000 was established by raising $250,000 from the Indo-American community. Ukabhai Solanki and the Doshis were the largest contributors. We were honored to give the first Sardar Patel Award to the winner. Later on, on many occasions I interacted with the prime minister and his friends, including the director of the Krishnamurti Foundation of America, Mark Lee and his wife Asha.

Vishal volunteered to hold the meeting at the former prime minister's residence in New Delhi. Mr. Gujral convinced UCLA Provost Dan Neuman how important it was for Indo-American community in southern California to fill the vacant chair. We were fortunate in that Provost Dan Neuman found a well-known scholar, Professor Sanjay Subrahmanyam from Oxford University. He is the son of the strategic analyst and adviser to many prime ministers of India, K. Subrahmanyam, and the brother of India's ambassador to America, S. Jaisankar.

With the leadership of Provost Dan Neuman, the initiative of cardiologist Tom Peters, and an entrepreneur Mohan Anand, we were able to raise $150,000 towards a music chair at UCLA, quite short of the money needed to establish a chair. Then out of the blue, I received a call from Dr. Mohinder Sambhi, who had recently lost his wife. He showed interest in establishing the music chair at UCLA in his wife's name, knowing that the Doshis had already established a chair in Indian history. I convinced Tom, Mohan, and Dan to accept Dr. Sambhi's proposition. Now Indians have two chairs at UCLA. In addition to these, Dan funded a center for Indian studies, known as the Center for India South Asia Studies (CISA) before he left the office. There are very few universities in America that have established a center to learn more about the Indian subcontinent.

As with UCLA, we established a close relationship of patronage with the Loyola Marymount University (LMU) in Los Angeles. I met Professor Christopher Chapple (Chris) of LMU sometime in 1990. Earlier I had met Professor Yajneshwar Shastri (Shastriji), then director of the school of psychology and philosophy at Gujarat University during an event at UCLA. We became good friends and I was quite impressed by his scholarship in Indic traditions. A visiting professor at LMU, Shastriji asked me to meet Chris for the same dedication to Indic traditions. Quoting Shastriji, "Chris is more Indian than most Indians in America. He is a strict vegetarian, expert in yoga practice, and removes his shoes outside his house." So I met him and agreed with Shastriji's assessment. Initially we supported Chris to bring scholars from India, specifically Shastriji from Gujarat University and Professor Billimoria for several years, depending on their availability.

In 2006, we endowed a professorship for Indic Traditions at LMU. The university also administers a $10,000 annual Bridge Builder Award program, meant to honor eminent personalities who have worked towards world peace and harmony by building a bridge between two opposites of a pair, for example, science and spirituality. Currently the Indic Traditions Chair at LMU is occupied by Professor Christopher Chapple. Recipients of the Bridgebuilder Award include Dr. Deepak Chopra, bridging spirituality and science; Conductor Zubin Mehta; world eminent writer and Buddhist Monk Thich Nhat Hanh; Greg Mortenson, the author and builder of schools and bridges in the remotest areas of Pakistan and Afghanistan; highly recognized world religions scholar Huston Smith; Dr. Vandana Shiva, the ecofeminist crusader; Dr. Karan Singh, Crown Prince of Kashmir; and the latest awardee in 2014, Rupert Sheldrake, a prominent scientist and naturalist.

In 2012, we established a professorship in Consciousness Studies at the California Institute of Integral Studies (CIIS) in San Francisco, a university focused on graduate studies and research in spiritual psychologies founded by Haridas Chaudhuri, a disciple of Sri Aurobindo Ghosh. The current occupant of the chair is Professor Leslie Allan Combs. Professor Debashish Banerji, an eminent scholar of Sri Aurobindo's philosophy, and I have established a non-profit organization, Nalanda International to promote education of Indic traditions. Our friends Ukabhai Solanki, Bhupesh Parikh, and Ushakant Thakar have followed us in establishing endowments in different academic institutions in southern California.

As a former chairman of the National Advisory Board of the Ekal Vidyalaya Foundation of America, where I served for three years, I contribute funds every year to support close to twenty-five schools in India's tribal villages. We have sponsored and participated actively in the promotion of a variety of cultural and educational projects meant to enhance world understanding in South Asian psychological and spiritual traditions and to promote world peace, including a number of conferences in southern California. In 2002, with the support of Ukabhai Solanki, we held a weeklong Mirabai Festival honoring the 16th-Century Indian woman saint, co-sponsored by the Los Angeles County Museum of Art (LACMA), UCLA, and the International Global Ethics and Religion Forum. I was asked to chair the event.

During the decade of 1990, I came across an eminent scholar of Aurobindo Ghose, Professor Debashish Banerji. Following the '90s we became good friends and established a nonprofit institution, Nalanda International. Debashish, coming from the bloodline of Rabindranath Tagore, is currently the executive director of Nalanda International. I chaired the weeklong Tagore Festival in October 2010.

On my seventy-sixth birthday on December 12, 2012 (12/12/12 occurs only once every 100 years), Debashish wrote about his experience of interacting with me. His words are reproduced here, through which he tries to lift the lid of the ideas behind what I have called my Vanaprastha phase of life.

"I've known Navin for about twenty years. I met him when I was the president of the Sri Aurobindo Center in Los Angeles. The context was, he used to have a study group at his home where a number of people, he and his friends, studied the Upanishads and Vedanta. I found that very extraordinary because a number of householders in America, many of them rich people who could do many other things with their lives, were sitting down every week and conducting a really serious study of Indian philosophy. It's quite uncommon.

So I got to know him a little bit then, and over time, our friendship grew because I saw that he was a seeker; he wanted to know more about Indian philosophy and the practices leading to transcendence. Then gradually as he started getting a better grasp, he began writing and his own thoughts started crystalizing.

I think his ideas moved in two directions: one is Indian philosophy and transcendence, and the other is economics. Navin's philosophical background was deeply influenced by the Upanishads. Related to this, he sought out intelligent modern interpreters of Vedanta, and one of these who deeply influenced his thinking is the scholar of world religions, Houston Smith. Navin likes to repeat the fact that Houston Smith says that there are three major civilizations in the world: the European, the Chinese, and the Indian. They have each contributed something significant to humanity. The Europeans have taught humanity about Nature; the Chinese about ethics and society; and India has given the world deep psychology.

After he came across this kind of approach to Indian thought, Navin started looking at what we call Indian philosophy in psychological terms. He avoided talking about Indian thought in a sectarian way, as a religion, where one becomes cubbyholed into a narrow identity. He wanted to give it a universal appeal and felt that was possible through reformulating what it means to be human, in terms of a deeper psychology.

Navin's understanding of Indian thought associated with psychology has a number of sources, mainly the Upanishads or

Vedanta. From these teachings, he concludes that the human being is layered; each of us is made up of a number of selves. He identified the outermost layer as the somatic self, associated with the body and its own needs, its own drives, and a logic of its own; then the psychic self, constituted of the intuitive mind (feelings, intuitions, beliefs), and the intellectual (logical, scientific) mind. The sub-layer of the psychic self, at the deepest level, is the philosophical self at the doorstep of the spiritual self. He believes the spiritual self is non-local, meaning beyond Nature, and is at the deepest level of consciousness.

This is how Navin has obtained out of his studies a practical teaching, whereby each of these selves should be given its independence to explore what it is, but at the same time there should be an attempt to transcend from the lower selves to the higher selves.

For this, he feels that ethics plays a very important part. Based on Indian thought, he talks about *samskaras*: *samskaras* are good habits, because particularly at the somatic level we are made up of habits in which it is easy to remain stuck. This is one of the great problems of modernity, where we don't have ethical teaching and people tend to gravitate towards the habits that keep them stuck in the lower realms, without being able to rise to the transcendent levels and even explore the best that we can be capable of.

In a way, as you might recognize, this kind of idea is similar to Maslow's 'hierarchy of needs.' However there are other teachers who have derived such ideas from Indian philosophy; Sri Aurobindo talks about our different selves and the integration and transcendence of these selves. All these ideas have fed into Navin's understanding of the human being, which he has talked and written about, and which forms the existential foundation of his own life.

The other very important aspect of his thought is economics. As we know, he is a business person, has made money and invested money, but the back bone of his economic thinking really comes from Mahatma Gandhi. Thus we can say that his economics is a kind of Gandhian economics. The importance of Gandhi in his life cannot be overstated. He met Gandhi when he was really young. He was a child when India sought her freedom; Gandhiji was a great national icon at that time, almost like a god, and Navin had the opportunity to walk beside Gandhi. That experience left an indelible mark in his mind and what he calls his psychic self.

What he really got from Gandhi, as far as economics goes, is the idea that we have to train ourselves to live frugal lives; that there is a certain level at which we have to understand what our needs are, what we really need, and not go beyond our needs. All too often, human beings exceed their basic needs and become greedy at the individual level. That's where Gandhian economic thought connects with philosophical thought, and the notion of *samskaras*, being able to understand intuitively, psychically, and at the level of the body, what it means to lead a life that is not in excess.

That becomes an important aspect at the individual or personal level, and for Navin, I believe, that is how economics begins at home. On the other level, you have the large-scale machinations of the government. You have Wall Street, for example, and you have the government, which in his terms is really run by Wall Street, which makes policies that allow large companies and corporations to run amok and maximize their profits. And the way in which they do it is by creating a debt-oriented society that is encouraged to live on what could be called a hot air balloon, an economics of air. This is what we've come to right now and Navin diagnoses very properly that the government needs to exert its power of restraint in preventing large corporations from exercising unrestrained greed, and practicing economies where you sell things based on promissory notes of the future, things that you don't really have.

The other side of this is what can be done at the individual level. If human beings exercise restraint, they find themselves leading lives in which they not only don't hurt themselves, but give the world something sustainable. So he believes that individual freedom has to be exercised in responsible ways and government exists to allow that freedom. But at the same time there are conditions under which that freedom can really flower, and competition can be something that is good, that can be healthy and full of goodwill, if complemented by meaningful lifestyles based on transcendence. This is the kind of society he looks forward to with his economic thinking.

The majority of very rich people, for one reason or the other, spend money on somatic needs. They have not graduated to go beyond somatic needs. Navin is a philanthropist who values the education of Indic traditions. Navin's own life is very moderate. But at the same time, one finds that he uses whatever extra he has made in a different way from what others do as charity. Other philanthropists often give money to religious causes, or to the poor. As far as Navin is concerned, he believes that it is more important to give money to people that will enable them to become better human beings and move toward transcendence. It is higher education that he has chosen, and in higher education, it is those kinds of teachings or research that will enable human beings to find a better life for themselves, a higher quality of life. He often asks a question specifically to younger people. "What is one asset that is given to us when we are born, that needs to be spent very wisely?" The majority don't come up with the right answer. He then explains that we are given only one asset, apart from the human mind and body. We are given a lifetime, measured in years, months, days and hours, that needs to be spent wisely to support ourselves and our loved ones. Only a few fortunate persons will inherit wealth that can be exchanged for time. Time can be exchanged for money and vice versa, and money is used for almost everything including food, shelter, education, and pleasure. He would then add that we need to spend time productively for our needs and most importantly, to transcend towards the highest level of being.

He funds a number of institutions for this purpose: a chair at UCLA, and professorships at Loyola Marymount University and the California Institute of Integral Studies. Gradually Navin has come to the belief that one is best served in these goals by initiating one's own foundation. This is where Navin and I collaborated to found Nalanda International, a nonprofit foundation where the idea is to promote the well being of a higher nature, of a transcendent nature, through higher educational activities. Nalanda has a number of initiatives and accomplishments in this direction; it has moved into publishing, various outreach functions, and cultural functions, such as a weeklong Mirabai event and a Tagore event on Tagore's 150th birth anniversary, that maximize the notion of the human potential. We are moving towards starting our own university dealing with Indic studies, including all the Indian philosophical and spiritual traditions and how they ramify in society and culture.

For all his continuing contributions, Navin has been richly awarded with recognition and honors. In 2001, he received the Hindu Vibhusan Award from Pravisi Bharati. In 2007, he received a Sanmanapatram (Certificate of Honor) from his old alma matter, Gujarat University. On September 13, 2008 at the Los Angeles Festival of Sacred Music in Royce Hall, UCLA, he was honored as a Local Hero. Navin and Pratima were awarded the Haridas Chaudhary Award at the California Institute of Integral Studies (CIIS), San Francisco, in 2012.

Apart from his philanthropic and promotional activities, Navin is an original thinker in the area of human values, economics and world harmony. A published author, Navin has been a regular contributor to local newspapers on subjects of global economics and philosophy. His books, titled *Transcendence, Saving Us from Ourselves*, published by Ithaca Press, and *Economics and Nature,* published by Nalanda and D. K. Print World in India, braid human psychology based on Indic traditions with science, economics, spirituality, and his life experiences."

Navin and Pratima also received a very prestigious award from the Maharishi University of Management on October 5, 2014. The Maharishi Award has been given to a wide range of individuals over the past thirty-eight years since it was inaugurated, from Nobel laureates to leading figures in government, science, the arts, and business, to local community members whose names may not be so well known but who nonetheless have displayed the same spirit of service to humanity.

Ayurveda Conference at UCLA. Participants included Prof.D. R. Sardesai, Dr. Chapple, Vasant Laad, Dr. Vikram Kamdar, and Matra Mashruwala, 1999.

Dr. Sardesai; Dr. Reddy; former Prime Minister Gujral (keynote speaker); Dr. Ram Roy; Dr. Shrirupa Roy (first Sardar Patel awardee); Dr. Wolpert; and Mr. Doshi, 2000.

): From left: Dr. Vikram Kamdar, Mr. Doshi, Mr. Rashmi Shah, and Dean Debashish Banerji organized a weeklong Tagore event under the banner of Nalanda International in 2010.

): Participants of the Vedanta Conference at LMU include Professor Shastri, Professor Paranjape, Phil Goldberg, Professor Chapple, Professor Prabhu, Professor Bajpai, Professor Rita Sharma, Professor Leslie Allan Combs, and Professor Banerji, 2013.

Professor Chapple, Mr. Doshi, and Professor Shastri inaugurating the publication of Isavasyopanisad, edited by Dr. Yajneshwar Shastri and Dr. Sunanda Shastri, 2013.

India's ambassador to America, Lalit Mansingh, actor Amir Khan, and invited guests with Mr. and Mrs. Doshi during a celebration for Academy Award foreign film nominee Lagaan, 2001.

Mr. Doshi having lunch with former Prime Minister Inder Kumar Gajral, 2003, Krishnamurti Foundation Ojai.

India's President A. P. J. Abdul Kalam with Mr. and Mrs. Doshi, 2004, New Delhi.

From left: Navin Doshi; Mohan Anand; Dr. Mo Sambhi, who endowed the music chair; Tom Peter; and UCLA provost Dan Neuman, responsible for establishing the Center for India South Asia Studies (CISA). Dan Neuman and I helped raise over 150,000 dollars for the UCLA music department, 2009.

Mr. Doshi with Dr. Modi of Modi Xerox corporation and Author-Philosopher Dr. Deepak Chopra.

Pratima (center) with Mirabai dancers Daksha Doshi Mashruwala (also Mr. Doshi's niece) and Malika Sarabhai (right), 2005.

CHAPTER 12

BRIDGING INDIA WITH AMERICA FOR BALANCE AND HARMONY

I often wonder if there is some purpose in life for all of us, just as light shines with a purpose. There is an important insight about light; I call it a quantum connection between Purusha and Prakriti. The speed of light is changeless and is associated with changeless Purusha. The changing attributes of light like velocity and color are associated with ever-changing Prakriti. Light is a beam of photon particles or packets of energy, which we cannot see. Light helps us to see and discover everything in Nature. Light therefore, in every sense, is seeing, and at a much higher level of mind, is enlightening. Light is pure action with purpose, and is attached to nothing. Light initiates the creation of matter, energy, space, time, and all of us, including you, the reader of this book.

I have concluded that we all have a purpose, whether we recognize it or not. The purpose of my life, as I perceive it, even in a miniscule way, has been to aid in global movements to bridge India and America to bring about balance, harmony, and complementarity for the benefit of humanity.

I was born in India, a subcontinent with many thousands of years of history (scholars would argue even tens of thousands), and landed in a country that is a polar opposite in so many different aspects, geographically for sure. On at least three, maybe five, different occasions, I could have died but did not.

The fourth event occurred during a trip to Mount Abu, a hill station in the state of Rajasthan. I believed I was cured from malaria when I was about thirteen years old. I went along with my two classmates, Kishore Shroff and Chandu Kothari, against the advice of my mother to Mount Abu, a Jain pilgrimage place and a resort. Our family doctor, Dr. Patadia, was noncommittal. On arrival, I came down with a high malaria fever. Luckily, one of the mothers living with us in the Dilwara Jain Temple gave me quinine pills to control the fever, which it did after three days. My mother could not recognize me, I was so darkened, ailing and skinny.

The fifth event occurred during our trip to Kumarakom, Kerala in 2000. I had a high fever due to the extreme heat and dehydration. While walking alone from the entertainment ground to our room in the dark, I fainted and fell down, hitting my chin on the rail of a short wooden bridge I was crossing. I was taken to hospital because of profuse bleeding under the chin from a three-inch cut that needed to be sewn. The combination of the fever and the accident caused me to faint twice during the night. Pratima cried and prayed for my survival. Pratima, like Savitri, prevented Yamraja (the God of death) from taking me away. Some would say it was just luck that I survived these sicknesses and accidents. I would argue that there was a purpose for me to live, and I believe that it is true for all of us.

I consider myself to be fortunate and lucky to be blessed with a good memory that has helped me to recall experiences I have had from the age of about five. I am fortunate also that I was born during the period of India's freedom movement under the leadership of idealist and realist giants like Gandhi, Patel, Tilak, Bose, and Nehru.

I am again fortunate that I received the right *samskara* and right education given to me by my larger family, including my parents, grandparents, brothers, and school teachers.

It was Socrates who stated, "By all means marry: If you get a good wife, you'll become happy; if you get a bad one, you'll become a philosopher." I must be very lucky because I have a wonderful wife, a very happy marriage, and I am a student of philosophy, contradicting Socrates' statement. Forrest Gump in the movie of the same name says that life is a box of chocolates with many wonderful chocolate-like experiences. I claim in his words that Pratima has been the sweetest and tastiest chocolate in my life. Add to this sweet taste the irresistible flavor of our wonderful children, Rahul and Sonya, and their children.

I consider myself to be fortunate that there were many angel-like people who helped me in many different ways. My maternal uncle Vadimama was responsible for removing potential obstacles before my marriage with Pratima. My father's friend and partner Shyamjibhai helped me start the textile business. Dr. Cam Knox and Dick Salvinski assisted me in getting jobs at Acoustica and TRW when I needed them. I had wise advice from industrialist Arvindbhai Mafatlal that I should return to America in '71. I was fortunate that I failed the PhD oral examination in '70 at UCLA, saving years of further education. I was fortunate that I left TRW, and acquired wealth in my enterprises during the right time in the '80s and after. During that period, the wealth of the bottom 90 percent (mostly middle-class wage earners, and retirees) had been shrinking, while the wealth of the top one percent rose. So I was catapulted from the bottom 90 percent to the top one percent of the population in matters of wealth acquisition. Even today, I am lucky to have had so many good friends for over thirty-five years, and friends from academic institutions during the last twenty years.

My brother Jitubhai and I were lucky that we did not get into trouble in matters of our weakness particularly during middle life, being susceptible to women. My father and eldest brother each had a mistress which created clashes within the family. I suspect they also suffered due to the additional responsibility to support a second family. All Doshi men (that includes me) had weaknesses in this matter, including my grandfather and one uncle who, I was informed, would visit prostitutes occasionally. My grandfather fathered seven babies, of whom five survived. My father was responsible for nine babies; three from my mother and two from Deepak's mother survived.

I was always curious about my ancestral genetic makeup. Test results show that I am 97 percent Asian; 91 percent from the Indian subcontinent, 6 percent East Asian, and 3 percent Melanesian. As described in Chapter One, my ancestors probably traveled to Burma (now Myanmar), Java and Sumatra and other South East Asian countries. The relationship of my ancestors with East Asian women could be the cause of my 6 percent East Asian genetic makeup.

Nayan Chanda in his book *Bound Together* gives the chronology of human migration going back some 50,000 years. Our ancestors, originating from Africa, migrated to India some 30,000 to 40,000 years ago. Migration to other parts of the world occurred later. India was trading with Mesopotamia (now Iraq) over 4,000 years ago. There is sufficient evidence that the Sindhu-Saraswati civilization blossomed at least 5,000 years ago; Hindu texts, like the Vedas and Upanishads, came into existence over 3,000 years ago. Prince Siddhartha attained Bodhi and became Buddha 2,600 years ago. King Ashoka convened the Buddhist council and dispatched missionaries in all different directions 2,300 years ago. Buddhism reached China during the 1st Century BCE. Buddhism arrived in Japan in the 6th Century CE. There is no historical evidence that Indian warrior kings invaded outside the greater Indian subcontinent.

In the words of historian H. G. Wells, Indians were content with their existence in an environment where Nature provided the necessities of life without working too hard. They had plenty of time to contemplate and ponder about matters other than the necessities for existence. They did not see any need to go out of the subcontinent to conquer other lands. They had time to think about and go deeper into all different matters, including spiritual freedom, sexual pleasure, and material abundance. British historian Arnold Toynbee admired Eastern psychological and philosophical achievement so much that he predicted the future with a statement, "A thousand years from now humanity will remember the 20th Century, not by WWI and WWII, or by the technological discoveries, but by the beginning of the process of integration of the East and the West." I believe his prediction is coming true. I would like to claim, in a miniscule way, to be one of the contributors in an ongoing integration of East and West.

I am not aware of any place in the world where the most powerful men, as Buddha did, would give away power and wealth to discover the path of Nirvana, a permanent state of blissful mind. The middle path realized by Buddha was an extraordinary insight of the time. His vision, removing all the complexities of the Upanishads, was a simple path of transcendence to Nirvana. In Mahatma Gandhi's words, spoken while visiting Sri Lanka in 1927, "He made words in the Vedas yield a meaning to which the men of his generation were strangers. He gave life to the teachings that were buried in the Vedas with overgrown weeds." There are corollaries to the middle path of moderation, and avoiding extremism in matters of austerities and pleasure. I also derive a sublime message of bridgebuilding between two polarized views, and come up with a middle ground of moderation for balance and harmony. All other statements like, "Anything in excess is poison," or Bohr's application of the word "complimentarity" (from the word "complement"), came much later.

There is another insight of Buddha, and that is of *sunyata*, meaning nothingness. Zero, nothingness, or *sunyata* is associated with Nirvana in the Buddhist tradition. The state of Nirvana is achieved when there is not a single desire left to be reborn. Moksha, in the Vedic tradition, is also a state of mind with zero desire. Zero and infinity have the same significance in all of the Indic traditions. When we observe the sky, we think of a void, nothingness, a huge shape of zero, a circle, or a space of infinite dimension. So in essence, zero and infinity, the two extremes of numbers, have the same significance, and can be associated with the Hindu perception of all-pervading nirguna (zero attributes) and anantaguna (infinite attributes) as equally primordial and equivalent descriptions of Brahman.

The story of Srinivasa Ramanujan tells of the astonishingly fruitful cross-cultural collaboration between this young mathematical genius and his mentor at Cambridge, G. H. Hardy—a relationship that turned the world of mathematics upside down. Ramanujan is supposed to have mathematically interpreted Brahman, the Absolute Reality, in both the ways described by Adi Shankara in the 8th Century. Nirguna Brahman implies zero attributes and zero manifestation; anantguna implies infinite attributes and infinite manifestation. However the ratio of zero to zero and infinity to infinity is unity. Unity in the realm of Nature implies unification of atman with Brahman. The number nine is a very auspicious number in the Vedic tradition because of its unique attributes. So there are four mahaanka, meaning four great numbers — zero, infinity, nine, and unity. Two pairs, zero and infinity are boundless, and one and nine bear in some ways boundaries.

India is a world within a world, or a subcontinent, with a high population density even during the time of Alexander of Greece. Archeologist Mark Kenoyer, during the Sindhu-Saraswati Conference sponsored by the Doshi endowment at LMU in 2009, informed us that Alexander was shocked to see such a densely populated country. That brings me to the story of Alexander and his search for a yogi. Greek scholars had heard about yogis and suggested that Alexander bring back one.

The stories about Alexander in India, which I gathered from two websites, are quite enlightening. When Alexander was busy conquering the world far and wide, he came at last to India. When he was about to return to his country, he remembered that his advisors had asked him to bring a yogi to them. They had heard a lot about yogis and were very desirous of seeing one, meeting him, hearing him speak, and receiving his blessings. Alexander was told that yogis dwelt in the forest.

In quest of a yogi he went to a forest. Sure enough, he found one sitting underneath a tree in deep meditation. He waited patiently until the yogi opened his eyes, which shone with a strange, mystic light. Reverently, Alexander requested the yogi to accompany him to his country, Greece, saying, "I will give you everything you need or ask for. But pray, do come with me. My people would love to meet you!" The yogi quietly answered, "I need nothing, I am happy where I am." This was the first time that anyone had turned down Alexander's request. He could not control himself and flew into a rage.

Unsheathing his sword, he thundered, "Do you know who is speaking to you? I am the great king Alexander. If you will not listen to me, I shall kill you, cut you into pieces!" Unperturbed, the yogi answered. "You cannot kill me. You can only kill my body. And the body is but a garment I have worn. I am not the body. I am that which dwells within the body and is unseen."

The yogi continued, "You say you are a king. May I tell you who you are? You are a slave of my slave!" Stunned, Alexander asked, "How am I a slave of your slave?" In a voice tender with compassion, the yogi explained. "I have mastered anger. Anger is my slave. See how easily you gave way to anger. You are a slave of anger, and therefore, a slave of my slave!"

For over 2,300 years, travelers from the most powerful countries on earth have come to India in search of her priceless spiritual wisdom. When Alexander the Great was returning home after his unsuccessful invasion of India, the most valued treasure that he had with him was not gold, jewels, silks or spices, but his guru (spiritual teacher), the yogi Kalyana, called "Kalanos" by the Greeks. The story of his initial contact and discussion with Kalanos is quite interesting.

Alexander's thirst for knowledge was real, so he invited Kalanos to Takshila for a philosophical discussion. According to the Greek historian and biographer Plutarch, Alexander himself framed a few questions. Some of these questions and the yogi's answers are as follows:

> *"Which are more numerous, the living or the dead?"*
> *"The living, for the dead are not."*
> *"Which has got a higher number of animals, the sea or the land?" "The land, for the sea is only a part of the land."*
> *"Which is the cleverest of all beasts that man should fear?" "That one with which man is not yet acquainted (man fears the unknown)."*
> *"Which existed first, the day or the night?" "The day was first by one day."*
> *"How may a man make himself beloved of all?" "A man will be beloved when possessed with great power and does not make himself feared."*
> *"How may a man become a God?" "By doing that which is almost impossible for a man to do."*
> *"Which is scarier, life or death?" "Life is scarier since it bears so many evils."*

Alexander was surprised by these answers. Kalanos smiled and added, "Impossible questions require impossible answers."

The sage accompanied Alexander to Persia. The long hard travel and changes in the climate became difficult for the seventy-three-year-old yogi. In India, Kalanos had never been ill, but when he lived in Persia, all strength ultimately left his old body. In spite of his enfeebled state he refused to submit to an invalid regimen, and told Alexander that he was content to die as he was, which would be preferable to enduring the misery of being forced to alter his way of life. Alexander, at some length, tried to talk him out of his obstinacy, but to no avail. Kalanos realized he had to find his own way to pass on, so he yielded to Alexander's request. He gave instructions for a funeral pyre to be built under the supervision of Ptolemy, son of Lagus of the Personal Guard. Kalanos embraced many of his close companions before leaving for his cremation but refrained from bidding farewell to Alexander, to whom he simply remarked: "I shall see you later in Babylon." Alexander died a year later in Babylon. The Indian guru's prophecy was his way of saying that he would be with Alexander both in life and death.

Some say Kalanos was escorted to the pyre by a solemn procession — horses, men, soldiers in armor, and people carrying all kinds of precious oils and spices to throw upon the flames; other accounts mention drinking cups of silver and gold and kingly robes. He was too ill to walk, and a horse was provided for him. He was incapable of mounting it, and had to be carried on a litter, upon which he lay with his head wreathed with garlands in the Indian fashion. He sang Indian songs, which his countrymen declared were hymns of praise to their gods. The horse he was to have ridden was of the royal breed of Nisaia and before he mounted the pyre he gave it to Lysimachus, one of his pupils in philosophy. He distributed among other pupils and friends the drinking cups and draperies that Alexander had ordered to be burnt in his honor upon the pyre.

At last he mounted the pyre and with due ceremony laid himself down. All the troops were watching. Alexander could not but feel that there was a sort of indelicacy in witnessing such a spectacle — the man, after all, had been his friend; everyone else, however, felt nothing but astonishment to see Kalanos give not the smallest sign of shrinking from the flames. We read in Nearchus' account of this incident that at the moment the fire was kindled there was, by Alexander's orders, an impressive salute: the bugles sounded, the troops with one accord roared out their battle cry, and the elephants joined in with their shrill war-trumpeting.

This story and others have been recorded by reliable authorities; they are not without value to those who care for evidence of the unconquerable resolution of the human spirit in carrying a chosen course of action through to the end.

When the Chinese traveler Xuanzhang attended a huge religious gathering, the Kumbha Mela in Allahabad in 544 AD, he recounts that Harsha, king of Northern India, gave away the entire wealth of his royal treasury to monks and pilgrims attending the event. When Xuanzhang prepared to return to China, he declined Harsha's offerings of jewels and gold. Understanding that his spiritual development was more valuable than worldly wealth, he accepted instead 657 religious manuscripts. Likewise, through the science of yoga, India has given the West a far more valuable gift than all the material wealth or technology the West could give in return. Even today, India offers great inspiration to those persons who seek oneness with God, and through yoga anyone can find the direction he or she needs to succeed.

India's spiritual heritage is legendary. Throughout the millennia, India has been blessed with more masters (rishis) — persons who during their lives on earth have merged their souls with God — than any other country in the world. There are many well-documented stories of their miracles.

The famous master Trailanga Swami, who lived in Benares during the late-19th Century, displayed miraculous powers that cannot be dismissed as myth. Until recently, there were living witnesses to his amazing feats. Many persons witnessed him drinking the most deadly poison with no ill effects. Thousands of people saw him levitating in a sitting position on the surface of the Ganges for days at a time. He would even disappear under the waves for long periods, finally to reappear unharmed. Though Trailanga seldom ate, he weighed over 300 pounds. The yogi never wore any clothing and was arrested by the police for his nudity on several occasions and locked in a cell. Each time, even with posted guards, he unexplainably escaped and could be seen walking on the prison roof, his cell still locked. The police had no clue as to how he did it.

I have witnessed with my own eyes, when I was a student in Khalsa College, Mumbai in '54, a yogi who stayed in a sealed, solid wooden box placed underground for a whole week. First, a square hole about ten feet deep was dug. Then placing the open box in the hole, the yogi was helped to lie down in it; the box was sealed and the hole was filled up with dirt. A week later the dirt was removed, the box was opened, and the yogi was lifted out of the box and made to sit on a chair, coming slowly out of hibernation.

About 400 years ago, Dara Shikoh, the eldest son of Shahjahn, the fifth Moghal emperor of India, completed the translation of fifty Upanishads from their original Sanskrit into Persian in 1657. His translation is often called Sirr-e-Akbar (*The Greatest Mystery*), where he states boldly in the introduction his speculative hypothesis that the work referred to in the Qur'an as the "Kitab al-maknun" or hidden book is none other than the Upanishads. His most famous work, Majma-ul-Bahrain (*The Confluence of the Two Seas*), was also devoted to a revelation of the mystical and pluralistic affinities between Sufic and Vedantic speculation. Dara's translation of the Upanishads was further translated into Latin, French and German in the early 19th Century. Ever since then, the interest of European scholars in Vedic philosophy and yoga was ignited. European scholars searched for the roots of Western civilization during and after their colonies were established. A few scholars, including Voltaire, proposed India; British imperialists shot it down, because India was the crown jewel supplying resources including soldiers to fight their wars. So they established the roots in Greece. However Greek scholars even now are in concurrence with Voltaire.

Many Western scholars made their journey to India to learn and discover something new and different for their own benefit.

The psychoanalyst Carl Jung came to India in the late '30s to discover solutions to problems in Europe caused after WWI. Jung was delighted to find that his ideas of archetypes were corroborated in Indian philosophy. He was extremely receptive to the conflicting stimuli of Indian philosophy. Irish Poet William Yeats, though aging and approaching seventy, visited India to learn about Indian traditions including the Upanishads. He became a student to learn about incarnation, meditation, and Patanjali. Yeats was one of the most productive English poets of his time. Many Westerners came to meet Mahatma Gandhi, such as Madeleine Slade, or to learn more about him, like Martin Luther King Jr. Travelers like Christopher Isherwood, a novelist, found mental peace due to the non-discriminative Indic philosophy in matters of homosexuality.

Jeffery Paine has described interesting stories of many travelers to India in his book, *Father India.* I recall giving two books to President Clinton, *Father India* and *Revenge and Reconciliation,* written by Rajmohan Gandhi in February 2000 just before Clinton was to visit India. President Clinton assured me before departing that he would read the books. Our son, Rahul in a 2014 conference of cardiologists, met the president and informed him that his father had given him a couple of books. His response was, "I remember, and I have read them." I presume he read *Father India* for several reasons. It is a book that gives a "birds-eye view" of India in a short time for men on the go.

Jeffery Paine devoted a whole chapter about Mahatma Gandhi with the title "The Gandhian Century" in his book. *TIME* magazine had a poll to select the Man of the Millennium in 2000. Einstein and Gandhi were voted first and second. (See Appendix B for statements of world leaders about Mahatma Gandhi.) I have always thought of Gandhi as the man who evolved as one of the greatest karma yogis. Gandhi was battling for India's independence, but he was also fighting to liberate the British from their own materialist psychology of colonialism. He wanted to be balanced to resolve the issue while maintaining friendship with the British without burning the bridge between India and the United Kingdom.

Gandhi described seven social sins, which included almost all of human endeavor:

> Politics without principles,
> Wealth without work,
> Pleasure without conscience,
> Knowledge without character,
> Commerce without morality,
> Science without humanity, and
> Worship without sacrifice.

Every activist in these fields wanted to consult with him, because he had thought through problems and their solutions at every level, micro to macro and in the in-between layers of human existence.

The exemplary character and governance of Rama, an Indian king supposed to have lived more than 10,000 years ago, has made his legend the most popular textbook on moral living and righteous polity. As a nationalist ideal in colonial India, the concept of Ramrajya or "rule of Rama" was first projected by Mahatma Gandhi. Gandhi announced that Ramrajya would be brought once Independence arrived. By using the Ramrajya slogan, Gandhi implied an ideal governance (without being communal) where values of justice, equality, liberty, and voluntary renunciation are followed. To quote Gandhi on Ramrajya, he wrote on February 26, 1947, "Let no one commit the mistake of thinking that Ramrajya means a rule of Hindus. My Rama is another name for Khuda or God." Obviously this meant an ideal society where everybody follows a code of righteous living and maintains a state of inner contentment, with all their essential needs being met.

Historically, Ramrajya, according to many scholars, meant that the state (Rajya) was ruled by an ideal philosopher-king, the sole legitimate governing agency wielding power. This philosopher king imposed limits on his own exercise of power for the greater happiness of the people, and to evade tyranny that could be caused by moral outrage or self-righteousness. The actions of the benevolent philosopher king were always for the good of every citizen. The chapter on Ayodhya, from the Ramayana, gives a majestic description of Ramrajya, where peace, prosperity and tranquillity reigned, for there was no one to challenge the seat of Ayodhya, literally the land without wars. In understanding this ideal today, where ideal kingship is so alien to us, we need to see what Gandhi saw as the democratic gift of Ramrajya. One can say that in such a state, attention is also given to building *samskaras* and orientation towards moksha among the population, so that they regulate themselves from within.

Samskaras are ethical behaviors obtained by training physical urges and impulses right from early childhood. One may promote *samskaras* in a society by making individuals aware that the good of all is conducive to the good of oneself. Selfish greed, which seems to bring personal advantage at the cost of others, ultimately leads to harm to the self, because all things are interconnected. In a global world, this is easy to see, but not so easy to teach. It is due to the greatness of ancient India that it created a civilization based on such values. Part of its success lay in the orientation towards moksha described in the Vedas, or "selflessness," the liberation from bondage of all kinds that became the supreme virtue.

In recent times, people from all over the world met and experienced yogis, like Vivekananda, Aurobindo, and Maharishi Mahesh Yogi. The story of Aurobindo I consider in some ways similar to the story of Buddha. Aurobindo Akroyd Ghose (the middle name was given by his hosts in England) was probably one of the most brilliant graduates of Cambridge, sweeping all the relevant academic prizes. He mastered European languages and literature ranging from ancient Greek to contemporary French, and composed poetry in the English, Latin and Greek languages. His physician father believed that one had to be British to be successful. Aurobindo's first language was English, and he had never learned an Indian language. His father meticulously made sure that his seven-year-old son, born in India, was not influenced by any Indian or anything Indian. Aurobindo was never exposed to any Indian religion, and did not visit India throughout his educational years. It reminds me of Siddhartha's father not wanting to have his son be influenced by the reality of suffering.

At the age of twenty-one, Aurobindo returned to India to work in the princely state of Baroda, traveling by ship. When inaccurately news was reported that his son's ship had sunk, the father, as had happened with King Rama's father Dasharatha, died of heart failure. Once back in India, in quick succession Aurobindo mastered Bengali, Marathi, Gujarati, and Sanskrit as well as cultural traditions his father had forbidden. Aurobindo remade himself by replacing his English name. Philosophically he became a firebrand revolutionary, determined to eject the British from India. In 1908, Aurobindo was jailed along with a group of extremists who had tried to assassinate a district judge, Douglas Kingsford. Incarcerated for a year with a probable verdict of capital punishment ahead of him, Aurobindo plunged into yoga and experienced the beginnings of the decisive revelations and spiritual experiences that would occupy him for the rest of his life. At the end of the year, he underwent trial but was not convicted, thanks to the expert defense of his counsel, the famous barrister and nationalist C. R. Das, and the upright verdict of the judge C. P. Beachcroft. It is interesting to note that Aurobindo and Beachcroft were contemporary students at Cambridge University and took the Indian Civil Services together. In these exams, Aurobindo came first in Greek, while Beachcroft came second, while ironically, Beachcroft did better than Aurobindo in Bengali. Many historians feel Aurobindo's release was at least partly due to "old boy favoritism" on the part of his colleague.

Aurobindo lost his interest in politics and revolution, thinking it to be too Western, and immersed himself deeper in yoga and spirituality. Escaping from the British authorities, he sailed for the French enclave of Pondicherry. Mirra Richard, a French woman, impressed with Aurobindo's philosophy, as his followers would say, cultivated a platonic relationship and spiritual collaboration with him. An Indian man and a French woman, rejecting nationality, race, and ideology, were able to create a utopia on earth. They put Pondicherry on the map of global culture. President Woodrow Wilson's daughter, living in Pondicherry in the '30s was able to attract Henry Ford's interest in Aurobindo's philosophy. She was one of the early Western bridgebuilders, when she envisioned dynamic America as a groom and visionary India as a bride.

Aurobindo, philosophically and insightfully, is responsible for fusing the Eastern thought of transcendence with the Western thought of evolution. Unlike Gandhi's vision of eternal unchanging truth, Aurobindo's insight was of human evolution associated with the changing Prakriti. Aurobindo adopted Social Darwinism not to differentiate among the races, as Europeans did to rule over colonies, but to transcend towards the whole of human consciousness. He argued that man is capable of becoming Buddha or Christ through evolution. Aurobindo's manifesto, "Man is a transitional being, and is evolving," rebuked the Europeans who thought themselves to be final and superior human beings. A German physicist, Ulrich Mohrhoff, has concluded and accepted Aurobindo's finding that there is non-local quantum connection between individual subjective consciousness and the all-pervading objective super-consciousness. He also accepts that not only our mind but consciousness itself is layered and has discrete poises rising towards the greater consciousness and wholeness pioneered by Aurobindo. Debashish Banerji, the foremost scholar of Aurobindo, has written a wonderful book about him, *Seven Quartets of Becoming*, for those scholars who want to learn about Aurobindo's deep philosophy and teaching of yoga.

There is a great story of the emergence of Maharishi Mahesh Yogi, who had prominent followers including the Beatles, scientist Buckminster Fuller, and leading thinkers of the day, Hans Selye and Jonas Salk. Maharishi Mahesh Yogi's message is very simple, comparable to the message of Buddha. Stress is rampant in our fast-moving society, so his message of introspection employing transcendental meditation was presented as the right path to cope with it. The roots of his teaching, like those of Gandhi and Aurobindo, are from the Vedas. Unlike Gandhi, both Aurobindo and Maharishi, a graduate in physics, practiced jnan yoga that included science as part of their teaching. Maharishi also employed modern technology to promote his message. Like Gandhi, Maharishi was a karma yogi, a man on the go, a man of action spreading his teachings to as wide an audience as he could assemble.

Perhaps the most striking feature of Maharishi's meditation technique is the simplicity and effortlessness of the practice. His message resembles that of J. Krishnamurti about the mind that is conditioned in time. Conditioning causes the continuous, non-stop flow of thoughts. Transcendental meditation (TM) is initiated effortlessly, seated in a quiet environment repeating an appropriate mantra. Sound is an important element of the practice. The first objective is to reduce the flow of thoughts. In time, TM practice will ultimately have no historicity, no images, no memory, and no thoughts. The objective, practicing TM at the highest level, is to experience the fourth state of mind (turya awastha), the state of pure consciousness. The three other states are light sleep with dreams when only the mind is active; an awakened state when both body and mind are active; and deep sleep when both the body and mind are inactive. The reason that we feel freshest after a deep dreamless sleep is because we are closest to atman or pure consciousness when we are at the deepest level beyond body and mind. However, the fourth state is even superior because the mind becomes pure consciousness in sync with super-consciousness.

Both Aurobindo and Maharishi think of consciousness as layered, and the meditator needs to transcend from layer to layer to arrive at the final state of consciousness. Maharishi believed that three kinds of empirical tests are relevant in matters of meditation: personal experience, scientific research, and confirmation with the ancient historical records. (See Appendix B for statements of luminaries about Maharishi.) Maharishi translated the Bhagavad Gita with his own commentary, first published in '67. Both Mahatma Gandhi and Maharishi were given state funerals by the government of India after they had passed away. It is amazing that the simplest messages, like Buddha's message of the middle path to obtain nirvana, Gandhi's message of non-violence to obtain freedom from British, Nelson Mandela's message of forgiveness to obtain the rule of democracy for all, and saint's message of Maharishi and Krishnamurti of simple meditation to become stress free have been so beneficial to humanity.

That reminds me of another Gita, known as the Ashtavakra Gita. King Janaka, father of Sita of the epic Ramayana, was a wise philosopher king who held a sabha, a gathering of scholars and saints, periodically. One day he recited his dream of the previous night in the sabha. "I was losing the war fighting the enemy, and I was trying to escape on a horse while enemies were chasing me. I was wounded, hungry, thirsty, and my enemy was about to kill me. I realized that it was just a dream when I opened my eyes. So tell me, which state of my mind is the true state? Is it the current state with all of you around me, or the dream state? Or is it the state without any dreams?"

Those men who responded stated the current state to be true. The king was not satisfied. Then a deformed man, Ashtavakra, with all kinds of handicaps including his speech, entered the sabha. He claimed in his barely understandable speech, "I have an answer for you, my king." Everyone started laughing at his speech and deformation, thinking how can such a man have the right answer? They were all equating appearance with knowledge. The king knew better and was ready to listen to his answer, that the true state is neither of the states, but a fourth state.

Ashtavakra described the fourth mental state, also known as turya, thus: "You are really unbound and action-less, self-illuminating and spotless already. The cause of your bondage is that you are still resorting to stilling the mind. You are unconditioned and changeless, formless and immovable, unfathomable awareness, imperturbable — such consciousness is un-clinging. You are not bound by anything. What does a pure person like you need to renounce? Putting the complex organism to rest, you can go to your rest." The king was pleased and accepted his answer. Ashtavakra reminds me of the modern-day genius of cosmology Stephen Hawking, with a deformed body and multiple handicaps. However we have overcome such barriers for Dr. Hawking employing modern technology, enabling him to communicate lucidly.

I have been fortunate to meet realized yogis, and experience their grace and blessings during my lifetime. My father took me to Swami Nityananda and his disciple Muktananda of Ganeshpury many times in the '50s. I listened to a discourse given by Swami Chinmayananda at USC in the '70s. These are experiences beyond the realm of natural human faculties. In the recent past, I have met modern sages and bridgebuilders like Huston Smith, Thich Nhat Hanh, Rupert Sheldrake, and John Hegalin. I am a lifetime student, and a student of life, and I am learning in my old age from these sages and many more.

The last intellectual push for pan-Asianism was promoted nearly a century ago by Rabindranath Tagore, a Nobel laureate. He was well received on tours to China and Japan, where he urged people to counter Western imperialism with Asian spiritualism. However, he did not succeed then. There is no doubt about the perception among Western intellectuals like Carl Jung, among others, that spiritualism is strongly associated with the East, particularly with India. The international headquarters of the Theosophical Society (an organization to unite world traditions) was transferred from New

York to Adyar, Chennai, in the late 1870s because Adyar had one of the largest forests of banyan trees. Later, under the leadership of Annie Besant, the group discovered in Adyar a Christ-like young boy named J. Krishnamurti with an aura of selflessness.

The banyan tree is found both physically and spiritually in nearly all Asian countries. The tree is sacred in Hindu theology; for instance, we often see the god Shiva meditating under the shade of such a tree. It is often called "The Tree of Life" or "The Tree of Knowledge." It is simple to understand the former, its symbolism of eternal life, when considering its visual appearance of unending expansion. Vishnu is also said to have taught beneath a banyan, bringing the knowledge of philosophy and science to the people. The bodhi tree, under which Buddha attained enlightenment, was a banyan by another name. A British magazine, by naming a column "Banyan" in 2009, may have recognized that India is at the root of all Asian (perhaps of all the world) civilizations, as many scholars of genetic research have hypothesized.

Not only is the banyan tree sprinkled throughout the various countries' mythology, religion, and daily life, but the science of the tree itself is representative of the perpetual growth and vastness of Asia's branches. After the dispersal of seeds from the banyan fruit, the roots erupt from the soil and spread laterally. Asia contains more than half the world's population, based on the latest census. The people themselves span worldwide in respect to geographical location, political power, and cultural influence. Like the roots of the banyan, the massive Asian population grows strong and comes to resemble the core trunk from which it originated, extending to all corners of the earth, much farther than one could imagine. The roots simultaneously lengthen and cling to the host trunk and remain attached for its life span, continually adding to the trunk, the core, the ancient tradition, and creating new life elsewhere.

The tree's roots are not the only parts to spread far over the land, for the branches are just as far-reaching. Even the parts of the world that are not home to Asian people are still "in the shade of the banyan tree," being affected by the continent and its inhabitants, however indirectly. The shade is immense, but through the leaves, here and there, the sky shines through — its shade does not smother or trap one in darkness.

How do I distinguish India, a world within a world, and America, at thetop of the world materially? Because there are so many unbalanced pairs of opposites causing difficulties for the majority of Americans, so much polarization in almost every field of human endeavor, I believe America needs to become even more closely associated with India, where human roots originated. Men of wealth and power in both countries need to shift their focus from acquiring more wealth and power to introspection and meditation to experience everlasting bliss. I envision flourishing banyan trees small and large with their roots in India, spreading east and west into different countries, ultimately ending in America as a jungle of thick large banyans, complementing the other trees of the region, like the tall redwoods and sequoias.

Currently, in 2014, the world is going through a serious cyclical crisis. The technology of the Internet and wireless communication has helped unite peoples of the world. After the Industrial Revolution, competition among colonial powers brought WWI and WWII. A transition occurred for the better after the wars; the rise of nationalism brought freedom to the colonies. The victor of WWII, America helped to remove colonialism. To be sure, wars are not good; millions of people have died during the World Wars and the smaller wars afterwards. Today great powers are polarized, and they are fighting financial and cyber wars. America is trying to protect its hegemony over the world using modern technology. I believe the 19th- and 20th-Century strategy of "divide and conquer," the strategy of the British, Bismarck, and the American neocons, needs to be scrapped.

Very rarely do we consider multiple big powers a sign of anything but war and discontent, but it does not have to be so. For years the world has lived with its countries in discord and at each other's throats for survival, influence, and affluence. How many years will it take to see that this way of dealing with other cultures and peoples hasn't been and is still not working? It is about time that we try something else. Every country is unique, and no country is "exceptional," if the meaning of the word is "superior" or claims to have more rights than other countries. Peoples and countries are equal in the eyes of international law. America needs to go back to the immortal quotation of Thomas Jefferson, first used in the U.S. Declaration of Independence, that "All men are created equal" at least in the eyes of the law. It has to apply to all countries as well. There cannot be a "unipolar" world, where the strongest makes rules for its advantage. There are ways a big power can use its advanced technology in the name of freedom and multiculturalism, and yet control resources of countries similar to what the colonial powers did. Even today, fairer wages of people in third world countries are rare at every level.

Western power needs to be in balance and harmony with the growing Eastern power. The two opposite powers need to complement each other and go beyond and transcend for the benefit of the whole of humanity. The cooperation of materially advanced countries should have a goal to eliminate poverty in developing countries in Asia, Africa, and South America. Resources need to be used for the good of humanity, not for war hardware. Pharmaceutical, biotechnology, nanotechnology, cyber and cognitive technology developed in the advanced nations of the West, together with the technology of introspection and transpersonal development in which non-western cultures have long histories and India has an unbroken tradition, could provide the needed growth, both material and mental, for the betterment of humanity.

Rahul with President Clinton, 2013.

From left: Myself, (the late) Sunil Aagi, and President Clinton, 2000.

): Doshi family with Dr. and Mrs. Chopra, the recipient of the Bridge Builder award, 2005.

From left: Professor Sardesai, Bridge Builder award recipient Professor Huston Smith and myself, 2011.

From left: LMU Professor Strauss, Pratima, Navin, Dr. Sheldrake, LMU Dean Crabtree, LMU Professor Chapple, and Dr. Hegalin, 2014.

Family photo: Pratima and Navin Doshi with Rahul's family (left) and Sonya's family (right), 2012.

POSTSCRIPT:

Today (February 13th 2016) the humanity and the world seems to be in a more dangerous state than in all the previous decades of my life, more even than during the Cuban Missile crisis of 1962. There was a report on February 13th that Russia warned Turkey that Russia is prepared to use tactical nuclear weapons to defend Russian military assets in Syria from Turkish attack. NATO currently has amassed the largest ever armed resources around the western boarder of Russia, more so than the invading force of Hitler against the Soviet Union (now Russia) during WWII. Any such conflict could escalate into a full scale nuclear confrontation between Russia and America, since Turkey and America are members of NATO. Is it a Kabuki dance played by America and Russia? Even if it is, there is a chance that it could result in a catastrophe.

A transition is occurring right in front of our eyes from a unipolar (Western Power) to a multipolar (add China and Russia) world. We forget that China and India were leading world powers in terms of almost every human endeavor during the 16th century. However civilizations are naturally cyclical just as any organism and organization. Among all human traditions, the cyclical attribute of Nature is best represented by the dance of Shiva, or Nataraja as described by Art historian Ananda Coomaraswamy. The cyclical movement we are witnessing is the receding West and rising East.

China and India saw a long period of decline from 17th through the 19th century. However what China has accomplished in the last several decades is unparalleled in human history. The spectacular rise of China was greatly facilitated by shortsighted Washington policy, influenced by the Wall Street. America imported vast quantities of cheap consumer goods from China eliminating manufacturing jobs of higher wages, and as a result destroying the middle class in America. The net worth of middle class American family has been going down since 1985, while the same is rising for the top ten percent.

China now is the largest economy measured in terms of purchasing power parity. It is difficult for "exceptional" America to assimilate the profound consequence of this shift. China's GDP growth has slowed down to around seven percent, but it still is much higher than the GDP growth rate of Western countries. The private and government debt burden of Western countries is a resisting force to their GDP growth rate.

I also see multiple polarizations in so many human endeavors including economics, politics, religious traditions, judiciary, and media. Polarization occurs where there is little or no middle grey between two black and white extremes; there is no bridge to compromise and reconcile. For example the middle class (grey) is reduced to insignificance in America. According to the New York Times, the "richest 1 percent in the United States now own more wealth than the bottom 90 percent".

It is not just one crack- like right versus left or east versus west, but multiple cracks radiating from the center towards the periphery. One piece could fragment into, not just two, but multiple pieces. It is an indication of a very high probability of formation of a tsunami in the not too distant future. The world population is rising but there are not enough jobs for graduates coming out of schools. Current demographics and environmental problems are not conducive to the growth of enough food for the masses. Malthus, who predicted starvation due to an exponentially rising population as opposed to linear food production, may have missed his timing but still could come out right in predicting human starvation.

The decline of the West is a mathematical certainty, as it has happened to any world power of the past. The leveling of all power poles could take a year or even much longer such as 40 years. However there is an increasingly profound sense of malaise permeating in the West. The political process apparently is patently hijacked by Wall Street bankers and the Military Industrial Complex as we were warned by the late President Eisenhower during the 1950s. It is estimated that the current world power is being held by no more than five thousands oligarchs. Europe is trying to absorb the migration from the Middle East, where there is no hope of feeding its masses or creating enough jobs for the exploding population of epochal proportion. European institutions seem paralyzed in an ineffective, anarchic, and noisy, also known as political correctness.

Religious fanaticism has been in existence ever since the religion was discovered. There are several decade long periods in the past when it stayed essentially harmless. Today the West is apparently using the same fanaticism for its own political gain. There is sufficient evidence that America along with Saudi Arabia created Al Qaeda and ISIS. Thinkers and journalists of suffering countries convincingly describe America as an Empire of Chaos, first invading then leaving their destroyed countries. European outlier journalists believe that America has hijacked EU foreign policy with disastrous results.

America's response to a rising China is to create anti-Chinese alliances, including remilitarization of Japan. The Obama administration has pushed Russia away by placing economic sanctions and declaring Russia to be America's enemy number one. Every American president of the past ensured that Russia and China do not become strong allies. Obama has succeeded doing exactly the same, pushing Russia to become China's strongest ally.

When Chinese leader Xi Jinping visited Central Asia and Southeast Asia in September and October 2013, he raised the initiative of jointly building the Silk Road Economic Belt and the 21st-Century Maritime Silk Road. The 'belt' includes countries situated on the original Silk Road through Central and West Asia, India, the Middle East, and Europe. The initiative calls for the integration of the region into a cohesive economic area through building infrastructure, increasing cultural exchanges, and broadening trade. I would argue that America, as an equal partner, should participate in such projects and in the economic and human development of any country desirous to do so.

The total death due to all causes including famine during WWII is estimated to be around 80 million, about 3 % of the world population. Russia and China suffered the most with death toll exceeding 26 and 20 million each respectively. India suffered less but still lost over 4 million due to the Bengal starvation, thanks to Winston Churchill. He knowingly engineered the famine in 1942-43 by transferring vast quantities of food grain from India to Britain. After the war, world leaders recognized the result of the grid of power and wealth. Gandhi's philosophy of non-violence was appreciated world over but implemented after the war; good things happened including the establishment of United Nations, an institution set up to secure world peace. Indo-Americans of my generation were very fortunate to be born in India and be influenced by great leaders and philosophers of India. Those who came to America saw the best of both, eastern and western worlds. There was some hardship in the beginning, but a good life followed with some lucky breaks. There has been a constant improvement in life comforts and material wellbeing, thanks to the technological development of last several decades.

So how do we go back to the good old days and keep improving going forward? I come back to the vision of the Buddha. To me, the only way out of this worsening situation is the middle path of the Buddha and bridge building between all extremes and contraries. We must make every effort to compromise, reconcile and bring back the balance harmony and complimentarity.

BRIDGING INDIA WITH AMERICA FOR BALANCE AND HARMONY

APPENDIX A

SPEECHES BY MR. DOSHI AT DIFFERENT OCCASIONS

Address by Mr. Doshi accepting the Chaudhuri Award for Distinguished Service, CIIS, 2012

Address by Mr. Doshi Accepting the Maharishi Award, October 5, 2014

Address by Mr. Doshi to Bridgebuilder Awardee, Rupert Sheldrake, LMu, September 2014

Foreword by Navin Doshi Written for the Memorial Volume Honoring Professor S. R. Rao, Based on the Opening Speech at the Sindhu-Saraswati Conference at LMu, 2014

An Open Letter to the Prime Minister of India, 2014 Address by Chief guest Navin Doshi at BAPS Temple, June 2013

Address by Navin Doshi, Chairman of the Nalanda Confluence Institute, August 2012

Address by Mr. Doshi to Bridgebuilder Awardee, Huston Smith, 2011

Address by Mr. Doshi to Bridgebuilder Awardee, Vandana Shiva, 2010/11

Address by Navin Doshi to Bridgebuilder Awardee, Greg Mortenson, 2009

Address by Mr. Doshi to Bridgebuilder Awardee, Thich Nhat Hanh, 2008

Address by Mr. Doshi to Bridgebuilder Awardee, Zubin Mehta, 2007

Address by Mr. Doshi to the First Bridgebuilder Awardee, Dr. Deepak Chopra, 2006

World Sacred Music Festival with Their Local Heroes Kicks Off at uCLA, September 13, 2008

CIIS President Subiondo with Mr. and Mrs. Doshi outside the event hall, 2012.

Address by Mr. Doshi accepting the Chaudhuri Award for Distinguished Service, CIIS, 2012

President Subiondo and friends, greetings and good evening. Pratima and I are very honored receiving this prestigious award ... we hope to do more, certainly in matters of education, to make us more deserving recipients. It is amazing how the world is getting smaller and smaller every passing day, thanks to the Internet, GPS, fast aeroplanes, Google, YouTube, and so on and so forth. We had invited for this occasion my old college mate and very accomplished friends, Kumar and his wife Shela Patel. Shela replied they could not make it because Kumar was to be inducted this week into the Science Hall of Fame in Washington, D.C., adding that their Hindu wedding ceremony in 1962 was performed by a Vedic scholar, Dr.

Haridas Chaudhuri. So we do have multiple connections with the Chaudhuri family and CIIS.

The world is not just getting smaller and smaller, but there is more realization that we are one family; each one of us are cousins, some distant, some closer. We have two parents, four grandparents, eight great-grandparents, and so on. The total population of Homo sapiens is a little over seven billion. If we were to multiply the number two, thirty-three times, where each multiplication represents one generation, the product comes out to be about eight billion. The implication of this simple exercise is that … every human being is at least your 33rd cousin.

So what do we need to do to get even closer, more united? I suspect we could do it by educating ourselves through introspection, by discovering brighter and brighter light. We are all ignorant in many ways. Even Einstein, in spite of his brilliance, exhibited his ignorance in matters of quantum mechanics when he made the statement that "God does not play dice." There is a story about him: after his death, he meets God at Heaven's Gate. Being curious, he asks the question, "I am puzzled, my Lord; is Schrodinger's equation valid? You would not introduce uncertainty in the workings of Nature, would you?" After a pause, God answers, "My dear Albert, you must play dice, since I do not play favorites. If I had only certainty in Nature, life would be so dull, boring; sports would not exist; women would not be able to play games with men."

There is a Gujarati poem, "Rakh na ramakda, mara Rame rampta rakhya re, Mrutyu lok ni mati mathi manav thai ne avya re …, rakh na ramakda." A rough translation is that we humans, made of earth's clay, must keep playing the game of life that God wishes us to play. Joseph Campbell in his book, *The Power of Myth*, recites a story of an American visiting India to learn more about God. He asks a question of Swami Rama Krishna: "Why is this world so cruel? There is so much pain, sorrow, destruction; people die without any reason! God is supposed to be loving and caring!"

After a pause, the saint answers, "Who are we to ask that question?" Often we ask questions showing our ego and ignorance.

So the game, as I perceive it, is to keep playing the game but keep transcending with good karmas, and discover brighter light. The light in every sense is an instrument, a conduit, to discover God. Einstein did have a quantum connection with Brahman to discover the Theory of Relativity. The quantum connection gave Einstein the insight that only the speed of light is constant; everything else, including time, space, matter, and energy is not.

The sun in the Upanishads is described as Sutratma that like a needle pierces all the Jivatmas or individual life souls, like all of us in this hall. Each of us, the life soul, has to realize oneness with the cosmic wind and the sun; if not, the life soul cannot cross the frontiers of death and will not experience immortality. To me, the Tibetan Buddhist concept of death is attractive. They believe that when I die, I will face the brightest light, and I am supposed to hold it. If I succeed, I will attain Nirvana. If not, I will face the light with receding brightness. The point of equilibrium depends upon the quality of my karmas.

Our endeavors are to keep learning and help others learn to get rid of darkness. I hope together we can design more projects to enlighten more students. Rest assured, Joseph, I will do my best so that I will be able to hold the brightest light possible after I die. Thank you, and Namaste.

Address by Mr. Doshi Accepting the Maharishi Award, October 5, 2014

Respected Raja Ram Dr. Nader, Dr. Hagelin, and friends,

Good afternoon. Pratima and I would like to express our deepest gratitude for the honor of receiving the Maharishi Award. I hope we are receiving this award purely on a merit basis and not because my dearest friend Michael Busch used his influence.

The people responsible for establishing this university are truly great visionaries and I cannot thank them enough for giving this gift to humanity. I am not aware of any other university outside of India that has its roots deep into the Vedic tradition.

European scholars were searching for the roots of Western civilization during and after their colonies were established. A few scholars, including Voltaire, proposed

India; British imperialists shot it down, because India was the crown jewel supplying resources including soldiers to fight their wars. So they established the roots in Greece. However, Greek scholars were in concurrence with Voltaire. That brings me to the story of Alexander of Greece and his search for a yogi. Greek scholars had heard about yogis and suggested that Alexander bring back one.

From left, Dr. John Hagelin (USA chief), Raja Ram Dr. Nader (World Organization chief), Pratima, Navin, Peggy and Michael Busch, October 2014.

In quest of a yogi, Alexander went to a forest. Sure enough, he found one sitting underneath a tree in deep meditation. He waited patiently until the yogi opened his eyes. Reverently, Alexander requested the yogi to accompany him to his country, Greece. "I will give you everything you need or ask for. But pray, do come with me. My people would love to meet you!" The yogi quietly answered, "I am happy where I am." Alexander could not control himself, and flew into a rage. Unsheathing his sword, he thundered, "I am the great King Alexander. If you will not listen to me, I shall kill you, cut you into pieces!" Unperturbed, the yogi answered, "You cannot kill me. You can only kill my body. And the body is but a garment I have worn. I am not the body. I am that which dwells deep within the body unseen."

The yogi continued, "You say you are a king. May I tell you who you are? You are a slave of my slave!" Stunned, Alexander asked. "How am I a slave of your slave?" In a voice tender with compassion, the yogi explained. "I have mastered anger. Anger is my slave. See how easily you gave way to anger. You are a slave of anger, and therefore a slave of my slave!" Alexander did find a Kalyana yogi in Takshila who went with him. Yogi Kalanos, as pronounced in Greek, was in his seventies and could not endure the hardship of the cold climate of Persia. He informed Alexander he would see him in Babylon and immolated himself, showing no pain. Sure enough, Alexander died in Babylon!

I am not aware of any place in the world, where the most powerful men like Buddha would give away power and wealth to discover the path of Nirvana, a permanent state of blissful mind. The middle path realized by Buddha is an extraordinary insight of the time. His vision, removing all the complexities of the Upanishad, was a simple path of transcendence to Nirvana. In Mahatma Gandhi's words, "He made words in the Vedas yield a meaning to which the men of his generation were strangers. He gave life to the teachings that were buried in the Vedas." There are corollaries to the middle path of moderation, avoiding extremism in matters including austerities and other indulgences. I would also derive a sublime message of bridgebuilding between the two polarized views, and came up with a middle ground of moderation for balance and harmony. All other statements like "Anything in excess is poison," or Bohr's application of the words, the "complimentarity" of opposites, came much later.

There is another insight of Buddha, and that is of sunyata, meaning nothingness. Zero, nothingness or sunyata is associated with Nirvana in the Buddhist tradition. The state of Nirvana is achieved when there is not a single desire left to be reborn. Moksha, in the Vedic tradition, is also a state of mind with zero desire. Zero and infinity have the same significance in all Indic traditions. When we observe the sky, we think of a void, nothingness, a huge shape of zero, a circle, or a space of an infinite dimension. So, in essence, zero and infinity, the two extremes of numbers, have the same significance, and can be associated with the Hindu perception of all pervading nirguna (zero attributes) and anantaguna (infinite attributes) Brahman.

The story of Srinivasa Ramanujan is also a story of the astonishingly fruitful cross-cultural collaboration between this young mathematical genius and his mentor at Cambridge, G. H. Hardy—a relationship that turned the world of mathematics upside down. Ramanujan is supposed to have interpreted Brahman, the absolute reality, in both ways, as described by Adi Shankara. Nirguna brahman implies zero attributes and zero manifestation; anantguna implies infinite attributes and infinite manifestations. However the ratio of zero to zero and infinite to infinite is unity. Unity in the realm of Nature implies the unification of atman with brahman. Number nine is a very auspicious number in the Vedic tradition because of its unique attributes. So there are four mahaanka, meaning four great numbers — zero, infinite, nine, and unity — just as we have four Vedic mahavakyas.

In the words of historian H. G. Wells, Indians were content with their existence in an environment where Nature provided the necessities of life without working too hard. They had plenty of time to contemplate and ponder about matters other than the essentials for existence. They did not need to go out of the sub-continent to conquer other lands.

About three hundred years ago, Darasiko, the eldest son of Shahjahn, the 5th Moghal emperor of India, had translated the Upanishads into the Persian language, which was then translated into the German language. Ever since then, the interest of European scholars in Vedic philosophy and yoga was ignited. In recent times, people from all over the world have met and experienced yogis, like Vivekananda and Maharishi Mahesh Yogi. I have been fortunate to meet and experience their grace and blessings during my lifetime. I had an opportunity to walk with the great karma yogi, Mahatma Gandhi, for an hour and a half in 1944. My father had taken me to Swami Nityananda of Ganeshpury many times in the '50s. I was fortunate to listen to the discourses given by Swami Chinmayananda in the '70s. These are experiences beyond the realm of all natural human faculties. Maharishi Mahesh Yogi's message is very simple, and comparable to the message of Buddha. Stressfulness is rampant in the fast-moving society of ours, so his message of introspection employing transcendental meditation is the right path to deal with stress.

I often have wondered if there is some purpose in life for all of us, just as light shines with a purpose. There is an important insight about light; I call it a quantum connection between Purusha and Prakriti. The speed of light is changeless and associated with changeless Purusha, and the changing attributes of light like velocity and color are associated with ever-changing Prakriti. Light is a beam of photon particles, or packets of energy; we do not see light; light helps us to see and discover everything in nature. Light therefore, in every sense, is seeing, and at a much higher level of mind, enlightening. Light is pure action with *purpose*, and it is attached to nothing. It is light initiating to create matter, energy, space, time, and all of us in this audience. And yes, therefore we all have purpose in our lives.

Through Maharishi, I have seen a purpose for me in bridging India and America together, in every way polar opposites, for the benefit of humanity with balance, harmony and complementarity.

Pleasures experienced by the outer body are momentary; they do not last long. We need to discover ourselves and connect with atman, residing at the deepest level of our layered body for Sat-Chit-Ananda, the true everlasting blissful state of mind. That is the true message Maharishi conveyed to us.

Pratima and I intend to spend the rest of our lives to spread his message in this world of ours.

Thank you, and Namaste.

Address by Mr. Doshi to Bridgebuilder Awardee, Rupert Sheldrake, LMu, September 2014

Good evening friends, welcome. One of the poignant quotes of Professor Huston Smith, a recipient of the year 2011 Bridgebuilder Award, is, and I quote, "Institutions are not pretty. Show me a pretty government. Healing is wonderful, but the American Medical Association? Learning is wonderful, but universities? The same is true for religion … religion is institutionalized spirituality." Apparently the field of science is also institutionalized; hard boundaries are drawn based upon bias and beliefs.

Dr. Rupert Sheldrake has categorized ten of them in his most recent book, *Set Science Free*. I wholeheartedly agree with him, and would like to comment on four of them supporting his critique through the lens of the Indic tradition. The laws of nature are fixed; not true, according to Indic tradition. Prakriti, meaning Nature, is always changing; it is never absolute. When materialists build walls around science, evolution stops. Science can never be complete, since every law needs to be kept in check as we gain more knowledge and experience.

Nature is purposeless, and evolution has no goal or direction; again not true. There is an important insight about light, I call it a link between Purusha and Prakriti. The speed of light is changeless and associated with Purusha, and the changing attributes of light like velocity and color are associated with Prakriti. Light is a beam of photon particles, or packets of energy; we do not see light; light helps us to see and discover everything in Nature. Light therefore, in every sense of the word, is seeing, and at a much higher level of mind, enlightening. Light is pure action with *purpose*, and it is attached to nothing. It is light that came down to create matter, energy, space, time, and all of us in this audience. And yes, we all have purpose in our lives.

Mind is inside the head; again, not true. Mind has no location in the space-time continuum. Mind, as I understand, is linked to all-pervading consciousness. We could call it a quantum or morphic connection.

Materialists also believe in upward causation, meaning they believe the primacy of matter over mind, and is equated to consciousness. Eastern traditions believe in downward causation where consciousness, that is Brahman, is the highest state of being, followed by the mind and the body, which is matter.

There are many more beliefs in the West that, at least to me, seem so irrational. Even today, when you Google to find the origin of zero, you will be surprised that several sites do not acknowledge India, though the United Nations has declared it to be India. Archeologists have proven using modern technology including genetics, that there was no Aryan invasion or migration of any kind into India. However they still keep teaching the Aryan invasion theory in schools both in the U.S. and India.

There is a war going on between materialists like Richard Dawkins, the author of *Selfish Gene*, and idealists like Rupert Sheldrake and John Hagelin, also internationally known authors. Fortunately there are more joining the ranks of idealists, but unfortunately materialists control the purse, as happened during Galileo's time when the Roman Catholic Church was controlling the purse. The church never accepted Galileo's Heliocentrism, meaning that planets revolve around the sun. He was persecuted and put under house arrest.

Today things are reversed. We are having this discussion in LMU, a Catholic university welcoming an open mind and breaking unnatural boundaries. We have two scientists in this gathering, Dr. Sheldrake, a biologist, and Dr. Hagelin, a physicist. I compare them with Darwin and Galileo, breaking boundaries to go beyond. In some ways they are freedom fighters like Gandhi and King, fighting to free the domain of philosophy from the shackles of hard materialists.

As a student of life, I wish to describe my understanding of our existence and "gurus of sciences"; please correct me wherever you find flaws in my understanding.

The work of a few physicists, in the mold of idealists, implies an affirmation of the Vedantic tradition that there is an ultimate self-conscious reality. This reality is the world and the cosmos we live in, but it is also the consciousness that contains and penetrates the cosmos in its totality. This ultimate reality is, subjectively speaking, infinite bliss, and objectively speaking, is infinite in quality and value that expresses and experiences itself.

This follows the top-down framework of the Vedantic kind with quality, value and consciousness rooted in the very heart of reality, as opposed to the bottom-up framework of the materialist kind. I also interpret that there is a nonlocal, meaning beyond the realm of perceivable space and time, quantum connection between individual subjective consciousness and the all-pervading objective super-consciousness. It has also been accepted that Nature within and without is fractal, meaning it is layered like an onion, in which each part contains the whole.

The implication here is that, not only our body and mind, but consciousness itself is layered and has discrete poises rising towards greater consciousness and wholeness. Sri Aurobindo pioneered this subject and claimed that humanity is on the evolutionary path of transcendence towards the ultimate reality.

The morphic field, as I understand, implies that collective memories within species are inherited, and the field establishes interconnectedness. We know we have two parents, four grandparents, eight great-grandparents, and so on. The world population is about eight billion or so. When we multiply two, thirty-three times, the number is larger than eight billion. The implication here is that any of us are at least a 33rd cousin of any other person. So we are connected genetically.

We know that Nature is layered, and so are we. My body is the undergarment of the garment I am wearing. When all the layers are removed, what remains at the deepest level, is atman, the individualized self-perception of Brahman. Atman is identical in all of us, so we are identical at the deepest level.

Resonance implies being in tune. Can morphic resonance under certain conditions unify humanity, just as resonance does in an optical laser, when photons spontaneously conform into a fine non-diverging, one-color beam of light? Vedic pandits at Maharishi University chant en masse to create an environment for peace. Could that possibly create a unified morphic resonance among all of us at the deepest level? Could it create paths to transcend towards becoming the realized superman that Aurobindo, Maharishi, and Nietzsche described?

So Dr. Sheldrake, it does not matter how you grade me, but this evening you are the man of the hour, receiving this year's Bridgebuilder Award.

Thank you, and Namaste.

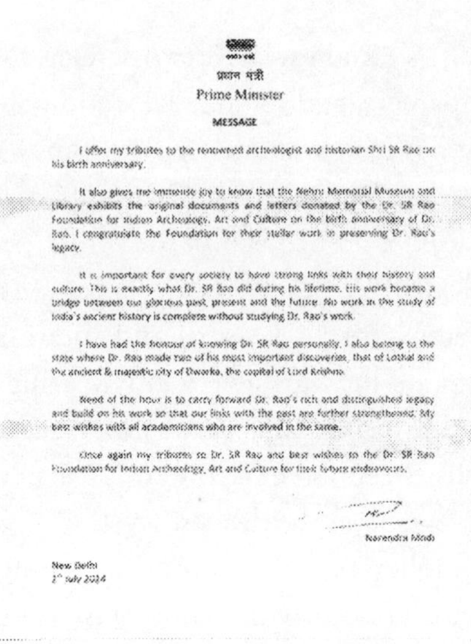

प्रधान मंत्री

Prime Minister

MESSAGE

I offer my tributes to the renowned archeologist and historian Shri SR Rao on his birth anniversary.

It also gives me immense joy to know that the Nehru Memorial Museum and Library exhibits the original documents and letters donated by the Dr. SR Rao Foundation for Indian Archeology, Art and Culture on the birth anniversary of Dr. Rao. I congratulate the Foundation for their stellar work in preserving Dr. Rao's legacy.

It is important for every society to have strong links with their history and culture. This is exactly what Dr. SR Rao did during his lifetime. His work became a bridge between our glorious past, present and the future. No work in the study of India's ancient history is complete without studying Dr. Rao's work.

I have had the honour of knowing Dr. SR Rao personally. I also belong to the state where Dr. Rao made two of his most important discoveries, that of Lothal and the ancient & majestic city of Dwarka, the capital of Lord Krishna.

Need of the hour is to carry forward Dr. Rao's rich and distinguished legacy and build on his work so that our links with the past are further strengthened. My best wishes with all academicians who are involved in the same.

Once again my tributes to Dr. SR Rao and best wishes to the Dr. SR Rao Foundation for Indian Archeology, Art and Culture for their future endeavours.

Narendra Modi

New Delhi

1st July 2014

A letter from the Prime Minister.

Foreword by Mr. Doshi Written for the Memorial Volume Honoring Professor S. R. Rao, Based on the Opening Speech at the Sindhu-Saraswati Conference at LMu, 2014

The memorial volume honoring Professor S. R. Rao had its origins in a conference on Sindhu-Saraswati civilization held at Loyola Marymount University on February21 and 22, 2009. It was sponsored by the Bridgebuilder Endowment of the Loyola Marymount University and Nalanda International, both of which I have the good fortune of founding and supporting. The conference was meant to be a reappraisal featuring the most recent research on the subject, looked at from different disciplines, but it was also meant to be a felicitation for Professor S. R. Rao, who was eighty-seven years old that year, and had traveled to Los Angeles from India to attend the conference. At eighty-seven, he was remarkably well kept and his mind was as sharp as a razor. No one could forget his enormous contributions to our understanding of this earliest civilization of South Asia, his discovery of a large number of its sites, his revolutionary excavation of the port city of Lothal in the '50s and '60s, his opening of the field of Marine Archeology and its use to establish the existence of Krishna's underwater city of Dwarka in 1979–80, and his continuing work on the decipherment of the Sindhu-Saraswati script, showing it to be a Sanskritic language. On the occasion, Professor Rao spoke of his most recent work on the script, with detailed reasoning on his decipherments. In 2013, Professor Rao departed from the physical plane, but his legacy continues in a many-directional advance towards the establishment of many of the intuitions he had about this civilization. This volume represents some of that large body of work that continues in the vast shade of his banyan-like erudition and eminence.

The essays here represent the state-of-the-art in research on Sindhu-Saraswati civilization, an amazing settlement that flourished 5,000 years ago, establishing itself as the largest and most sophisticated urban culture in history. The ruins of this impressive civilization are twice the size of the Egyptian and Sumerian societies combined. The fact that these proto-historic remains exist today in two nations separated by a common partition, makes one pause to consider how so much of our world is divided and even antagonized by differences of religion, economics, philosophy, and politics. It makes us rewind into our own origins and also fast-forward to the increasing technological prowess of contemporary humans and their ability to probe their own hidden pasts. If we travel thus back in time, we discover that each of us comes from a common ancestry that makes us all related. Through genetic studies, we know today that the most distant we are to anyone in the world is a 50th cousin.

We could ponder our earliest ancestors originating in Africa and imagine the first tribes of Homo sapiens migrating from there to Asia, to India, and on to Indonesia and further east. Concurrently, we would see these same ancestors parting and migrating north to China and America in the east and to Europe in the west. We could imagine how future generations from this common origin began to divide into many tribes. Soon the tribes lost the knowledge of their origin and taking each other to be different, began warfare for domination. Later, rulers arose with the imperial urge to control large territories and many peoples, and spread into empires that colonized most of the world. Abridged histories are written, often by the rulers of the time or the nations that dominated those moments in our past. Still, these nations, these civilizations all started as one.

As we return to recent times, our eagerness for knowledge has brought us the discovery that we are all intimately connected. Through the Internet, cell phones and GPS systems, our physical and cultural separations are giving way to the possibility of a knowledge of unity. This "body of humanity" is expanding its awareness in every field of human endeavor. This conference on the Sindhu-Saraswati civilization is another example of this expansion of knowledge. Though ostensibly we turned our gaze on the antiquity of South Asia, the ancestors of the peoples of the Indian subcontinent, it was in reality another chapter of the story of a common humanity that we gathered together to decipher, in the spirit of Professor Rao's archeological excavations on earth and sea, an excavation without bias for universal knowledge.

Both in piecing together the stories of the different peoples of the earth, and in the disciplinary approaches taken to gather these stories, we resemble the blind men of Hindustan spoken of in the Upanishads, each with their fixed belief in their interpretation of the elephant that confronted them. This has been the story of specialization in the modern world. But as we enter the 21st Century, we find ourselves embarking on a new curve of the circle, the inward curve of integration. The way here is to collaborate and synthesize the results of the varied knowledge workers, attempting to provide an integral description from their piecemeal knowledge. Professor Rao set the example for this spirit, utilizing varied tools — intuitional, hermeneutic, technological and cross-disciplinary — to arrive at a coherent understanding of the province of knowledge he set for himself. The papers in this volume are marked by this spirit of synergy and coherence. Evidence is probed for consistency; inconsistent results are reexamined. Integration of diverse approaches obtained from different fields of endeavor are attempted to bring forth the true image of the invisible "elephant in the room," the vast civilization that disappeared along with the missing river Saraswati.

Finally, though Professor Rao's passing is a great loss for all of us, I am heartened to see so much goodwill and enthusiasm by present-day scholars who have submitted their research to honor their great forerunner; and most of all, the work done by Professor Rao's daughter, Dr. Nalini Rao, for her tireless efforts in approaching the scholars for the conference and later editing their papers to consolidate the present volume. My thanks go out to her. My thanks also go to Professor Debashish Banerji, executive director of Nalanda International, for his organization and scholarship that have gone into the conference and this volume; and to Professor Chris Chapple, Doshi Professor at Loyola Marymount University, for arranging for the conference venue and helping with the complex logistics.

Navin Doshi, Los Angeles

Mr. Doshi with the future Prime Minister of India December 2013.

An Open Letter to the Prime Minister of India, 2014

Dear and respected Shree Narendra Bhai Modi:

I want to express my gratitude for seeing me and spending half an hour of your precious time, a few months before the election on December 3, 2013. I had then expressed my strong desire of your becoming the next prime minister of India, because the country needed the change in leadership so badly. I am sure that the majority of Indians, inside and outside of India, are jubilant that you will occupy the desired position within days. I do appreciate that you let me express my views for over 20 minutes on two evils, corruption and inflation, that people in India are suffering from.

Now I would like to express a few more thoughts about what the country needs in order of priority, or you could take action simultaneously. First, we must collectively provide the means to take care of every Indian, his/her somatic self (human body), the mother of the intellect, and the intuitive mind that leads to the path of transcendence. India needs to provide water, energy, and the right education, the education of the heart.

Such education will help us to create an exponentially increasing population of what Sri Aurobindo dreamed of as the supermen of the future, selfless enlightened beings like Rama, Krishna, Buddha, Mahavir, Nanak, and Gandhi. Such education will also help us to control the population. India needs to control the population, not by the force of law as implemented in China, but by using the right education and right incentives.

For providing water to Gujarat and Rajastan, we already have a project on the drawing board that needs to be implemented. The Kalpasar Project envisages building a dam across the Gulf of Khambat for generating tidal power and for establishing a huge reservoir for fresh water for irrigation, drinking, and industrial purposes. A 10-lane road link will also be set up over the dam, greatly reducing the distance between Saurashtra and South Gujarat.

The Gulf of Khambhat was identified as a promising site for tidal-power generation by UNDP expert, Mr. Eric Wilson, in the year 1975. Successive governments were then presented with the details of the possibility of a project, aptly named Kalpasar Project by its visionary Dr. Anil Kane, who conceptualized it in the '80s as a feasible project. In 1988–9 a reconnaissance report was prepared for the dam across the Gulf of Khambhat. The report concluded that, assuming sound foundation conditions, the closure of the gulf was technically feasible.

A state government release said the Rs 55,000 crore (US$ 11.7 billion) project, to be completed by 2020, will have a vast fresh water reservoir with a gross storage of 16,791 million cubic meters of water, with a 35-km-long dam across the Gulf of Khambhat connecting Ghogha in Bhavnagar with Hansot in the Bharuch District, reducing the distance between the two by 225 km. It will have a tidal-power generation house with an installed capacity of 5,880 MW. Another estimate was given by the government in October 2010, which stated the proposed dam be built just north of Bhavnagar in the west to Alandar in Dahej in the east. We need to look into such projects all around the Indian coastline. India is blessed with one of the longest coastlines compared to most countries, large and small.

In matters of energy production, India is blessed with an abundant supply of thorium. Thorium-based nuclear power is electrical power generation from nuclear reactors, fueled primarily by the fission of theisotope uranium-233 produced from the fertile element thorium. According to proponents, a thorium fuel cycle offers several potential advantages over a uranium fuel cycle —including much greater abundance on earth, superior physical and nuclear fuel properties, and reduced nuclear waste production. Proponents also cite the lack of weaponization potential as an advantage of thorium, while critics say that the development of breeder reactors in general (including thorium reactors that are breeders by nature) increase proliferation concerns. Since about 2008, nuclear energy experts have become more interested in thorium to supply nuclear fuel in place of uranium to generate nuclear power.

Some believe thorium is the key to developing a new generation of cleaner, safer nuclear power. According to an opinion piece by a group of scientists at the Georgia Institute of Technology, considering its overall potential, thorium-based power "can mean a 1000+ year solution or a quality low-carbon bridge to truly sustainable energy sources solving a huge portion of mankind's negative environmental impact. India is also blessed with natural gas that could provide energy for the immediate need of the country."

One of the immediate problems, so painful to the common man, is the rampant inflation. You need to work with Raghuram

Rajan, for whom I have high regard (I met him once briefly before he became chief of the Reserve Bank of India), by anchoring the rupee to another stable and friendly currency, or a selected precious metal. We need to remember that a gram of gold in 1947 was about a rupee, or a dollar. Today, the same gram of gold fetches about 2,700 rupees or about 42 dollars.

The black money of Indians stashed in Swiss banks is estimated to be about one-and-a-half trillion dollars. This money, if it is brought back to India by employing every trick, would be a windfall to the country's economy. The rupee as a currency should remain strong for decades to come. The dollar has been more stable because the great Western powers after WWII, supported by English-speaking Western countries, made the dollar a world reserve currency. The rupee should also become part of a future SDR (a future world currency devised by employing multiple currencies issued by IMF) whenever it comes into existence.

I also believe that the Non Aligned Movement of late Prime Minister Nehru has not helped to create strong friends. We must always be on the right side instead of being in a grey area, establishing our moral authority.

Why should we consider India as the center or mother of all civilizations, all traditions? Only in India, powerful kings like Buddha, Mahavir, and Asoka gave away wealth and power to transcend and discover the real human heart of love and compassion.

Do we remember what Mahatma Gandhi said about different religions? He said, "I am a Hindu, a Muslim, a Sikh, a Christian, a Jew, … all of them. Because I have an equal regard for each of them."

You could say, "I do agree with what Mahatma said." Let me elaborate a bit more. I admire the Muslim faith because of their devotion or Bhakti to Allah, similar to Bhakti Yoga. I admire the Buddhist faith because of their intellectual discourse on Nirvana, and the discovery of Sunyata or Zero or Nothingness, similar to the Niraguna Brahman of Vedanta; that I believe is the essence of Jnana Yoga. I admire the Sikh, and the Christian faith for their work ethics and love for their fellow human beings, similar to Karma and Raja Yoga. However, I am a born Hindu, and we believe in Sanatan dharma, the eternal seeking for God, respecting all of these faiths. Only in India have the principles of Sanatan dharma been practiced for millennia, welcoming people of all different faiths, even some persecuted."

Address by Chief guest Navin Doshi at BAPS Temple, June 2013

Early philosophers gazed at stars, and derived their inspiration looking at the Sun and beyond. Philosophers from many traditions started worshiping the Sun God in India and elsewhere; Moses came with the Ten Commandments, gazing at the sky. The Upanishads, a collection of philosophical texts written by unknown authors, considered the "last word" of the Vedas, were composed during this time frame. This was a spiritual quest gazing at the light of the cosmos, beyond the human self. For those early Homo sapiens, without the current knowledge of quantum physics, light that is changeless and not seen, but helps us to see with purpose, is intuitively accepted to be supreme. The primacy of light over mind, matter, and changing Nature was ingrained without any doubt.

Then the human focus shifted from the skies to the intellectual mind, within the human self. King David of Israel established laws for the Jews. In India, Kautilya gave *Arthasastra* to his king, millennia before Italian Machiavelli's book, *The Prince.*

Then the focus of humanity shifted to the intuitive mind, residing in the heart. Krishna in the Bhagavad Gita, described the path of devotion, also known as Bhakti Yoga. "Love thy neighbor," so preached the Christ. Many more saints elaborated on the heart, a symbol of love, during the expanse of time.

The human population increased in leaps and bounds. Malthus saw the human population multiply much faster than the food supply needed for the masses. The focus changed again; it came down to the stomach. Karl Marx and Gandhi saw the starving masses enslaved by the rich and powerful and by the colonial powers. They both believed in simplicity and singleness of purpose; they had their differences in matters of achieving the goal. More such leaders came on board all over the world. There were power struggles. Many wars, including two very destructive World Wars, erupted during the period of over 120 years.

But the focus changed again even lower, to the sex organs, thanks to Sigmund Freud. The Kama Sutra was composed in India centuries earlier. Today, the whole prosperous world seems to be enamored by sexual pleasures, broadcast during the late evening hours, along with crimes related to sex. Humanity seems to be descending down the ladder of the Kundalini chakras at this juncture.

But thank God, we have scientists like Einstein, Plank, and Schrodinger, and philosophers like Aurobindo, Emerson, and Neitzche. These philosophers went beyond intellectualism. They were all in line with the Eastern view that transcendence towards the selfless being has to be through intuition, introspection, and personal experiences. Einstein concluded, using complex mathematical equations and the human intellect, that everything is relative; time, space, matter, and energy are changeable, they are not absolute. Vedanta concluded the same, employing the intuitive mind and experience many millennia ago. But just as the speed of light is constant among all temporaries for Einstein, Vedanta postulated transcendence that was eternal among the permanence of the world. Statements like "Unity in diversity"; "There are many paths to the mountaintop"; "The truth is like many facets of a diamond"; and the story of the blind men of Hindustan prove my claim. Note that I am also a believer of scientist Rupert Sheldrake's findings of the morphic field. The morphic field, just as Vedanta claims, connects people, plants, animals, and the whole universe.

Modern technology should help us by employing the knowledge and wisdom that is good for the whole living organism called Mother Earth, and stop reinventing the wheel again and again. IBM estimates that every day we now generate 2.5 quintillian bits of data (that is one with eighteen zeros), and we have now fast computers to process this data.

So where do we go from here? I am a believer in strong deep roots, as I have written in my two books, *Transcendence* and *Economics and Nature.* The British, during their colonial rule, discarded the suggestion by French philosopher Voltaire establishing the roots of human civilization in India. However the British did not want to lose India, the crown jewel of their empire; they maintained the roots of Western civilization were in Greece.

We must claim the deepest roots of Homo sapiens that start in Africa. This is true physically, but philosophically, Vedanta can be seen as having the deepest, longest, strongest, and among the most prominent roots of human civilization.

Today, it seems to me that we are in the thickest night of Kali Yuga. There is a war going on between the instinctive and intuitive heart of the common people and the deceitful intellect of the power elites. The elite, among them some psychopaths, are able to trade hard labor, the skill of wage earners, and the stuff that has maintained a decent value over millennia, with digital and printed paper money of lesser value, employing their most advanced technology. However the laws of Nature categorically state that increasing complexity increases the chances of catastrophic black swan events.

When you see increasing polarization, the rich getting richer, a shrinking middle class, the poor getting poorer, such huge unemployment in younger generations the world over including Western countries, and literally anarchy in many developing countries, I wonder, where are the philosopher kings to bring social and economic fairness? If we are not careful, we could experience the kinds of anarchic revolutions that occurred in France, Russia, and China.

A great effort needs to be in place to educate kings and captains of humanity and future generations to change their mindset. The ancient Rishis of Vedanta claim that there are real paths to a much superior state of mind, as Buddha, Christ, and later philosopher saints like Nietzche, Sri Aurobindo, and Shri Pramukh Swami have explained. Yes, evolution may help humanity to transcend to Nietzsche's Overman or Aurobindo's Superman. As these two great philosophers have suggested, we are currently, like a bridge, between the world of animals and highly evolved, selfless, super human beings. But how can we make this evolution conscious?

Perhaps, we could construct a model for the mind based upon the Greek model for the body, namely the Olympics. Why not have an Olympics of the mind, possibly organized by organizations like BAPS, where we could have competition among students to become more compassionate and more charitable. How could we transform a selfish and deceitful intellect to an intellect subservient to a loving heart?

Thank you.

Address by Navin Doshi, Chairman of the Nalanda Confluence Institute, August 2012

To the assembled guests present to witness the signing of an agreement to establish a program of Hindu Studies at Claremont Lincoln University, President Campbell, Dean Clayton, honorable guests and friends, good afternoon.

Surfing on the CLU website, I was pleasantly surprised to find words that were uttered many millennia ago back in India — that religions have deep wells of wisdom that speak to the best within humanity … if we'll only stop, listen, and understand.

We are all descendents of Homo sapiens, who originated in Ethiopia, then migrated north and east around the Red Sea to Iran and India, and then on to Europe, China, and the Americas. This scenario is based upon recent discoveries made in the fields of archeology and genetics.

Historically, our ancestors protected themselves by staying in clusters or tribes. Cluster formation is very natural at every level;

blood clots are clusters at the micro level, just as galaxies are at the astronomical level. In time, great human civilizations appeared in different parts of the world. Great religions were developed employing life experience, intuition, and intellect.

Now, it seems to me the direction is reversing. We realize after all, that we are all human beings. Genetics and aeroplanes connect all of us Homo sapiens in the somatic realm; technology like cell phones, the Internet, Google, and GPS systems keep us connected in the psychic realm.

The world is not only increasingly getting smaller, there is a greater realization that we are one family; each of us is related, some more distant, some closer. We have two parents, four grandparents, eight great-grandparents, and so on. The total population of Homo sapiens is a little over seven billion. If we were to multiply the number two 33 times, where each multiplication represents one generation, the product comes out to be about eight-and-a-half billion. The implication of this simple exercise is that ... every human being is at least your 33rd cousin.

The earth is huge with its seven billion inhabitants. Humans have become a force of Nature reshaping the planet on a geological scale, at a far-faster-than-geological speed. A single engineering project, the Syncrude mine in the tar sands of Canada, involves moving 30 billion tons of earth, twice the amount of sediment that flows down all the rivers in the world in a year.

Geologists look at fossils and at other forces that have shaped the planet. Now a number of these scientists are hypothesizing that future geologists observing this moment in the Earth's progress will conclude that something very odd was going on. Scientists are increasingly using a new name for this new period in the earth's history. Rather than placing us still in the Holocene, a stable era that began around 10,000 years ago, geologists say we have moved into the Anthropocene: the age of man. The Anthropocene is different. It is one of those moments where a scientific realization could fundamentally change people's view of things. It means thinking afresh about the relationship between people and their world. Too many scientists still embrace the assumption that Nature can be studied in isolation from the human world, with people as mere observers. But this "objective truth" of Newton and Einstein is less and less relevant in the Anthropocene — we humans matter, more than ever in the past. The subjective truth of Tagore is becoming more relevant.

The sheer amount of biomass now walking around the planet in the form of humans and livestock handily outweighs that of all other large animals. The world's ecosystems are dominated by increasingly homogeneous crops, livestock and creatures that get on well in environments dominated by humans. Creatures less useful or adaptable don't survive: the extinction rate is running far higher than during normal geological periods. A planet that could soon be supporting as many as 10 billion human beings has to work differently from the one that held one billion people, mostly peasants, only 200 years ago. This outward expansion, together with the cultural evolution of the last 200 years, is due to the creative order-generating activity of the human mind, as I have described in my book, *Transcendence.*

The challenge of the Anthropocene is to use human ingenuity to set things up so that the planet can accomplish its planetary functions in the 21st Century. One message of the Anthropocene age is that we need to curtail the external, material growth and reverse the expansion to a growth within. Now each of us, which includes all of us in this audience, are the bearers of collective human experience.

What do we need to do to get even closer, more united, giving equal importance to our environment? I suspect we could do it by educating ourselves through introspection, by discovering a brighter and brighter light. We are all ignorant in many ways. Even Einstein, in spite of his brilliance, exhibited his ignorance in matters of quantum mechanics when he made the statement, "God does not play dice." There is a story told about him. After his death, he meets God at Heaven's gate. Being so curious, he asks the question, "I am puzzled my Lord, is Schrodinger's equation valid? You would not introduce uncertainty in the workings of Nature, would you?" After a pause, God answers, "My dear Albert, you must play dice, since I do not play favorite. If I had only certainty in Nature, life would be so dull, boring; sports would not exist; women would not be able to play games with men."

So here is one metaphor to consider. Think of CLU as a mountain and think of many paths leading towards the mountaintop. This mountaintop represents collective human experience, and each path is a personal journey towards the understanding of All. All religions, which have so long existed in isolation, can begin to recognize the others and discover the vistas they bring as complementary to their own.

Think of Phil Clayton, Rita, Debashish, Deepak, Chris, and many more as mountain guides, all available at the foothills of the CLU mountain. Vivekananda, whose 150th birth anniversary we will celebrate next year, saw a variation of this same vision, adapted from the Upanishads. He declared this in his famous address given at the Parliament of World Religions in Chicago in 1893. He saw all the religions of the world as many rivers that followed different paths to the same ocean. The significance of the mountaintop, tending to shrink towards a dot, implies the philosophy of the "Sunyata" of Buddhism, meaning nothingness or Advaita's Nirguna Brahmana. The significance of the ocean, tending towards infinity, implies the all-embracing Saguna Brahmana. These are both metaphors for the Transcendent Being that embraces all and is yet beyond everything.

Similarly, Mahatma Gandhi had a reverence, respect and acceptance of all traditions, as I described in my book, *Transcendence*. I presented this book to the former president of India, A. P. J. Abdul Kalam. Let me end with his quote in an email I received later:

"Dear Navinji, Thank you for your book. I am really moved by your last paragraph on Gandhi's spirituality. 'You may change the path to go around the obstacles, so long as the direction is towards the mountaintop, where all paths meet.' Beautiful and enchanting."

From left: LMU President David Burcham, Huston Smith, Mrs. Doshi, Professor Chapple, and Mr. Doshi, 2011.

Address by Mr. Doshi to Bridgebuilder Awardee, Huston Smith, 2011

Salmubarak or Happy New Year, friends. Today begins the New Year based upon our Indian tradition. First, I would like to congratulate President David Burcham for becoming the first non-Catholic president of Loyola Marymount University. LMU apparently is following the tradition of another great university that was established about 2,000 years ago in India. Nalanda associated with the Buddhist tradition, and LMU associated with the Catholic tradition, are universities dedicated to learning almost every aspect of human endeavor with an open mind. In the wonderful California climate, overlooking the Pacific Ocean, maybe having a glass of wine, where else can you learn, contemplate and philosophize on a subject of your choosing but here on this beautiful LMU campus?

Again, in my mind, today's recipient of the Bridgebuilder Award, Dr. Huston Smith, is a perfect fit for this award. Why? Because he has been building bridges both in time and in space domains not just for a few years but for multiple decades, not just at one place but in multiple continents, not just with one tradition but with multiple traditions. He reminds me of a chakra, a wheel with a hub and spokes. The Divine resides at the center and the spokes are the paths for God-realization. He has traversed almost all spokes of this chakra.

When I met him for the first time, I became his student and friend instantly. He is a ninety-plus-years sage with a vast experience of life, a sharp mind, and an ability to observe in minute detail. Being a student, I sent him my "thesis," my book *Transcendence.* A few days later, I received the following note from him:

"My dear new-found friend, I have spent an inspiring and uplifting Fourth of July weekend, not watching brilliant displays of fireworks in the sky but reading a brilliant display of profound, insightful, and inspiring ideas in your book. Among many accolades I read, I do not see one that jumps out of my mind. Please add to it that you are a very wiseman." When I read it, I was propelled to Cloud Nine. Only then, I felt that I had passed the test.

Now, a few words about my guru. If you Google his name, you can read the whole shebang about his accomplishments. So I will be very brief so that we have more time to hear him. Like the great scholar-mystics of all ages, Dr. Smith has been a beacon for the kind of scholarship that walks its talk through experience and personal practice. Introduced to Christianity and the Chinese traditions of Confucianism, Taosim and Buddhism from his childhood, Dr. Smith went on to explore Hinduism, Zen Buddhism and Islamic Sufism, studying each under a realized master for over 10 years until he arrived at their spiritual experiences. He has also made deep forays into shamanism and the use of psychoactive substances to induce occult or spiritual experiences.

Dr. Smith developed an interest in the Traditionalist School formulated by Rene Guenon and Ananda Coomaraswamy. This interest has become a continuing thread in all his writings.

In late 19th century India, there was a mystic whom Dr. Smith has often referred to in his talks and writings, whose inexhaustible thirst for the Divine pushed him to realize the Divine in every religious and sectarian tradition he found. This was Sri Ramakrishna, whose worldwide ecumenical spirit made him declare, "Jato mat tato path" or "There are as many ways to God as there are opinions." Truly Dr. Smith can be thought of as a living image of Sri Ramakrishna in our times. Radiant with the bliss of god-realization, Dr. Smith is a living example of the perennial philosophy that he espouses and which was announced in the great wisdom teaching of the earliest sacred text of the world, the Vedas: "Ekam sat viprah bahudha badanti." "There is one truth; the sages speak of it in many ways."

When asked whether all great religions lead to salvation, Dr. Smith's answer is an unequivocal yes. Religion, he says, is like a walnut. "The shell is exoteric, it's outside, visible. The kernel is esoteric, invisible. Both are important … Esoterically, religions are identical. Exoterically, they are different." Here is another of his very poignant quotes.

"Institutions are not pretty. Show me a pretty government. Healing is wonderful, but the American Medical Association? Learning is wonderful, but universities? The same is true for religion … religion is institutionalized spirituality."

My dear friend Huston, congratulations, and thank you for all you have done for humanity.

Address by Mr. Doshi to Bridgebuilder Awardee, Vandana Shiva, 2010/11

Good evening friends. I would like to describe two realities that seem to me difficult to reconcile. I hope Dr. Shiva will enlighten us with her realistic views informed by her idealistic vision.

Let me review what I believe we know about our existence within and without. First, the within. Based upon the works of at least two physicists, Amit Goswami and Ulrich Mohrhoff of Germany working independently and a pole apart, there is affirmation of the Vedantic view that there is an ultimate self-conscious reality. This reality is our existent world. It is also the consciousness that contains and penetrates the cosmos in its totality. This ultimate reality is, subjectively speaking, infinite bliss. Objectively speaking, it is infinite in any quality and value we can imagine that expresses and experiences itself. This follows the top-down framework of the Vedantic kind. Quality, value and consciousness are rooted in the very heart of this reality. This differs from the bottom-up framework of the materialist kind with no idealism associated with it. Note that the universe exists both by itself in the material sense, and for itself in the sense of consciousness. I also interpret it that there is non-local quantum connection between individual subjective consciousness and the all-pervading objective super-consciousness beyond the bounds of Nature. It has been accepted by scientists that Nature is fractal. It is layered like an onion within and without, and each part contains the whole.

The implication here is that not only our mind but consciousness itself is layered and has discrete poises rising towards the threshold of super-consciousness. Sri Aurobindo pioneered this insight and claimed that humanity is on the evolutionary path of transcendence towards the ultimate reality.

At this juncture, I quote Dr. Shiva: "Gandhi is the only person who knew about real democracy — not democracy as the right to go and buy what you want, but democracy as the responsibility to be accountable to everyone around you. Democracy begins with freedom from hunger, freedom from unemployment, freedom from fear, and freedom from hatred. Those are the real freedoms on the basis of which good societies are based." In such societies, adds Dr. Shiva, "The currency of Nature's economy is life, not money." I believe such societies would indeed be a fertile ground to realize the vision of Gandhi and Sri Aurobindo, based upon the unity we desire. However, there is another reality associated with human existence on our planet Earth that I am sure Dr. Shiva is quite familiar with. The earth is huge with its seven billion inhabitants. Humans have become a force of Nature, reshaping the planet on a geological scale at a far-faster-than-geological speed. A single engineering project, the Syncrude mine in the tar sands of Canada, involves moving 30 billion tons of earth — twice the amount of sediment that flows down all the rivers in the world in a year. Geologists look at fossils and other forces that have shaped the planet. Now a number of these scientists are hypothesizing that future geologists observing this moment in the Earth's progress will conclude that something very odd was going on. Scientists are increasingly using a new name for this new period. Rather than placing us still in the Holocene, a stable era that began around 10,000 years ago, geologists say we are already living in the Anthropocene, the age of man. The Anthropocene is different. It is one of those moments where a paradigm shift has occurred. It means thinking afresh about the relationship between people and their world. Too many scientists still embrace the view that Nature can be studied in isolation from the human world, with people as mere observers. There is no more the absolute objective truth of Newton and Einstein — we humans matter, more than ever in the past. The subjective cosmos of Tagore is becoming more relevant.

The sheer amount of biomass now walking around the planet in the form of humans and livestock handily outweighs that of all other large animals. The world's ecosystems are dominated by an increasingly homogeneous set of crops, livestock and creatures that get on well in environments tamed, controlled and exploited by humans. Creatures less useful or adaptable don't survive: the extinction rate is running far higher than during normal geological periods. A planet that could soon be supporting as many as 10 billion human beings has to work differently from the one that held one billion people, mostly peasants, only 200 years ago. This outward expansion, together with the cultural evolution of the last 200 years, is due to the creative order-generating activity of the human mind, as I have described in my book, *Transcendence.*

The challenge of the *Anthropocene* is to use human ingenuity to set things up so that the planet can accomplish its planetary functions in the 21st Century. One message of the Anthropocene age is that piecemeal actions can add up to planetary change prolonging or destroying human existence on the planet.

Another quote of Dr. Shiva associated with the reality of Anthropocene: "Globalized industrialized food is not cheap: it is too costly for the Earth, for the farmers, for our health. The Earth can no longer carry the burden of groundwater mining, pesticide pollution, disappearance of species, and destabilization of the climate. Farmers can no longer carry the burden of debt, which is inevitable in industrial farming with its high costs of production. It is incapable of producing safe, culturally appropriate, quality food. And it is incapable of producing enough food for all because it is wasteful of land, water and energy. Industrial agriculture uses ten times more energy than it produces."

Today we observe that people all over the world are revolting against the empire builders and exploiters of Nature and civilization, thanks to the reality created in the Anthropocene age. I consider Dr. Shiva an embodiment of Shakti, the conscious force that has become this cosmos and expresses itself through everything in it. Please, Dr. Shiva, enlighten us, guide us.

Address by Navin Doshi to Bridgebuilder Awardee, greg Mortenson, 2009

Good evening, friends.

India, Pakistan, Nepal, Bangladesh and Afghanistan are all part of a vast region known as the Indian subcontinent, a world within a world that stretches from the Himalayan Mountains down to the Indian Ocean, home to over a billion people. People of all races and religions live in this region, speaking hundreds of languages and dialects. Archaeologists have dated the first settlements of Homo sapiens on the west coast of the subcontinent to over 35,000 years ago, long before the Ice Age, and long before any humans reached the Americas. In ancient times, trade along the Silk Road route connected the peoples of Asia, Africa and Europe, bringing Buddhism and its message of peace and meditation, and early forms of Christianity to Asia and the Middle East. A thousand years ago, some of these people chose to embrace Islam, adapting it to the unique mountainous landscape.

Like the early explorers, Greg Mortenson first ventured into this highest area of the planet hoping to conquer K2, the world's second-highest mountain peak. On the way down, he discovered a village in dire need of things that we take for granted, namely education and medical care. By acquiring needed materials and money through hardship and determination, he was able to start his life's work with one school and one clinic. Along the way, he has built bridges, not only across a mountain chasm but between peoples of different faith, uplanders and lowlanders, Westerners and Easterners, rich and poor.

My wife Pratima and I are both from the Indian state of Gujarat, adjacent to Pakistan. Indians and Pakistanis are in reality the closest of cousins and have a common history, culture and traditions of many millennia. In fact, if Mahatma Gandhi's wishes had been followed, we would have been citizens of only one country.

Good and evil in the Eastern traditions are an inseparable pair of opposites, where evil is ignorance and good is knowledge. The only way to remove evil is through education. By helping these people who have fallen behind in so many ways over the past fifty years, Greg is showing the right way similar to what the early Buddhists did, employing the best of human attributes. Greg's schools and clinics are winning the minds and hearts of people, and I hope he extends his work all over the Asian subcontinent.

Recognizing his magnificent obsession to create a legacy of education and friendship, we recognize his magnanimity to humanity. In *Three Cups of Tea*, Greg says, "My friends' village in the upper Braldu Valley has no bridge. I'm going to help them build one." These few words make Greg the very essence of a bridgebuilder, so we are indeed honored this evening to present to him the LMU Doshi Bridgebuilder Award. Thank you.

From left: His Holiness Thich Nhat Hanh showing the award, Professor Chapple, LMU Vice President Rose, and Mrs. and Mr. Doshi, 2008.

Address by Mr. Doshi to Bridgebuilder Awardee, Thich Nhat Hanh, 2008

Good morning friends.

I take a lot of pride to be in the company of Venerable Thich Nhat Hanh. The initial letters of these four words also apply to a visionary, teacher, and Nirvanic humanitarian. TNH, a Buddhist monk, is a pacifist who has lived in exile from Vietnam for over forty years.

His Holiness Thich Nhat Hanh with the Doshis, 2008.

During the war in Vietnam, he worked tirelessly for reconciliation between North and South Vietnam. In that year of 1966, both the non-Communist and Communist governments banned him for his role in denouncing the violence he saw affecting his people. A Buddhist monk since the age of sixteen, Thich Nhat Hanh earned a reputation as a respected writer, scholar, and leader. He championed a movement known as "engaged Buddhism," which intertwined traditional meditative practices with active nonviolent civil disobedience. He also set up relief organizations to rebuild destroyed villages, instituted the School of Youth for Social Service (a Peace Corps of sorts for Buddhist peace workers), founded a peace magazine, and urged world leaders to use nonviolence as a tool. Although his struggle for cooperation meant he had to relinquish his homeland, it won him accolades around the world.

When Thich Nhat Hanh left Vietnam, he embarked on a mission to spread Buddhist thought around the globe. In 1966, when he came to the United States for the first of many humanitarian visits, the territory was not completely new to him; he had experienced American culture as a student at Princeton, and more recently as a professor at Columbia. The Fellowship of Reconciliation at Cornell invited Thich Nhat Hanh to speak on behalf of Buddhist monks, and he offered an enlightened view on ways to end the Vietnam conflict. He spoke on college campuses, met with administration officials, and impressed social dignitaries. The following year, Nobel Peace Prize winner Dr. Martin Luther King Jr. nominated Thich Nhat Hanh for the same honor. Hanh's Buddhist delegation to the Paris peace talks resulted in accords between North Vietnam and the United States, but his pacifist efforts did not end with the war. He also helped organize rescue missions well into the '70s for Vietnamese trying to escape from political oppression. Even after the political stabilization of Vietnam, Thich Nhat Hanh has not been allowed to return home. The government still sees him as a threat — ironic when one considers the subjects of his teachings: respect for life, generosity, responsible sexual behavior, loving communication, and the cultivation of a healthful lifestyle.

Despite the fact that Thich Nhat Hanh is nearing eighty-two, his strength as a world leader and spiritual guide grows. He has written more than seventy-five books of prose, poetry, and prayers. For at least a decade, Thich Nhat Hanh has visited the United States every other year; he draws more and more people with each tour, Christian, Hindu, Jewish, atheist, and Zen Buddhist alike. His philosophy is not limited to preexistent religious structures, but speaks to the individual's desire for wholeness and inner calm. Clearly, Thich Nhat Hanh is a human link with a prophetic past, a soft-spoken advocate of peace for the Buddhist community and the American citizen.

And today, ladies and gentlemen, we are here at Loyola Marymount University — a Christian college, to honor Thich Nhat Hanh — a Buddhist monk, with the Doshi Bridgebuilder Award, endowed by a Hindu family. Isn't it a wonderful event that acknowledges and reveres every human tradition? This to me is real bridgebuilding here at LMU. Thank you, Vice President Rose and Father Engh, and thank you, Chris and Bob.

This is where we must take a step back and look at our past. Going back tens of thousands of years, we see our oldest great-great-great-grandfathers originating in Ethiopia. The African tribes of Homo sapiens migrated to India, central Asia, then moved to the west to Europe, and to China, Alaska and the Americas. Ever since, we have been connected in some shape or form. And with today's technology of the internet, cell phones and GPS systems, we are more connected than ever. Humanity is now, more than ever before, transcending from individual consciousness and moving towards a unified consciousness. This is all part of evolution within and evolution without. And now we need to evolve within, that is, in the psychological domain at higher speed. This is where the wisdom of scholars, saints and philosophers like Thich Nhat Hanh (TNH) is indispensable to us. Pratima and I are greatly honored to present Thich Nhat Hanh with the Doshi Family Bridgebuilder Award for 2007–8.

Address by Mr. Doshi to Bridgebuilder Awardee, Zubin Mehta, 2007

Good afternoon, ladies and gentleman, and welcome to the second annual Bridgebuilder Award program. First and foremost, I would like to thank our friends, many of them also philanthropists who have helped the community and our countries, America and India, who grace this event. Who is a bridgebuilder and what is a bridge? Simply put, bridges are connections between different cultures and traditions, bringing them together.

These subtle bridges, for example, between India and America have come in various forms, from Dr. Martin Luther King Jr.'s advocating Gandhi's "ahimsa" to Ravi Shankar making "sitar" a household word. Today we have with us a man of extraordinary talent and charisma. A man who has fully comprehended and appreciated the Indian tradition that human existence lies within the multiple boundaries of opposites, like good and evil; simple and complex; noise and melody. He is a man who, by the facility of his music, has managed to balance these opposites in perfect accord, allowing them to complement each other.

Maestro Zubin Mehta with Mr. Navin Doshi, 2007.

From left: Mr. and Mrs. Doshi, Mr. and Mrs. Mehta, and Professor Chapple, 2007.

Starting out with the intention of studying medicine, Zubin Mehta found his calling and was a student of music by the age of eighteen in Vienna under Hans Swarowsky. With time, like a fine wine, Mr. Mehta's capabilities matured. He was appointed director of the Los Angeles Philharmonic Orchestra in 1962, and the New York Philharmonic from 1978 to 1991, the longest holder of this post. The Israel Philharmonic Orchestra appointed Mr. Mehta music director in 1977, and made him music director for life in 1981. After all, he is a Gujurati, also known as a "guju" or a "good Jew."

Mr. Mehta realized a long-time ambition in 1994, when he brought the Israel Philharmonic Orchestra to his birthplace, India. By conducting in Bombay and New Delhi, he helped bridge a political gap that had prevented the orchestra from performing there for three decades. His affection for the orchestra so close to his heart, combined with the love of his motherland, made this tour one of the most memorable events of his life. No wonder someone has stated that India is in his marrow.

In 2001, Mr. Zubin Mehta was awarded the Padma Vibhushan, a monumental civilian award in India. On December 26, 2005, the first anniversary of the Indian Ocean tsunami, Zubin Mehta performed at the Madras Music Academy in Chennai to raise funds for the victims. Zubin is in the company of a very few great achievers, like Gandhi and Nehru, also of Indian origin, by being portrayed on a cover of *TIME* Magazine. He is the only person from India honored at the Kennedy Center.

I would like to share an experience I had of Zubin while we were coming home on a Los Angeles–bound TWA flight sometime in the '70s. I initiated a conversation complementing him and talking about our native city Bombay while we were waiting for our luggage to arrive. When a man of his stature offered to help me carry a heavy bundle of textile samples, I was pleasantly shocked at his humility and friendliness. Zubin is obviously no prima donna, like the conductor in the movie *Once More with Feelings*, played by Yul Brynner.

Saints of all traditions believe that the substance of spirituality is Universal Love. Love binds humanity together and it also extends outwards to include much more. It is this love and this passion for his music that has made Mr. Zubin Mehta a notable bridgebuilder between the East and the West. The world needs more bridgebuilders whose rare, clear vision inspires us all.

Ladies and gentlemen, Maestro Zubin Mehta.

Dr. Deepak Chopra with Mrs. Doshi, 2006.

Address by Navin Doshi to the First Bridgebuilder Awardee, Dr. Deepak Chopra, 2006

Dr. Chopra, LMU Vice President Rose, and friends: First, I want to explain what bridgebuilding is and who is a bridgebuilder. Building bridges allows us to establish contact, communication, and helps us synthesize differences between two opposites. We must recognize that Nature has created pairs of opposites around us and also in every field of human endeavor. Pairs of opposites, for example, include good and evil, the north pole and the south pole of a magnet, and these opposites cannot be separated from each other. In face, evil is ignorance and the raw material of good. Every Indian tradition believes in balancing the opposites of every pair, maintaining harmony while complementing each other.

The truth is discovered in two different ways, intellectually in a state of being and by participating in a process. In the origin of science, there has been a reductionist approach based on division and analysis, conducted by an observer. An objective observer is a being separated from the rest of the world. Becoming, that is, participating, and experiencing through spontaneous revelation is another wayof discovering truth. The ultimate human goal is to unify everything including fundamental natural forces and certainly humanity. Truth therefore is the reason to discover or build a bridge between elements of every pair of opposites for unification.

When we think of a network or a web, there are nodes or centers and links connecting these centers. Links or bridges unify and make a network. Disconnected centers without links have littleor no value. Friends, I hope I have convinced you how important the links and bridges and their builders are for unification.

Now let us talk about a few examples of good bridgebuilders. Dr. Martin Luther King Jr. built a bridge to unify a divided America by introducing Mahatma Gandhi's ahimsa, that is, a movement of nonviolence as a cornerstone to his civil rights movement. By doing so, he also built a bridge between America and India. Music Maestro Ravi Shankar of India did the same by making "sitar" a household word among music lovers in America.

Among the first bridgebuilders in the early 20th Century was Swami Vivekananda, who participated in a conference of world religions and held the audience spellbound. His influence affected the writer Frank Baum, whose books included the American classic, *The Wizard of Oz*. Writer Dhaliwal convincingly argues that there is some influence of Indian scriptures in Baum's work.

Another early bridgebuilder between America and India was J. Krishnamurti, who was raised and educated by the Theosophical Society. Many of you may not know that the Theosophical Society initiated the process of building the Hollywood Bowl so that Krishnamurti could speak to a very large audience.

Late in the year 2004, former President Clinton, at the opening of the Clinton Library, declared that he plans to spend the rest of his life building bridges between two opponents. Before I say a few words about Dr. Chopra, our Bridgebuilder of the Year, I should explain a bit about our human selves. We all are constituted of many pairs of opposites, including body and mind, and within mind, there are intuitive and intellectual minds. These pairs must be in balance and in harmony to transcend to higher levels.

Dr. Chopra is acknowledged as a world leader in establishing a new life-giving paradigm that has revolutionized common wisdom about the mind and body. He has authored many books to bring balance and harmony within ourselves that have been translated into over 35 languages. Mikhail Gorbachev calls him one of the most lucid and inspiring philosophers of our time. Dr. Chopra perhaps may be one of the men responsible for bringing down the Iron Curtain, ending the Cold War. One could spend hours to describe his achievements, but I won't do it here. I will say only this: He is, in our opinion, the most deserving person for our first Bridgebuilder Award, and we are very fortunate that he has come here to accept it.

Namaste, and thank you.

World Sacred Music Festival with Their Local Heroes Kicks Off at uCLA, September 13, 2008

By Greg Heffernan

LOS ANGELES: This month for 16 days, the *2008 World Festival of Sacred Music—Los Angeles*will presentnearly a thousand artists performing in 41 sacred events of music and movement throughout Los Angeles. UCLA's Royce Hall initiated the city's program with an impressive lineup of five diverse groups of artists that covered the world. Saturday night's show included "Chirgilchn," an ensemble of deep meditative resonance of Tuvan throat singing from central Asia; Waldemar Bastos, whose defection from Angola to Portugal was reflected in his infectious Pourtuguese fado, Brazilian samba and Caribbean zouk; the Lian Ensemble who provided the art of improvisation which lies at the heart of the mystical heritage of classical Persian music; the eight-man Rupayan from Rajasthan that rocked thehall with hypnotic rhythms of Sufiand Qawwali music of the Indian Thar desert; and finally the intimate and supple collaboration between the award-winning American jazz guitarist Rob Levit and Emiko Susilo, a classical vocalist of extraordinary grace and depth whose voice, beautiful, clear-toned and with phenomenal range was nurtured and sculpted amidst the ancient temples of a Balinese village.

The word "sacred" actually came from His Holiness the Dalai Lama. "I might not have chosen that word myself," recalled Judy Mitoma, festival director, professor of world arts and cultures, and director of the UCLA Center for Intercultural Performance. "My definition might be quite different from yours." Ms. Mitoma was referring to the world's subjectivity and diversity, and Saturday night she emphasized the importance of this opening event.

In fact, the opening night reception, hosted by His Highness Prince Aga Khan Shia Imami's Council for the Western United States, also honored the "Local Heroes" Project, which included Indo-American and former student at UCLA, Navin Doshi, who has been a regular supporter of UCLA's South Asian history department and cultural events. "The Local Heroes project aims to challenge the standard definition of a hero and commends individuals that are at the core of our community. These selfless individuals donate their time and energy out of genuine concern for the present and future solidarity of their communities," said Judy Mitoma as each honoree was awarded a gift.

LMU Professor Paul Humphreys, who has helped organize the "Voices of the Way" show at Loyola Marymount University's Sacred Heart Chapel on September 20 as part of the festival, explained that the origin of the Sacred Music Festival came from the Dalai Lama himself. "It goes back to 1999 when the Dalai Lama approached a number of people, among them Judy Mitoma, my mentor and friend from my graduate school days here at UCLA, and there would be no better way to enter the millennium and honor the independence and diversity of all human kind than a festival like this."

Clearly the audience's enjoyment of the magical and musical venue of the evening indicated that song and dance from various parts of the world has a way of bridging differences and healing wounds. "I have always believed that human beings are called to move from being self-involved to being selfless, or to move from "ahum" to "ohm," reflected "Local Hero" Navin Doshi at the end of the show. "It's very difficult in life to do this but clearly music is a vehicle that allows the soul to transcend to a blissful state of unified or interconnected centeredness. Tonight's music showed this is possible." When asked his preference of performers, Navin quickly praised Rupayan from Rajasthan. "I know I may be partial, but you can't beat the Rajasthan music with the clappers, the flute, strings and drums. They had the crowd clapping and dancing in Royce Hall. I also liked the duet with Ron Levit and Emiko Susilo, as Emiko has an exceptional voice that is very moving." One of the final moments of the festival included all of the performers playing together on the stage. The mosaic of music from all over the world gave the audience a striking moment of seeing the talent and uniqueness of the human race in a melodic way most will never forget.

APPENDIX B

GANDHI AND MAHESH YOGI IN THE EYES OF WORLD LEADERS

Nobel Laureate Rabindranath Tagore: "At Gandhi's call, India has blossomed forth to new greatness,just as once before when Buddha proclaimed the truth of compassion and fellowship among all living creatures." It was Tagore who first addressed Gandhi as "Mahatma," meaning "Great Soul." Gandhi's focus went far beyond helping only his family; he wanted to help all the people of India. In a limited sense, it is similar to what Buddha did, leaving the family and looking to find the path for greater good for all of humanity. Richard Attenborough's particular inspiration to make afilm on Mahatma Gandhi was Gandhi's dictum, and I quote him: "It has always been a mystery to me how men can feel themselves honored by the humiliation of their fellow beings." The film was made in 1982, and we all know how popular it became. I recall that teachers took their students to see it for educational purposes.

General Omar Bradley, who served second only to General Eisenhower during the Second World War "Gandhi rejected the atom and grasped the Sermon on the Mount. He was a nuclear infant, but an ethical giant. He knew nothing about killing and much about living in the 20th Century."

Reverend Martin Luther King Jr.: "If humanity is to progress, Gandhi is inescapable. We may ignore him at our own peril." Replying to a Christian critic, he further stated, "It is ironic yet very true that the greatest Christian of the modern world was a man who never embraced Christianity." The author Mary King said, "Gandhi was a pioneer in leading eight difficult struggles; they are against racism, against colonialism, against the caste system, against economic exploitation, against religious and ethnic supremacy, for equality for women, for democratic participation, and for nonviolent methods."

In his Noble Prize acceptance speech, the Dalai Lama stated, "I accept the prize as a tribute to the man who founded the modern tradition of non-violent action for change—Mahatma Gandhi—whose life taught and inspired me. And of course, I accept it on behalf of the six million Tibetan people who have suffered and continue to suffer."

In 1981, 53 Nobel Laureates issued a manifesto calling upon national governments and international NGOs; I will quote part of it. "One way to combat the holocaust of hunger is to have the weak and powerless organize themselves and use nonviolent actions exemplified by Gandhi, then it is certain that an end could be put to this catastrophe in our time."

His actions and compassion, as can be seen from the above quotations, have touched the lives of hundreds of thousands, if not millions. Ronald Reagan, who was not considered to be the brightest by his nemesis, made a very perceptive remark about Gandhi's leadership. He stated, "Great leaders do not do great things themselves. They inspire people to do great things." Gandhi most definitely fitted Reagan's criteria of great leadership.

Arnold Toynbee also commented that Gandhi was "as much a benefactor of Britain as of his own country. Though he made it impossible for the British to go on ruling India, he made it possible for the British to abdicate without dishonor."

On the occasion of Gandhi's seventieth birthday in 1939, Albert Einstein said, "A leader of his people, unsupported by any outward authority: a politician whose success rests not upon craft nor the mastery of technical devices, but simply on the convincing power of his personality; a victorious fighter who has always scorned the use of force; a man of wisdom and humility, armed with resolve and inflexible consistency, who has devoted all his strength to the uplifting of his people and the betterment of their lot; a man who has confronted the brutality of Europe with the dignity of the simple human being, and thus at all times risen superior." Later, after his death, he added, " Generations to come, it may be, will scarce believe that such a one as this ever in flesh and blood walked upon this earth."

Gandhi was a true philosopher king and he was fortunate to have found the right nemesis in the British to be successful. One Gandhi quote reverberates with one of the ancients: "God and the devil both reside in our hearts," similar to the statement that good and evil are two opposites and cannot be separated, and the evil is ignorance, the raw material for good.

Maharishi in the Eyes of Luminaries

Paul McCartney of the Beatles: "Whilst I am deeply saddened by his passing, my memories of him will only be joyful ones. He was a great man who worked tirelessly for the people of the world and the cause of unity."

Times of India: "His unique and enduring contribution to humankind was his deep understanding of — and mechanics of experiencing — pure consciousness."

Roy Ascott: "Maharishi Vedic Science explains the potential for every human being to experience the infinite natureof transcendental consciousness, also defined as Being or Self, while engaged in the normal activities of daily life."

Author Jack Forem: "In his interpretation of the Gita, the Maharishi expressed several times that as man gains greater awareness through the practice of Transcendental Meditation, he gradually establishes a level of contentment which remains increasingly grounded within him and in which the mind does not waver and is not affected by either attachment or fear."

Educator James Grant: "Maharishi brought out a 'full revival of the Vedic tradition of knowledge from India' and demonstrated its relevance in many areas including education, business, medicine and government."

Buckminister Fuller: "You could not meet with Maharishi without recognizing instantly his integrity."

Author Chryssides: "The Maharishi tended to emphasize the positive aspects of humanity, focusing on the good that exists in everyone."

APPENDIX C

MY BELIEF, CONSCIOUSNESS, THE ULTIMATE REALITY

We humans have come a long way to learning and understanding nature within and without. Let me describe what I have understood about the Ultimate Reality, based upon the work of German physicist Ulrich Mohrhoff's mathematical quantum mechanics, American physicist Menas Kafatos who published the "Conscious Universe" in 1991and the work of Physicist Amit Goswami, working independently and geographically poles apart all agree on the basic premise of the primacy of consciousness. Several new book chapters and articles by Menas Kafatos, Deepak Chopra, Neil Theise, John Hagelin, and others make the same point through a variety of arguments.

Einstein's theory of Special Relativity proves that the mass and energy are convertible (E=MC2) and the space and time change depending upon the speed of the frame of reference. In General Relativity, the behavior of masses entering the space-time region in a collapsed state has been studied. For example, the density in a perfect non-rotating black hole goes to infinity, meaning space containing matter goes to zero, a singularity; the implication here is that the space vanishes and becomes irrelevant or at least it changes from ordinary space to a form unknown to us. Of course we still don't have a quantum theory of gravity so the limits of collapsed space as implied by General Relativity are still outside of current knowledge of physics. Another example of space becoming irrelevant is based upon an experiment conducted by a group of French physicists led by Alain Aspect in 1982 following the nonlocality correlations of quantum mechanics. Two correlated photons (light) influence one another far away from each other instantaneously without exchanging any signal. Though the experiment was conducted in our natural space-time domain, apparently their interaction was nonlocal, out of or beyond space-time domain.

Another way to look at the relationship of space and the matter in quantum language is that the matter of forms needs space to contain it as in case of the macro-world. However in the micro-world, certain quanta with integer or zero spin like photons are identical, massless, formless and undistinguishable; there is no space to contain them. Though they are many but they are numerically identical, and show the attribute of oneness. There is a clear sense that the actual number of ultimate constituents is one. Photons in a sense exist outside of space and time not only because we can put a vast number of them in the same space but also because of the theory of Relativity, for them space-time is instantaneous or non-existent: They get "there" in no time and "there" for them is everywhere the same.

The reality we experience in the macro-world of matter and forms from the micro-world of massless and formless quanta like photons can be explained employing top down causation implying supremacy of consciousness over matter, and the concept of manifestation. Manifestation implies almost instantaneous perception through sense organs, usually eyes, mediated by brain, recognized and perceived by the nonlocal mind. Manifestation of space, and matter of forms is the act of almost an instant appearance of image and almost an instant materialization demonstrating the power and purpose of light. I say almost, because the response of all human material faculty cannot be instantaneous; there is a finite time of response.

Quantum mechanics provides us a junction or a link between the manifested world of matter and forms, and the ultimate reality of Pure being which manifests the world or manifests itself as the world without losing its essential identity. The junction is constituted of formless numerically identical, non-visualizable non-local quanta transcending space and time, and local partially visualizable molecules forming macrostructures including living forms and objects of everyday life. The process of manifestation is a transition from numerical identity of unity to a distinctive multiplicity, a progressive differentiation of the undifferentiated. Recently Kafatos and Kak (2015) have shown that a veiling of nonlocality and the prevention of seeing inside a black hole create a classical world view. This is analogous to the *maya* principle of veiling of ultimate Reality found in Vedanta and Shaivism.

Why do we choose top down and not bottom up causation? Bottom up approach is basically materialistic and inadequate in finding roots, quality and value. Top down causation has its deep roots in human mysticism associated in almost all human tradition, going back to over three millennia. It is the framework, supported by quantum mechanics discovered more recently, and it adequately conforms to the reality of consciousness, providing deeper insights into the nature of evolution. Katha Upanishad, similar to an axiom, states that Chetan that is consciousness is primary and Jada or Prakrity (nature) as secondary. Corollary to that statement stated by Professor Hiriyanna is, “Everything that exists is either Life-force (Consciousness) or for Life-force”. The statement, “Things that can be known are those compatible with the existence of the knowers”, similar to the previous statement, is one of the interpretations of the Anthropic Principle stated by physicist Brandon Carter in the 1970s.

More than a millennium long philosophic tradition, known as Vedanta, affirms that there is an Ultimate self-conscious Reality relating to the world we live in, in three different ways. This Reality is the world and the cosmos we live in, it is also the consciousness that contains and penetrates the cosmos in its totality. This Ultimate Reality is, subjectively speaking, an infinite bliss, and objectively speaking, an infinite in any quality and value we can imagine that expresses and experiences itself.

This follows the top-down framework of the Vedantic kind with quality, value and consciousness rooted in the very heart of Reality, as opposed to the bottom-up framework of the materialist kind with no idealism or sentience attached to it. Note that the universe exists by itself, and nothing else, in the material sense; it is self-aware and exists for Itself in the sense of consciousness. The universe is conscious and this is a conclusion that quantum theory leads to according to Kafatos and Goswami. I also interpret that there is nonlocal, meaning beyond the realm of perceivable space and time, Quantum connection between individual subjective consciousness and the all-pervading objective super-consciousness, the Ultimate Reality. Please note that non-locality cannot be manifested; but it is implied as in the Aspect et al. experiments; it is beyond our gross body material existence, beyond the perception and apprehension of space-time and matter-energy of nature. Non-locality encompasses all of the nature and beyond. However it is nowhere in the natural world.

It has also been conjectured that the nature within and without is fractal, meaning it is layered like an onion, and in which each part contains the whole like in a hologram. The implication here is that, not only our mind, but Consciousness itself is layered and has discrete states rising towards greater consciousness and wholeness. Sri Aurobindo had pioneered this subject and claimed that humanity is on the evolutionary path of transcendence towards the Ultimate

Reality. For example, one layer we are familiar with is our own body constituted of millions of living cells. In words of Erwin Schrodinger, the discoverer of the mathematics (The wave equation) of quantum mechanics, "There is million fold democracy among these cells, functioning autonomously within the body. There is only one consciousness and there is no super cell associated with it". Schrodinger then raises the question, "How is it possible that we as individuals having the mind of our own can communicate and understand each other?" He, without any reservation, had accepted that in reality there is only one mind, one consciousness in totality expounded by Vedanta.

The primary state features a single conscious self, coexisting with the cosmos we live in. The subject in this state is wherever its objects are, and it is non-dual meaning there is no space or disconnect of any kind between the seer and the seen. The state that we are familiar with, arises when there are multitude of conscious selves becoming exclusive. Here conscious selves lose sight of its identity with other selves and with the single self of the primary state. When an individual conscious self loses the awareness of its oneness with the ultimate reality of the primary state, it also loses the awareness of infinite quality and the delight (Sat-Chit-Ananda) at the heart of its existence. In essence, evolution is a process in reverse, when the life evolves first and then the individual mind which, nevertheless, is still part of the infinite sea of Consciousness. Transcendence is the process of ascending from grosser states to subtler states as described by Maharishi Mahesh Yogi and Shree Krishnamurti. Humanity will ultimately arrive to the state of Ultimate Reality through the process of evolution, as predicted by Shri Aurobindo.

Mathematics is the golden key to communicable truth of reality of the natural world-maybe even beyond our limited bandwidth. The key to non-communicable truth is the mystic experience through yoga and meditation. There is a link between Shanti Sloka of Isavasya Upanishad and mathematics. The Sloka describes the "Supreme Whole" (Ultimate Reality, Brahman) is such that it remains whole, even if the whole is taken away out of it or added to it. This is by definition, the concept of mathematical infinity, developed in 19th century.

How is the Ultimate Reality described in the mystic tradition, specifically in the Upanishads? The Upanishads describe Brahman as Sat-chit-ananda—the true Absolute Ultimate Reality, which not separately but simultaneously is Sat, or Truth, Chit or Consciousness or Light, and Ananda or Bliss. They describe it as non-dual: That which is One-without-a second, That from which nothing is separate, That which is limitless, That which is brilliantly radiant, That which is changeless, That which is not conditioned by time, space and causation, That which is self-existent, That which is devoid of attributes, and That which is without a beginning or an end. It does not have any limits because it is beyond space, for limits of something or someone can only be cognized within the contours of space. It is changeless because change can only be conceived within the parameters of time. It is without a beginning or an end because the beginning or end can only be perceived within the confines of time and space. It is self-effulgent for It is Consciousness itself; its effulgence is not dependent on anything, for It is beyond causation. Because nothing in the cosmos is separate from the Brahman, It has manifested this universe from its own body, first engendering time and space and then entering into them, just as a spider creates its web from its own saliva.

In manifestation, Brahman manifests as a principle of Purusha and Prakriti, as enumerated in detail by the Sankhya philosophy. Purusha is the static principle and Prakriti or Nature is the dynamic principle. Purusha is the witness and static or unchanging principle which supports and gives assent or negates the workings of Prakriti, which carries its dynamic processes through three gunas: Sattva, Rajas, and Tamas. Sattva psychologically manifests in human beings as the force of truth, harmony, peace, right poise, equilibrium, intelligence, happiness etc. Rajas psychologically translates as the quality of action, energy, domination, possession, creation, will to fight, will to resist, and will to conquer. Tamas signifies indolence, inertia, unintelligence, sloth, and resistance towards change. All these gunas are present in each individual and are in flux—however the predominance of one or two determines the general character of an individual in that whether he or she will be sattvic, rājasic or tamasic. When an individual is under the influence of the modes of Prakriti or Nature, then his or her soul or Purusha is involved in the play; it is not free and it suffers or enjoys the play of the Prakriti as the case may be. Therefore the first step towards liberation or moksha involves separating the Purusha from the modes of Prakriti, and letting the witness and unchanging consciousness of Purusha, which is its natural characteristic, to emerge. The Purusha, then, instead of being involved in the constant subjection to Prakriti, is able to watch the movement of her different modes and can give sanction to the continuance or cessation of the play. Finding its union with the transcendental Brahman it can then find its complete liberation or moksha.

Thus in manifestation, the transcendental Brahman through Purusha and Prakriti reveals changeless or constant characteristics and changing or dynamic characteristics respectively. However, it is due to the greater similarities that the Purusha has with transcendental Brahman that it is considered Divine in the universe while Prakriti is not—the crucial difference being that Purusha is unchanging and constant whereas Prakriti or Nature is dynamic and changing.

The Divine or God in most major traditions is characterized by Light. The Brahmasutras and Upanishads define Brahman as self-effulgent, the Light from which all other lights are borrowed. One of the prayers in the Upanishads specifically speaks about taking one from falsehood to truth, from darkness to light, and from death to immortality equating the characteristic of the Divine with truth and light. Diwali, the festival of light, in most Indian traditions represent the triumph of good over evil or an attainment of nirvana in Buddhist and Jain traditions. Genesis explains that at the time of creation God said, "Let there be light" and from light all the possibilities of the universe appeared. Light in the eyes of a scientist is a beam of photons or packs of energy which our eyes cannot see. Light helps us to see and make the world visible and transparent. Light therefore, in every sense, is seeing and at much higher level of mind is enlightening. Light is pure action with the purpose of enlightening and is attached to nothing. Light initiated the creation of matter, energy, space and time of the macro-world in which we have evolved to the current state of humanity.

People who have had near-death experiences recount them as godly tête-à-tête with light. The Tibetan Book of the Dead contends that as soon as an individual dies, it has an encounter with "Clear Light of Reality." It is not able to hold that state because its karmic propensities bring it to lesser and lesser states until it is reborn. Ramakrishna, describing his experiences in featureless or nirvikalpa samadhi, stated that he saw an ocean of light having no beginning or end. Many mystics from different traditions have also experienced and recorded spiritual encounters as light. It is the life giving light of solar deity that we find in ancient Egypt, Chinese, Aztec, and Inca mythology. Even in movies like The Abyss and The Ghost, they project higher beings as self-effulgent.

Everything in Nature is changing and relative except the speed of Light. It is true that the velocity of light changes when it is approaching a black hole, but not the speed. Light, constituted of photons, has zero mass. The speed of light is not affected by the gravitational force exerted by a black hole--only the direction of motion as space-time is curved close to a black hole, is affected. From this we may say that the unchanging nature of the speed of light is associated with Purusha, and the changing nature of light direction is associated with Prakriti. Philosophically speaking this intuition of Einstein may be thought of a next great step in civilizational thought, perhaps heralding a new age leading from the modern preoccupation with the Science and Technology of changeful Nature to a search for the unchanging Source of consciousness and Being.

What about other physical constants like the Alpha or fine structure constant? Nobel laureate physicist extraordinaire Richard Feynman called Alpha a "magic number" and its value "one of the greatest mysteries of physics". A dimensionless number which goes by the symbol alpha must remain constant for our existence. If not, then stars, including sun, would not be able to sustain nuclear reactions that synthesize carbon and oxygen atoms and therefore the carbon based life would not exist. A new research in astrophysics, reviewed in Economist magazine dated September 4, 2010, has discovered that the Alpha may not be constant after all, but changing from place to place within the universe. Other physicists including Kafatos and Roy believe that all constants of nature may be changing. If their results hold up to scrutiny, they will have profound implications-for they suggest that the universe stretches far beyond what human telescopes can observe, and that the laws of physics, discovered by human beings, vary within it. Our material existence, if true in matters of the size of the universe, has become even more insignificant. The new research, however, does not change our connectedness with light. The speed of light remains unchanging at least in our part of the universe, and probably elsewhere.

Light holds a special place in relativity, in quantum physics and in the eternal monistic traditions of the East. It therefore remains the conduit to the Divine and connects it with Nature. All living souls in Nature, bounded within the space time continuum, are also connected with the gale of the sun, as described by Ananda Coomaraswami. The significance here is that we need to learn to live "Now", not in the past and not in the future. That would help us to transcend to higher states of mind. Recall "Now" is the common apex of both, past and future cones, in space-time continuum bounded within the confines of the speed of light. "Now" literally is at the threshold to escape the domain of Nature. When our mind stays on "Now", there are no thoughts of the past pleasure and pain and no thoughts of the future expectations and anxiety; the arrow of time keeps moving forward, but the mind without thoughts goes through the experience of action. The slope at the apex is the ratio of zero to zero which is one, or the speed of your choosing, or the speed of light. The subtlest mind of a realized Rishi is in the state of "Now" experiencing the bright light, escaping the confinement bounded by the speed of light. Apparently our existence at the apex "Now" may be a step away or in the ultimate state of Sat-chit-Ananda.

I suppose H. G. Wells was travelling in his Time-Machine by keeping his machine in the "Now" domain. Apparently "Now" also represents the middle path preached by Buddha. When someone would ask Yogi Berra, "What is the time?" He would answer with a question, do you mean "Now"?

The goal of a transcending philosopher is to acquire the highest mental state of being, the spiritual self. The insight here is to becoming selfless, egoless. This condition is quintessentially light like in quality, mass-less and approaching the attribute of changelessness. Here we need to focus on only the mind disassociating from the somatic self. Thoughts are similar to sub-atomic particles; thoughts jump discretely from one to the next or from lower to higher energy states similar to quantum jumps of sub-atomic particles. By identification with thoughts, our mental being also knows no rest and cannot know itself as an unchanging reality. Intuitively therefore, only a thoughtless mind could be egoless, and selfless. The highest yogic state is when all desires lodged in the heart have been dissolved. It is amazing and significant that Einstein was able to uncover the relative nature of Nature by associating light with the realm of the Divine, which happens also to be the view of the world's great religious traditions.

The fact that we perceive, communicate, and understand each other is due to our connection to consciousness. If we believe that mind could help heal the body, then consciousness is the cause. As explained earlier, Einstein's insight of connecting unchanging nature of light with the traditional view of the first glimpse of the Absolute is, I believe, one of the strongest proofs of the existence of the Absolute, the ultimate reality, the consciousness.

Printed in the United States
By Bookmasters